P9-BJO-951

Social Treatment

MODERN
APPLICATIONS
OF
SOCIAL
WORK

A
SERIES
EDITED
BY
JAMES K.
WHITTAKER

CHICAGO

ABOUT THE AUTHOR

James K. Whittaker is Associate Professor in the School of
Social Work, University of Washington. He is a frequent consultant on child care training both in the Seattle area and
nationally. Professor Whittaker previously taught at the University of Minnesota where he received his Ph.D. A frequent
contributor to professional journals, Professor Whittaker is co-
author of *The Other 23 Hours: Child Care Work in a Therapeutic Milieu* (with Albert E. Trieschman and Larry K.
Brendtro, Aldine, 1969), and *Children Away from Home: A
Sourcebook in Residential Treatment* (with Albert E. Trieschman, Aldine, 1972).

Copyright © 1974 by James K. Whittaker

First published 1974 by
Aldine Publishing Company
529 South Wabash Avenue
Chicago, Illinois 60605

ISBN 0-202-36011-3 cloth; 0-202-36012-1 paper
Library of Congress Catalog Number 71-172856

Printed in the United States of America

Social Treatment

an approach to interpersonal helping

James K. Whittaker
University of Washington

 ALDINE PUBLISHING COMPANY

Contents

To my mother, Julia, and my late father, Brendan,
for all the help along the way.

Preface

This is a book about people helping people, for that is what social work is—a point too easily lost amidst the technical jargon and abstract conceptualizations that engulf much of present-day social work practice with individuals, families, and small groups. This is not intended as carping criticism, merely as recognition of the fact that in their desire to perfect the means of helping, social work practitioners and theoreticians (present company included) sometimes lose sight of its fundamental purpose, which is, in the words of Jane Addams (1910), "the raising of life to its highest value." In our present highly technical, impersonal culture, this simply stated goal perhaps has greater import than when it was first pronounced.

The primary purpose of this volume is to provide an introduction to interpersonal helping in the context of social work practice. A secondary objective is to develop a framework for interpersonal helping, called social treatment, which will constitute a conceptual coatrack on which to place all of the various methods and strategies of helping currently practiced.

A note of caution: This book does not attempt to synthe-

1

size or integrate present methods of intervention with individuals, families, and small groups. At this point in time,
such attempts appear premature. In this book I intend something far less grandiose: to provide a reasonable and orderly
way of proceeding through an area of knowledge often be-
wildering in its complexity, while attempting to avoid the
twin pitfalls of overspecificity on the one hand and simplistic reduction on the other.

Chapter 1 examines the concept of remediation against
the more encompassing issues of social reform and environmental protection. The impending environmental crisis will
require a totally new view of the relationship of human
beings to the rest of physical nature. Similarly, the remediation of social problems is likely to require radical changes in
our existing social institutions. Both factors create problems
for the social work practitioner. These will be explored along
with some possible strategies for conflict resolution.

Chapter 2 explores several issues of critical importance to
present social work practice: client advocacy, service delivery systems, professionalization, and competing technologies
of social treatment.

Chapter 3 offers the following definition of social treatment as a conceptual framework for interpersonal helping
and examines its essential components:

> Social treatment is an approach to interpersonal helping which
> utilizes direct and indirect strategies of intervention to aid in-
> dividuals, families, and small groups in improving social func-
> tioning and coping with social problems.

Finally, the multiple roles that social work practitioners perform are introduced: treatment agent, advocate-ombudsman, broker of services and resources, and teacher-counselor.

Chapter 4 examines some of the major knowledge bases of

social treatment, including psychoanalytic theory, social learning theory, social systems theory, and humanistic-existential approaches. Each is explored in terms of its internal value framework and view of man, as well as implications for practice.

Chapter 5 develops the social treatment sequence: intake, assessment and social diagnosis, determination of goals, selection of a social treatment plan, establishment of a working agreement, sustaining social treatment, evaluation, termination, and aftercare. Each phase of the social treatment sequence is explored in terms of basic objectives, worker activities, client perspectives, and resources.

Chapter 6 examines the range of helping activities that practitioners undertake indirectly on behalf of their clients. Topics include bases of practitioner power, system foci for indirect intervention, indirect helping roles, and community services.

Chapter 7 explores current trends and future directions in social treatment practice.

In the Appendix, a framework for evaluating methods of interpersonal helping is developed, and twenty-one approaches to social treatment are briefly introduced and resource bibliographies provided.

To give proper acknowledgment to all who had a hand in shaping this effort is unusually difficult, since they essentially include all who played a part in the development of my own stance toward social treatment practice. A special debt of gratitude is owed to Ralph L. Kolodny and Albert E. Trieschman, colleagues and former clinical supervisors whose vision extends beyond the fifty-minute therapy hour; David Wineman, who gave real-life meaning to the concept of client advocacy; Edwin J. Thomas, who introduced me to social learning theory; and Clarke A. Chambers, who made social welfare history come alive. More recent indebtedness is owed to Scott Briar, whose own writing on social work practice has been a catalyst to my present effort, and to William C. Berleman for many fruitful discussions on social welfare issues. Former students at the University of Minnesota and the University of Washington aided immensely in providing critical commentary on many of the concepts and methods of social treatment presented in the text. Curtis D. Harstad, Asbjörn Osland, and Joyce Osland made many useful suggestions on the first draft of the manuscript and compiled much of the source material contained in the Appendix. Their collective efforts are deeply appreciated. Marla Guindon typed the first draft of the manuscript and Elaine Scherba supervised the preparation of the final draft and offered many useful suggestions along the way. The book would not have been completed on schedule without her considerable efforts above and beyond the call of duty. Finally, it is customary at this point for authors to express gratitude to patient and longsuffering spouses and children for long hours spent away from hearth and home during the preparation of the manuscript. Such acknowledgment is not fully warranted here, since in our current design for living, family time is never allowed to be overshadowed for too long a period by professional commitment. Accordingly, this book always finished second. Thus absolved of that particular obligation, I here express in a more general sense my gratitude to my wife, Kathleen, and our children, Matthew and Patrick, for having full, active, and productive lives of their own and for providing support and encouragement in ways less obvious. In short, I thank them for simply *being*.

1

Dilemmas of the Helping Person in an Age of Ecological and Social Crisis

Increasingly, members of the helping professions are being asked to address themselves to what the historian Crane Brinton has called "the Big Questions": From whence have we come and where are we going?

At no other time in recent history have the concept of interpersonal helping and the professions dedicated to implementing that concept come under such intensive scrutiny. Two forces would appear to be at least partially responsible for this questioning: the increasing popularity of large-scale, macro interventions designed to effect changes within organizations and communities and the growing concern with environmental protection and ecology.

Many within the helping professions have argued persuasively for one particular type of treatment over others: family mode versus individual mode; group approach versus one-to-one encounter; long-term versus short-term treatment; professional versus nonprofessional practitioner. Indeed, the dialogue carried out in the professional literature,

This chapter is adapted from an earlier journal version: Dilemmas of the mental health practitioner in an age of ecological crisis, *Mental Hygiene*, in press.

at conferences, and in actual practice has undoubtedly had a beneficial effect on the remedial field generally, and in many instances has resulted in a more informed and innovative practice. But while many have energetically argued the case for one or another type of treatment, until relatively recently few have called into question the whole notion of remediation per se.

The profession of social work, with its long history of providing help to those in need when they need it, finds the notion of moving from an individual case approach to a more community or institutionally focused form of intervention particularly discomforting. Yet the growing body of literature critical of the effectiveness of case-by-case intervention; the proposition that if pathology in fact exists, it lies within our societal institutions and not within those individuals who have difficulty adapting to them; the increasing fascination of government and private funding sources with larger and more basic forms of social intervention—all these must cause the professional helping person, regardless of his particular theoretical or practice orientation, to feel that all is not entirely well.

At an even more basic level a potentially more far-reaching conflict would appear to be emerging between the concerns of environmental protection and those of social welfare, whether achieved by micro or macro intervention. If the controversy between small- and large-scale intervention for purposes of human betterment is only now in its nascent phase, the conflict between the forces of conservation and those of social welfare is still in embryo. W. C. Berleman paints the scenario vividly (1972, p. 229):

In our time two small armies of crusaders have declared war each upon its particular heathen. One band is bent upon a "war on poverty," while the other is thinly arrayed about the ravaged citadel, Earth, hoping to preserve it. Probably neither group now sees the other as representing "the foe," but suppose the ranks of social reform stumble frontally upon the conservationists' picket line, would there be rejoicing or would battle ensue?

We may hope that together, these two sets of conflict—between individual helping and larger scale community or societal intervention and between social welfare concerns and environmental concerns—will produce in the future a rethinking and reordering of priorities based on a single value framework that extends from the broadest planetary concerns to the narrowest of individual problems This rapprochement would appear to be light-years away, however; for the present the professional social worker faces a series of dilemmas that strike at the core of what he is supposed to be about: helping individuals, families, and small groups to help themselves. Let us take a look at some of the particular problems and pitfalls faced by the professional social worker.

Areas of Potential Conflict

REMEDIATION VS. PREVENTION

The first dilemma has already been alluded to: how does one continue to justify any form of teatment or remediation when massive social problems like poverty, inferior education, and urban blight so clearly demand large-scale programs aimed at basic systemic change? Aren't any efforts directed toward remediation just futile attempts to apply band-aids when what is needed is major surgery? This is the position taken by some social activists who view pathology as societal and not individual. They would have us direct our efforts at change not at individuals and families, but at the unjust and inadequate social systems in which those individuals are caught. Thus communities themselves or social organizations become the targets for change, ultimately resulting in the remediation of individual problems.

Beyond this hue and cry for less individual treatment and more community treatment or social action is heard the even louder call of the environmentalists. Enhancement of social welfare and amelioration of human misery, they argue, simply cannot be based any longer on the notion of an infinitely expanding technology and economy, which will provide whatever measures of improved social welfare are deemed desirable. The notion of more and more people sharing in the good life and increasing consumption may, in fact, produce such a drain on renewable and nonrenewable resources that the planet will suffer irreparable harm. Thus social welfare measures must no longer be predicated on the concept of a cornucopia of resources awaiting only the guiding hand of the social reformer to direct its boundless contents to a greater multitude, but rather on Kenneth Boulding's (1966) notion of "spaceship earth," with its limited amount of life's basic resources, which, once depleted, are gone forever. Finally, at least implicit in the argument of the ecologically concerned is the judgment that certain problems, such as overpopulation and the rape of the environment, are so pressing, so ubiquitous, and so much at the root of all other human problems that they deserve the highest priority in the hierarchy of concerns and should command the major share of resources.

Hence the professional social worker interested in interpersonal helping finds himself in a kind of no man's land between those who argue for more social action and large-scale system intervention, on the one hand, and those who cry for an even more basic attempt to deflect society's present collision course with the physical environment, on the other. When posed against such ominous problems requiring such massive resources, the argument for remedial efforts with individuals pales considerably and the helping person engaged in such efforts must feel increasingly uncertain that what he is doing is any longer justified. In sum, the basic question appears to be: Can one continue to make a case for social treatment? The answer is yes.

While it is clear that justification for any form of remediation or interpersonal helping has come under intensive scrutiny in recent times, it is equally clear that much of the criticism would have us jettison the whole because of malfunctions in some of the parts. It is undoubtedly true that radical changes in our social welfare system are needed and that these changes will require a concerted effort at social action on the part of professionals and nonprofessionals alike. Furthermore, it appears evident that efforts at individual helping have not brought about these needed changes, and in fact have contributed at least partially to the problem by attempting to help individuals adjust to essentially pathological social conditions. Finally, in a certain sense, the entire field of interpersonal helping can be accused of merely ministering to the symptoms of the problem while leaving the root causes untouched.

What is easy to argue in the abstract, however, becomes more difficult to defend in the specific. Who will presume to deny help to the family in a state of emotional crisis, or the juvenile offender frustrated in his attempts to cope with the world around him, or the lonely young adult who is terrified of social relationships yet longs for warmth and acceptance? On what grounds will help, however inadequate, be denied to these individuals? Without question, the provision of temporary remediation to these symptoms will not solve the basic problems of family disorganization, poverty, inferior education, and anomie which underlie the specific manifestations. But in carrying forward the banner of social reform, can we ignore completely those who have already felt some pain?

At another level, even given the most enlightened and pro-

gressive social institutions, it is naive to assume that the society will be free of all individuals requiring treatment or
help. Too often social activists fall into the trap of explaining all individual problems as socially determined: simply
modify the environment and the problem will disappear.
Suffice it to say that this kind of logic blunts individual differences and underplays the function of organism in the
paradigm stimulus-organism-respnnse.

The solution to this first dilemma would appear to lie in a
more socially conscious and informed helping professional
who will link his remedial efforts with those of the social ac-
tivist which are directed at more basic reforms. Exactly how
this rapprochement comes about is of course the nexus of the
dilemma. But difficult as this "both/and" approach may be
to implement, it is far more desirable than the simplistic
"either/or" view that holds that improved social conditions
will do away with the need for all remedial helping, or that
individual treatment is all that is needed to solve society's
problems. The major difficulty occurs when we mistakenly
ascribe the goals of one to the other. Interpersonal helping
will not of itself bring about needed reform in our social institutions, nor will improvements in those social institutions
do away completely with the need for remedial efforts.

VALUE QUESTIONS

A second dilemma lies in the potential clash of professional
values with some of those set forth by the ecological movement. For example, in supporting the notion of a limited
family size, perhaps enforced by government sanction, is not
the professional compromising the basic principle of the client's right to self-determination? What is a moot point in
the abstract becomes an increasingly uncomfortable reality
for those professionals charged with counseling clients in
the area of family planning. Some ecologically minded persons would argue that it is not simply a question of individu-

al freedom to have as many children as one can care for adequately, but that the ability of society to absorb the increasing number of children, each taxing the already dwindling supply of nonrenewable resources, should be the primary factor in the decision.

At what point, then, should the "rights" of society supersede those of the individual? The professional social worker may soon be forced to choose between the individual client's right to self-determination in matters of family size and a policy of limitation that may be ecologically sound but which infringes upon individual rights.

The issue of overpopulation as a global problem will shortly have to be faced by every professional, for it appears as a major concern of many ecologists (Ehrlich & Ehrlich, 1970; Berelson, 1969; Harkavy, Jaffe, & Wishnik, 1969; Blake, 1969). "Population control," as population biologist Paul Ehrlich says, "is not a 'panacea' but 'absolutely essential'" if the problems now facing mankind are to be solved. "Whatever your cause, it's a lost cause without population control" (Ehrlich & Ehrlich, 1970, p. 111).

More recently, Barry Commoner (1971) has disputed Ehrlich's claim of the centrality of population pressures as a major causative factor in the environmental crisis. Commoner argues rather that the particular nature of post–World War II technology, with its enormous dependence on synthetic, polluting materials, and the profit system that supports that technology represent the major threats to the biosphere. The implications in either case are clear: improved social conditions can no longer be purchased at the expense of the basic life systems of earth, water, and air.

But if the professional social worker reads Ehrlich and Commoner, he also hears the numerous voices of those who view population control as a means of controlling the poor and oppressed by limiting their number. Indeed, at a time when the notion of power and equal participation in the

larger society is becoming less of an illusion and more of a
reality for many low-income and minority groups, to speak
of limiting births to a group that already finds itself under-
represented is to run the risk of being labeled racist or eli-
tist. One wonders what arguments, what rationale will be
available to those helping professionals who find themselves
at the precarious point of contact between the disenfran-
chised seeking to grow in strength and numbers and those
who would seek to limit population or consumption. In a delicate and infinitely complex area of controversy, the question
for the professional social worker may be simply reduced to:
Whose side are you on?

For the individual professional and his national association, a related dilemma concerns the norms and guidelines to
be used in planning interventive strategies. A step in the
direction of short-term gain may, for reasons already alluded to, prove ecologically unsound in the long run. On the other hand, even if one accepts the rightness of working on underlying ecological problems, how are we to deal with the
victims of the many other problems that beset society—poverty, racism, inferior education, mental illness, and so on?
Even further assuming some consensus on the hierarchy of
problems confronting us, at what level should they be at-
tacked? Given limited manpower and financial resources,
should greater attention be paid to the young or to those who
have suffered longer under the yoke of social problems? What
might have been armchair discussion even a few years ago
now becomes daily reality for the legislator, private foundation executive, and professional social worker forced to decide where to direct already scant resources and plagued with
the underlying fear that what they can do will have virtually
no effect anyway.

For all practitioners and especially for those just beginning their careers, the knowledge that what they are capable

of doing *can* make a difference is becoming increasingly rare. Buffeted from all sides by an awareness of his own limitations, by the exhortations of the environmentalists and the social activists, and by the demands of his clients, the professional social worker must at times feel as if the value framework within which he operates is as outdated as the taxonomy of psychiatric labels that he discarded long ago as being irrelevant to his practice. What steps are to be taken, then, to overcome these considerable difficulties?

In the past two decades the technology of interpersonal helping—the various treatment modalities, strategies, and techniques of individual change—have undergone considerable investigation and have emerged greatly strengthened and refined. Perhaps it is now time to turn with equal vigor and resolve to a careful examination of the values underlying that technology. In light of what many feel to be the impending environmental crisis, it would be well to reexamine our long-held belief in the individual's right to self-determination and to see how this articulates with the needs and demands of an increasingly densely populated world.

On a broader scale, the value base that underlies social welfare generally must be reexamined. Are we in fact, as Berleman (1971) has suggested, basing our social welfare goals on the premise of an ever expanding economy with limitless resources? If this is true, as it appears to be, how do we bring our goals for both large-scale and individual change into harmony with the principle of a sound ecology?

When the various dilemmas of the helping person in an age of ecological and social crisis are examined, the answer often seems to lie not with the creation of new technology—we are fully provided for in that area—but in the creation of a new value framework that can relate itself to the extremely complex problems of our age, an "age of perfect means and confused goals," as Albert Einstein said.

WORKING WITHIN THE SYSTEM

Another problem for the practitioner concerns his locus of practice. How does one continue to work within the system (in this instance, the social welfare system) when in many instances the most serious pathology lies not within individual clients, but within the very social service network of which the professional is a part? Can one retain professional integrity and uphold a primary allegiance to clients in a social welfare bureaucracy that may at times dehumanize clients or base priorities on organizational expediency rather than on client needs? In short, when the helping professional becomes a part of the social welfare establishment, does he not run the risk of placing allegiance to the organization before allegiance to clients?

Clearly the professional code of ethics would speak forcefully against this type of compromise in principle. But the question here is not really one of intent. The issue is whether or not segments of our social welfare system have gotten so large, so unwieldy, and so far diverted from their original purposes that professional practice within them almost automatically runs the risk of becoming organization-centered rather than client-centered.

Assuming for a moment that this were a reality even for a single social welfare bureaucracy, what should be the decision of the professional social worker regarding practice within that system? To work within the system would almost certainly mean that some professional values would be compromised, if only in the sense that the professional would have to cooperate in some degree with the policies and practices of the organization. On the positive side, some clients could receive much needed service and the professional could work vigorously for change within the system. This course may prove to be particularly frustrating, however, for if the professional's views are alien to the system and his values too outspoken, he may be asked to leave and his clients will then be deprived of much needed service. On the other hand, too cautious a position vis-a-vis internal change will undoubtedly bring the professional into conflict with his own value system and code of ethics.

Another alternative for the professional social worker would be simply to refuse to work within a system that engaged in dehumanizing practices toward clients, or placed organizational needs before client needs. He could always choose to practice his profession elsewhere. But what of his clients? Do they have a similar choice? In choosing not to participate, the professional may in fact be depriving clients of the services they need. Professional ethics may be upheld, but at what cost?

The situation is further clouded by the fact that issues and problems such as these are seldom clear-cut. Who is to determine when an organization is serving its own needs at the expense of clients, and by what criteria will such a decision be reached? Perhaps the organization even acknowledges unfair policies and inadequate practices and invites the practitioner to join it in bringing about needed changes. The nagging question remains, however: How effective will his efforts be once he himself has become a part of the very organization he seeks to change?

In sum, are we speaking here of a hypothetical dilemma or of a present reality for the professional social worker? The wealth of literature on the shortcomings of our present social welfare system would seem to suggest that we are dealing more with fact than with fancy.[1] Greatly overburdened by gigantic case loads, hamstrung by punitive regulations, and in practice often guided more by the way the client fits

---

1. See, for example, Cloward & Piven (1971); Rein (1970a); Brager (1968a, 1968b); Epstein (1970); Polsky, Claster, & Goldberg (1970); Briar (1968); Etzioni (1969).

the organizational structure than vice versa, the social worker is often forced to offer clients what he knows to be inferi-
or service.

To cite but one example, can we truly speak of offering
treatment or rehabilitative services in settings where clients
are not there of their own volition? One could argue that a
client might choose to participate in a treatment relationship within the context of an involuntary setting, but what
of instances where participation in treatment is mandatory?
Is this still to be considered professional practice, and if so,
what of the client's right to self-determination?

It is clear that there is no easy answer to this dilemma if
one accepts the premise that all existing social welfare institutions are helping to maintain the very problems they were
designed to alleviate and are treating only symptoms. The
problem with this position, taken to its extreme, is that it
leaves precious few alternatives open to the concerned professional other than nonparticipation or revolution. For
even if one chooses to work outside of the established agency
structure, one must of necessity think of operating within
the framework of some social organization—an organization
susceptible to the same kinds of "disease processes" as the
more established social welfare organizations and agencies.
Finally, the question of clients' needs comes again to the
fore. Are clients equally free to leave the established structure, and if not, are they likely to be deprived of needed
services if professionals leave the traditional social welfare
organizations?

In reality, two separate circumstances would seem to pre-
vail. In the first, the system may have simply reached the
point where the sheer number of clients to be served, arbitrary or capricious policies, dehumanizing practices, or a
number of these in combination have made it virtually impossible for professional services to be rendered. In such
cases the only proper course for the professional social

worker would seem to be to leave and do everything in his power to lead or support efforts to see that such policies or practices are eliminated. In the second instance, where a few dehumanizing practices exist along with some that are acceptable, the professional should move to expose such practices and seek remedies through advocacy action on behalf of the clients involved.

Clearly the commitment to client advocacy required by the professional's code of ethics presupposes a strong and viable machinery within the professional association to support and investigate such advocacy action and to provide legal assistance to professionals who may be putting their positions on the line.

TARGETS FOR CHANGE

A related dilemma concerns the degree to which the notion of a target philosophy is still viable in professional practice. Until recently it was sufficient for the helping professional to justify his practice by pointing to the fact that he was working on a piece of the overall web of social problems. Given his limited scope and insufficient resources, he would aim for a specific target: working with emotionally disturbed children, or counseling families, or treating the mentally ill. Presumably enough pieces were receiving professional attention to suggest that the problem as a whole was being addressed.

But how valid is this concept of target philosophy today? Have not many of the social problems we face been shown to be interrelated? Are not all of our social institutions, including social welfare institutions, in need of a basic and total restructuring? Can the helping professional continue to be content with the knowledge that he is working on a part of the problem if he truly believes that basic structural changes in the delivery of helping services are called for? Might it not be better to work toward the realization of those changes in lieu of offering direct services to a select group of clients? Finally, if the professional continues to work toward his specific target, believing as he does that basic systemic changes in the social welfare system are needed, is he not contributing to the illusion that the overall problem is really being met through a multitude of individual piecemeal efforts?

Again the questions posed by this dilemma do not readily yield answers. It is of course true that in addressing ourselves to specific targets, we may neglect the overall problem. In addition, there is some justification to the notion that in operating on specific target populations, helping professionals have perhaps inadvertently supported the mistaken notion that more basic underlying societal problems were being addressed. On the other hand, it would appear equally correct to say that in addressing any problem, one necessarily has to speak about specific targets for change. Otherwise, we run the risk of getting caught up in the rhetoric of reform without ever having addressed the question of planned change.

What we do *not* need are more narrowly focused clinicians who have no awareness of or apparent interest in their clients outside of the weekly treatment encounter. We should shun with equal resolve those who speak loudly of the need for more basic societal change, but whose fascination with their own rhetoric precludes their ability to discuss specific means to specific ends: targets for change.

In sum, it is safe to say that the notion of a target philosophy is still valid, but the definitions of the targets need revising. Specifically, do many of our existing problem categories make sense anymore in light of what we now know about the interrelatedness of social problems? Do the categories "dependent," "neglected," "delinquent," "mentally ill," and "socially maladjusted" continue to make sense, and if not, what better ways are there of defining these problems?

Each of the existing problem categories comes complete with its own network of helping services designed to remedy that particular problem. If, as many have suggested, the way in which we now go about defining problems is based on false assumptions or outmoded analyses, then perhaps these very categories themselves should become targets for change. Times and problems change (though perhaps not so quickly as our perceptions of them), and this is all the more reason to take a long, hard look at our present system of defining problems and to see how well that system fits with the reality of the current situation.

PROFESSIONAL ROLE DEFINITIONS

A final dilemma for the helping professional concerns his commitment to social action. Given the maze of problems besetting our social welfare system and the particular dilemmas faced by the practitioner operating within that system, is it any longer possible to separate social concerns from professional life? There has been traditional support for the position that helping professionals should be committed to social action, but this has usually been translated to mean working through the social action arm of the professional organization or some similar group. In short, social action was fine if it occurred after professional responsibilities to clients had been discharged. But what if now the professional defines at least some of those responsibilities as requiring social action on behalf of his clients? Can he incorporate such activity into his professional helping role, especially when it may bring him into conflict with his agency or with the community? With rapidly changing definitions of service, the time to cease working with the client in a direct treatment relationship and to begin working on his behalf in an advocacy relationship is extremely difficult to decide.

Finally, what of the professional who views his responsibilities as lying only within the context of his direct treat-

ment relationship with the client? He eschews the path of
social action on behalf of clients and practices what he
knows best: individual treatment. Increasingly the question
becomes: Can one be a professional helping person and remain uninvolved?

It should be clear from all that has been said that the professional social worker cannot relegate social action exclusively to after-hours times when responsibilities to clients
have been discharged. Indeed, those very responsibilities
may impel the worker to take up intervention on behalf of
his client. Rein (1970b), Wineman and James (1969), Briar
(1967), Brager (1968a), and H. Miller (1968) are among
those authors who have spoken to the specifics of the integration of a worker's broad social consciousness with his
professional helping role. Of particular importance here is
the concept of the worker acting as advocate on behalf of the
civil rights of his client. Advocacy of this type is not only in
harmony with the professional code of ethics, but required
by it (Ad Hoc Committee on Advocacy, 1969, p. 21).

There are, of course, some potential pitfalls in the adoption of advocacy stances by professional helping persons.
Promotion of one client's interest might be at the expense of
another, as in the case of scarce resources, and not all of the
problems concerning the legal sanctions available to the
worker who initiates an advocacy action, as well as those
that may be potentially used against him, have been fully explored.

Despite the problems in setting up the machinery for advocacy actions—and this would appear to be the crucial factor—it is clear that a narrowly focused treatment agent interested only in his client's emotional state and unmindful of
the social conditions that have an impact upon him is as out
of touch with the realities of the time as he is in basic disagreement with the professional code of ethics.

Summary

Current social problems requiring radical changes in our existing social institutions, together with the environmental crisis that will ultimately require a totally new view of the relationship of human beings to the rest of physical nature, serve to create dilemmas for the professional social worker dedicated to interpersonal helping with individuals, families, and small groups. The debate no longer focuses solely on what type of remediation works best, but on whether or not any form of remedial effort is justified when such massive preventive measures are needed. In facing these multiple dilemmas, the professional helping person may find that his value system no longer matches the real-life situations he faces and is of as little help in actually solving problems as the psychodiagnostic nomenclature he long ago discarded as meaningless.

It is clear that much will have to be changed in the field of interpersonal helping if it is to retain its vitality. These needed changes include a greatly expanded view of the professional helping role, a reconceptualization of problem categories, a rethinking of the basic values that underlie interventive strategies, and an integration of the efforts toward individual change with larger ends of the social reformer and the environmentalist. In short, the helping professions have come full circle until they now view themselves as the targets for much needed change and in doing so recognize the considerable strengths of the client as well as the numerous weaknesses.

Such a mandate is clearly staggering in its implications and will require professional social workers, both individually and collectively, to engage in the deepest soul-searching and the most wrenching kinds of change. What ray of hope

will encourage the already overtaxed professional to undertake such introspection and implement such change? Of
course the mere press of events will provide some motivation, but perhaps the greater portion will come from that
long-absent sense of purpose and engagement which awaits
those who at least attempt to find answers to the "Big Questions." Dickens' description of times long past may be most
illustrative of our current state. In a curious sense, these are
"the best of times and the worst of times."

ADDITIONAL SOURCES

Ehrlich, P. *The population bomb*. New York: Ballantine Books,
1968.

Farvar, M. T., & Milton, J. P. *The careless technology*. Garden
City, N.Y.: Natural History Press, 1972.

Fuller, R. B. *Operating manual for spaceship earth*. New York:
Pocket Books, 1972.

Kahn, A. J. The societal context of social work practice. *Social
Work* 10, no. 4 (1965):144–55.

Kindelsperger, K. W. Public welfare: Taxpayer's advocate or recipient's advocate? *Public Welfare* 27, no. 4 (1963):361–65.

McHarg, I. *Design with nature*. Garden City, N.Y.: Natural History Press, 1971.

Mitchell, J. G., & Stellings, C. L. *Ecotactics: The Sierra Club
handbook for environment activists*. New York: Pocket
Books, 1970.

Piven, H. The fragmentation of social work. *Social Casework* 50,
no. 2 (1969):88–94.

Social Welfare and Human Rights. Proceedings of the XIV'th
International Conference on Social Welfare, New York: Columbia, 1969.

Soleri, P. *Arcology: The city in the image of man*. Cambridge:
M.I.T. Press, 1969.

Turnbull, C. M. *The mountain people*. New York: Simon &
Schuster, 1972.

2

Issues in Social Treatment

Having briefly addressed some of the "Big Questions" confronting the field of social welfare, let us turn our attention to several somewhat more circumscribed issues related to social treatment. Several such issues have a direct impact on the nature and delivery of helping services. It is therefore crucial that the social work practitioner understand the ramifications of these issues, as they will probably have a considerable influence on the type of helping service he is able to render.

In what is admittedly an arbitrary choice, four areas will be explored: issues of client advocacy, issues of service definition and delivery, issues of professionalization, and issues of competing technologies of helping. To be sure, these are not the only issues facing social work practitioners, but they are representative of the kinds of issues that touch all professionals involved in interpersonal helping. The point of view taken vis-à-vis these issues represents less a definitive answer in each instance than a statement of the critical elements involved.

Client Advocacy

Broadly speaking, the concept of client advocacy has always
been a key element in social welfare practice. Indeed, the
early history of social welfare is replete with illustrations of
individuals such as Jane Addams, Dorothea Dix, Lillian
Wald, Homer Folks, Julia Lathrop, and numerous others
who added eloquence and strength to the pleas of the poor,
the oppressed, and the troubled.[1] These class actions—undertaken on behalf of women, children, the mentally ill, the
incarcerated, and others—were supplemented by individual
acts of advocacy undertaken on behalf of individual clients.
The helping person was to act as the advocate for his client
in dealing with the host of societal institutions that had an
impact upon him: courts, public schools, hospitals, the
business community. Mary Richmond, the chief architect of
what came to be known as social casework, spoke of the
"friendly visitor" intervening on behalf of a family with a
child having problems in school. (Richmond, 1889, p. 79) and
later wrote of the need to interrelate social movements with
neighborhood case work (Richmond, 1930, p. 287).

Thus advocacy was seen generally as an indirect intervention of the practitioner on behalf of his clients. A worker negotiating a plan of payment for a client's debts or helping
him to secure employment or seeking help for him from other agencies was in effect acting as an advocate for specific
client needs. While this type of advocacy action has always
been an accepted part of social work practice, certain forces
caused it to diminish in importance until recent times.

In the beginning, it was relatively easy for the social

1. For a richly detailed account of early efforts at client advocacy
and social action, see Chambers, (1967).

worker (or "friendly visitor") to determine when a family needed collateral action undertaken on its behalf. The widow being evicted from her tenement, the father in need of hospitalization, the child in trouble with the law were part of the daily experience of the friendly visitor. Since she alone usually constituted the available help and because of her proximity to and familiarity with her client's total life situation, it was natural for her to intercede with the landlord or arrange for medical care or talk with the judge of the juvenile court. Later on, as services became more specialized and as social agencies grew in size and complexity, the opportunity for the worker to intervene on behalf of her client was lessened. Increased case loads meant less time spent with individual clients, less home visiting, and more office appointments. Newly developing specialties within the social welfare field meant that each individual worker was seeing only a piece of the client's total problem. Finally, the standardization of procedures necessitated by these two factors made individual advocacy action on the part of the worker very difficult.

Another factor contributing to the diminution of client advocacy had to do with the orientation to treatment adopted by the social work profession in the late 1920s. Implicit in the psychodynamic model was the assumption that many problems were the result of internal psychological difficulties and therefore the solutions could more easily be found in the fifty-minute therapeutic hour than in any environmental manipulation on the part of the worker. Adjustment became the goal, insight the means.

An early social welfare pioneer, speaking on the effects of the "new psychology" on social welfare practice, related: "To a very large extent they have substituted the concept of personal inadequacy and individual maladjustment for the theory of the responsibility of the environment" (Chambers,

1967, p. 95). It was ironic that at the very time when individual clients most needed representation and advocacy, social work was turning its attention from social concerns to
psychological ones. Chambers observes (1967, p. 96):

> It is probably incorrect to conclude . . . that social work had
> "gone psychiatric in a world which had gone industrial" . . .
> But this movement away from reform toward adjustment, to-
> gether with the growing specialization within social work, the
> increasing bureaucratization of its functions, and its passion
> for professional stature, undoubtedly contributed greatly to
> the quieting of enthusiasm for broad social action.

While generalizations on such a broad subject are at best
tenuous, it is probably fair to say that, in the main, efforts at
client advocacy and social action generally assumed a rather
low profile in social work from the late 1920s to the early
1960s. At that time there began to appear in the literature
and professional conferences an increasing concern for the
civil rights of clients and a renaissance of interest in the
techniques of social action and environmental manipulation
to secure and ensure those rights.

What precipitated this interest in what had been the early
concern of the social work profession? Undoubtedly many
factors were involved: the civil rights movement of the late
1950s and early 1960s; the realization that perhaps many
client problems were less related to individual pathology
than the result of social system "disease"; and, finally, the
increasing awareness on the part of social work professionals that many of the social welfare bureaucracies within
which they operated often had deleterious effects upon individual clients.

Wineman and James explain the problem this way: (1969,
p. 23).

There are prisons with and without walls. A prison is here de-

fined as a social arrangement in which a captor-captive relationship exists. Public assistance, probation, and parole agencies are prisons without walls. All forms of incarceration are
prisons without walls. . . . Captor-captive states are inherently
inimical to the human condition because they jeopardize the
humanity of both captor and captive.

Wineman and James go on to catalog various forms of
dehumanization that may occur in captor-captive settings
(1969, p. 25): physical brutalization psychic humiliation,
sexual traumatization, condoned use of feared indigenous
leaders for behavioral management, chronic exposure to pro-
gramless boredom, indiscriminate mixing of all types of in-
mates with varying pathologies, symptom-squeezing forms
of punishment, enforced work routines in the guise of vocational training, and violations of privacy. The authors voice
a special plea that schools of social work make a concerted
attempt to identify those settings where dehumanizing practices exist and make every attempt to bring sanctions
against them.

Other authors—notably Briar (1967), Specht (1972),
Rein (1970b), and Brager (1968a)—have addressed themselves to the problem of incorporating advocacy stances into
the professional helping role. As we saw earlier, the professional code of ethics and the National Association of Social
Workers' Ad Hoc Committee on Advocacy (1969) would appear to require advocacy actions on behalf of individual
clients where they are deemed indicated. Quoting Briar, the
Ad Hoc Committee on Advocacy describes the caseworker-
advocate who is "his client's supporter, his adviser, his
champion, and if need be, his representative in his dealings
with the court, the police, the social agency" (p. 17).

The committee goes on record as saying that the worker's
obligation to his client takes primacy over his obligations to
the agency when the two interests compete with one another.

If the commitment to an advocacy stance is clear in principle, the implementation of that principle has been anything
but simple and clear-cut. For the most part, professional
schools of social work have not adopted models of client advocacy. One suspects that this recalcitrance is due in part to
the rather limited arsenal of sanctions available to professional schools in initiating advocacy actions. Other problems
in implementing advocacy machinery are more basic: What
is to constitute sufficient grounds for an advocacy procedure? How will dehumanizing practices be distinquished?
Who shall constitute the fact-finding body—the professional
school? the national organization? a committee of professionals and clients? Finally, what will be the legal implications of advocacy actions? Will they in fact become legal
proceedings, and if not, how can they keep from becoming
either star chamber proceedings or meaningless rituals?

These and other problems for the social work practitioner
remain unsolved. Neither the professional schools nor the
professional organizations have spoken definitively on the
matter. Yet the professional is bound by his code of ethics to
protect the rights of his client and to serve his ends above
those of the agency. Most professionals would subscribe to
the code of ethics and agree that their primary allegiance is
to their clients. The problem lies in attempting to define just
how that allegiance becomes operational and what sources of
support are available to the professional in carrying out his
responsibility. If professional schools and associations require the practitioner through his code of ethics to become
an advocate for his client, then it is incumbent upon them to
specify under what conditions and with what support such
action should be taken. The issue of what client advocacy actually means remains a dilemma for the social work practitioner and his professional associations.

Definition and Delivery of Helping Services

The way in which remedial services are defined as well as
the manner in which they are delivered has a great deal to
do with their eventual impact on individual clients. Rein
(1970a) notes that the vendors of helping services (the social welfare agencies) define an individual's problems, the
helping services he requires, and the moral attitudes appropriate to his situation. Rein further speaks of at least four
competing views of the overall network of helping services
(1970a), p. 50):

1. A *production delivery system*, where the customer
   (client) purchases a product (helping services).
2. A *helping process*, aimed chiefly at malfunctioning
   clients or patients.
3. A *humanitarian effort*, in which the practitioner is
   committed to the notion of personal care to victims.
4. A *social control* orientation, which molds the deviant
   into more socially acceptable modes of behavior.

There are two apparent problems with a system so defined. In the first instance, the client as the recipient of the
helping service may reject the label given him by the social
welfare system. This is true in many areas of social welfare,
but is nowhere more clear than in public welfare, where
clients increasingly view themselves as entitled to welfare
payments by right, not out of any paternalistic concept of
charity. Similarly, in the field of mental health, the view of
the malfunctioning client or patient as needing to be "ad-
justed" to his environment is being supplanted by the notion
that environments themselves are often in need of modification. Change efforts, according to this view, should be direct-

ed with equal vigor at "sick" systems and at malfunctioning clients. Clearly one whole thrust of the community mental health movement is to bring the professional helper closer to the client's life space, where he can offer remediation to both individual and environment.

Finally, whole categories of individuals heretofore labeled as clients in need of help reject the notion that because an individual falls within that category he is necessarily malfunctioning. Such categories include homosexuals, drug users, and unwed mothers. Each group has very vocal proponents who would bridle at the notion that anyone who is a homophile or who uses drugs or bears a child out of wedlock is, by definition, malfunctioning. Indeed, they would rightly point out that society's attitude toward each of these groups has changed greatly in recent years. Yet the fact remains that there are whole networks of helping services based on the assumption that such individuals are malfunctioning. These services are now faced with an ever growing number of potential clients who view their condition as less a matter of pathology than a reflection of personal choice and life style.

Another problem lies with the service delivery system that preaches one value stance but practices another, or is based on a mixed value orientation. An example of the former would be the public welfare department, formally charged with aiding society's victims, which considers itself mandated to exercise social controls to force clients into living patterns it considers more acceptable. Some service delivery networks would appear to have a mixed mandate. Szasz (1965), Goffman (1961), and others have written of the various ways in which psychiatric treatment (particularly involving hospitalization) is often used by the courts as a means of social control. Involuntary hospitalization under the guise of treatment becomes the "sentence," often meted out without benefit of due process. Aside from the considerable legal implications of such practice, the ethical questions raised for the social work professional who is put in the position of delivering the helping services to the involuntary client are numerous. Basically, the question comes down to this: Can we truly speak of offering treatment to those who have not requested it and who are coerced into the treatment relationship?

A related problem of definition involves the traditional triad of services: mental health, corrections, and welfare. At the federal and state levels, this trichotomy has been the norm until relatively recently. Typically, each of the three areas has its own large state bureaucracy, each vying with the others for the same limited resources and personnel, often with little coordination of function.

This division of resources, personnel, and function was based on the assumption that there were clearly identifiable groups of clients in need of the services thus categorized. Increasingly, however, it has become clear that clients seldom fit neatly into one of the three categories, but frequently fall between the cracks and have a multiplicity of problems requiring involvement of all three service areas. Another possibility is that the type of service a client eventually receives —and the label that accompanies that service—may be determined more by chance than by a careful differential diagnosis.

Consider, for example, the latency-age child from a multiproblem low-income family who is frequently truant, is involved in petty thievery, has marked learning difficulties in school, and is poorly supervised at home. If this child comes first to the attention of the juvenile court for truancy and minor law violations, he may well be given the label "predelinquent" and eventually go the route of detention facility and state training school. On the other hand, if the case first comes under the scrutiny of the public welfare worker, then "dependent-neglected" will be the label, and the path may

take him to a temporary foster home and from there to a
group care facility. Finally, if the child should fall into the
purview of the community mental health worker, the diagnosis may be "emotionally disturbed" and the plan include a
stay in a residential treatment center followed by a return
home.

If this hypothetical example in any sense approximates
reality for some children or other groups of clients, then
perhaps it is time to reexamine the ways in which we have
traditionally defined services. An umbrella organization encompassing the entire range of specialized services might
make more sense than the current triumvirate of mental
health, corrections, and welfare. More basic even than this
would be a rethinking of the way in which we currently define problems. Can we continue to separate "emotional" and
"delinquent" problem behavior from more fundamental
problems like poverty? Just as the illness model in mental
health has been questioned vigorously in recent years, so
also must the various other ways in which we define problem
behavior be carefully examined. In defining a problem as
"delinquency" or "dependency and neglect," we have gone a
long way toward shaping the form of organization that delivers the helping services, and thus to a certain extent have
markedly influenced the actual helping services that are delivered to the client.

Another issue of service delivery involves the effect of
agency structure on social service practice. A large, central-
ized social welfare bureaucracy made up of countless positions and functions has the effect of breaking up the client's
problem into many small pieces, each handled by a different
specialist. Thus for the multiproblem family there is one
worker to see about financial assistance, another to aid in job
finding, a third for counseling, and so on. A service structure
that might make sense in terms of organizational expediency
and the division of labor hypothesis may make little sense to

the family that does not have such neatly encapsulated and well-defined problems. In fact, the division of labor hypothesis in people-serving organizations, as in others, would appear to be based on the assumption of uniform raw materials undergoing uniform procedures and resulting in uniform end products—an assumption easily questioned when one thinks of the wide range of individual clients, each with a particular complex array of problems requiring special handling.

The answer, of course, would seem to lie in the creation of organizational structures that permit the professional to see more than just a segment of the client's problem and ensure that helping services are oriented more toward client needs than organizational expediency. The correct answer to this problem has so far eluded the social welfare establishment, but will most surely involve decentralization of service units, broadened definition of worker function and indigenous workers, increased flexibility in rules and regulations, and a much more concerted attempt to supply aid to the client at the moment of greatest crisis.

Professionalization

Among the helping professions generally, and particularly in the profession of social work, intensive efforts have been made to achieve the same degree of professional stature and recognition as the older, more firmly established professions. This drive toward professionalization has had both salutary and deleterious effects upon social work practice. These effects continue to have an impact on the delivery of remedial services and are therefore worthy of some examination.

In his 1929 presidential address to the National Conference of Social Work, Porter R. Lee, a distinguished social work educator, gave what many consider an amazingly accurate description of the shift that was occurring within the

field. Lee spoke of social work's shift from a "cause" orientation to a "functional" orientation. In essence, he was describing a shift away from broad social reforms and legislative emphases, which had characterized the earlier progres-
sive era, to an emphasis on social welfare programs designed
to fulfill specific functions. While depicting the essential differences between a causal and functional orientation, he
gave voice to what must have been the thoughts of many of
the old reformers who were dismayed at the lack of social
concern among the newly emerging professional social workers. He said (1929, p. 5):

> . . . Zeal is perhaps the most conspicuous trait in adherents to
> the cause, while intelligence is perhaps most essential in those
> who administer a function. The emblazoned banner and the
> shibboleth for the cause, the program and the manual for the
> function; devoted sacrifice and the flaming spirit for the cause,
> fidelity, standards and methods for the function; an embattled
> host for the cause, an efficient personnel for the function.

In a concise analysis of the period, Chambers (1967, pp.
88–106) describes the move toward professionalization.

> Insofar as social workers focused upon new methods and tech-
> niques, especially in casework and in the new and exciting
> field of psychiatry, their attention was concentrated on proce-
> dure and the adjustment of the individual to his environment,
> rather than on the transformation of the social environment
> within which the individual lived.

The new profession required specialization, which would
have the effect of narrowing the field of vision for all but a
few discerning social workers. "Enthusiasm for reform,"
Chambers notes, "was not high among the qualities making
for success in research, theoretical or applied." Some costs

in this new concern for professionalization were to be expected (1967, p. 93):

> For many social workers the new path toward social betterment had become scientific and constructive rather than emotional and charitable. A kind of professional myopia, then, was often the consequence of specialization. . . . social workers had come to concern themselves with means rather than ends.

For the many professional specializations born in this period—psychiatric social work, medical social work, family social work, child welfare work—great emphasis was placed on explaining their particular roles and functions in relation to other professions. One observer concluded from an analysis of the papers of the Association of Medical Social Workers during the 1930s that their singular concern, pursued with an apparent unawareness of the economic depression of the period, appeared to be the fact that physicians failed to understand their role in the hospital.

The focus inward, the concern with standards of professional practice and admission into the professional association, had beneficial effects as well. The growth of graduate professional social work education, the establishment of the Academy of Certified Social Workers (ACSW), and the move toward professional licensing for social work practitioners have all been steps forward. In addition, refinements in technique have undoubtedly raised the level of practice in social work. But one can question—as many have—whether or not the ill effects of the drive for professional status have outweighed the good. The narrowness of vision that often accompanies specialization of function, the tendency away from a concern for social reform, and the mistaken belief that professionals alone possess the requisite skills for interpersonal helping have all, to one degree or another, been by-products of social work's push for professional status. Unfortunately, the movement toward increasing specialization of worker function, coupled with the effects on service delivery of large-scale social welfare bureaucracies, tended to remove the professional a step further from the social and emotional problems of the client he was serving.

In the child welfare field in the late 1920s, for example, the social worker's role in the child caring institution was much more closely aligned with that of the consulting psychiatrist and psychologist than with the group life personnel (Whittaker, 1971). Social workers in children's institutions were to collect social histories, work with families, and sometimes counsel individual children, but working in the group living situation and consulting with the child care staff on daily problems of group living were seldom seen as any function of theirs. One suspects that social workers viewed themselves as having more to gain in prestige by relating upwardly to the medical profession than downward toward the housemother and child care worker. Recent studies, however (Polsky, 1962; Trieschman, Whittaker, & Brendtro, 1969), have suggested putting the professional person much closer to "where the action is" in the child care institution: in the group living situation.

Recent trends in social work have added new dimensions to the whole drive toward professionalization. The growth of undergraduate social work programs, the acceptance of B.A. social workers as full voting members in the National Association of Social Workers, the trend toward the use of indigenous workers and nonprofessional personnel, and the renewed interest in broad social action and reform have changed considerably the goal of a profession singularly dedicated to the perfection of techniques for interpersonal helping delivered exclusively by graduate trained professional social workers. Another factor involved in social work's reexamination of its basic goals and purposes has been the proliferation of other professional groups that have intruded on what has traditionally been the territory of social work. Notable among these are urban planners, community development specialists, and family life educators. These, together with the whole host of specialists in the community mental health and neighborhood organization and health organizations generated by the government programs of the early 1960s, have made many both within and without the profession of social work wonder just what its function will be in the future.[2]

Social work as a profession has progressed greatly since Porter Lee's "cause and function" speech, yet today it finds itself in far stronger currents that those of the 1920s. Struggling to find its proper place in the broader field of social welfare, social work is torn between those who argue for increased emphasis on professionalization, improvement of techniques, and elevation of standards and those who argue for a frontal assault on the root causes of society's most blatant problems: poverty, inequality, and urban blight. It is curious to note that if the position of the former could currently be characterized as traditionalist, then the latter must certainly hark back to an even earlier time in social work when cause, not function, was the guiding principle and, to use Lee's words, "zeal and enthusiasm" for social change ruled, rather than "standards" and "method" for the social program. What at first appears the most radical stance for the profession of social work today—advocacy of broad social action and legislative reform—may in fact be the most traditional of positions. One hopes that the ultimate direction chosen by the profession will include the best of both

2. For a sociological analysis of social work's concern with professionalization, see Toren (1969).

approaches, for cause and function are integrally related, and effective solutions of social problems will require attention to both.

Competing Technologies of Interpersonal Helping

From the beginning, practitioners of social work have disagreed about the most efficacious methods of dealing with the social and emotional problems of their clients. The early efforts of the friendly visitors consisted largely of offering suggestions on homemaking, good nutrition, and simple health measures. These visitors, often volunteers, for the most part viewed the problems of the poor as environmentally determined. The remedy, or treatment, often consisted of "putting the family out of immediate need" and making them "permanently self supporting" (Richmond, 1899, p. 191).

For an early practitioner-writer like Mary Richmond (1917, 1930) the route to problem-solving lay in a carefully executed "social diagnosis" or inventory of the client's life situation. From this accumulation of facts would flow a plan of treatment. The emphasis continued to be on social problems that yielded to various forms of environmental manipulation: the widowed mother in need of support, the deserted family, the neglected child, the homeless man. For Richmond, social treatment consisted of "those processes which develop personality through adjustment consciously effected, individual by individual, between men and their social environment" (1922, p. 98). Briar (1971, p. 1239) notes that this rather imprecise definition would later be interpreted in terms more psychological than sociological.

With the growth of professional education for social work, the decline of the friendly visitor in favor of the paid caseworker, and the shift in emphasis from cause to function, social work practice found itself passing into what one writer called "a psychological phase" (Jarret, 1918, p.290). This corresponded with the flowering of the mental hygiene movement, originated by such pioneers as Adolf Meyer, Henry Goddard, William Healy, Augusta Bronner, Douglas Thom, and Richard Cabot, and nurtured by the importation of the newly developed psychology of Freud. What the mental hygiene movement and in particular Freudian or psychodynamic psychology offered the fledgling profession of social work was an entire new organization and technology for treatment. Problems were now seen as the results of internal psychological conflicts more than of social conditions. Individual clients were helped to "adjust" to society and work out problems in the context of an insight-oriented therapeutic interview session. The mental hygiene movement also contained a ready-made structure for the new professional social worker to operate within: the psychiatric team. Basking in the glow of reflected status from the psychiatrists and clinical psychologists, the psychiatric social workers became, as one writer notes, the Brahmins of the profession (Briar, 1971).

If the new movement away from social concerns and legislative reform in favor of a more psychologically oriented approach to problems was a bitter pill for many of the old reformers to swallow, the trend nevertheless continued in the twenties. In fact, the major argument over the succeeding decades had more to do with which particular school of psychological thought the social caseworker identified with rather than whether or not a psychological orientation to client problems was valid.[3]

Over the last two decades one observes in social treatment a kind of pendulum effect: one method of treatment reigns

3. For an account of the argument between the functional school and the diagnostic school, see Briar (1971, pp. 1239–40), and Lubove (1965, pp. 115–16.

supreme for a period, only to be supplanted by another. In the absence of any overall conceptual framework for interpersonal helping within social work, the debate often assumed a kind of either/or quality, with proponents of a particular method of treatment taking an all-or-nothing stand.

Currently, we are witnessing such debate in two areas: family treatment and behavioral modification. The techniques proposed by Satir, Ackerman, and others for treating the family as a unit and conceiving of the problems of any of its members as family problems have achieved widespread acceptance in the field. Many agencies practice family treatment almost exclusively, often patterned after the model of a particular theoretician. Other modes of helping are eschewed in favor of the unitary approach. In the area of behavioral modification, the lines of debate are even more sharply drawn between those who view the eradication of problem behavior as paramount and those who stress aiding the client to develop insight and awareness. Edwin J. Thomas and his associates at the University of Michigan have probably accomplished more in translating the principles of social learning theory for social work practice than any other group of scholars. Thomas views his approach as "sociobehavioral"—that is, one that makes use of techniques derived from behavior therapy, behavior modification, and other areas of behavioral science (Thomas, 1971, p. 1228).

Within the profession, the debate over the use of behavioral techniques has taken essentially two directions: an *ideological* argument, which questions the very use of such techniques within the profession's ethical framework, and a *technological* argument, which questions the efficacy of behavioral techniques and the validity of the research that supports them. Often these two arguments become hopelessly confused. The debate in professional literature indicates how far we are from a unified theory of interpersonal helping.[4]

Ironically, few would claim that any particular method of treatment could encompass the wide range of clients' social and emotional problems. The great challenge is to develop a system that ensures a good fit between the technology of interpersonal helping and client problems. This means, for the theoretician and the practitioner, a more open and less ideological stance regarding treatment; less fervor to declare, *a priori*, universal applicability for their technology and more concerted effort to see when and where it works best. The recent past history of interpersonal helping in social work shows the folly of subscribing uncritically to one particular theoretical orientation: psychodynamic psychology. At a point in time when new and promising methods of helping —such as behavior modification—appear on the horizon, we would do well as a profession to move critically and incrementally. Otherwise, we run the risk of merely substituting one set of dogmatic beliefs for another.

Summary

It is clear that issues of client advocacy, service delivery, professionalization, and competing technologies of interpersonal helping are far from any permanent resolution. Together with the broader issues of remediation versus environmental protection, they reflect the changing world that the social work practitioner will inhabit for some time to come. Given this fact, what sort of stance toward interpersonal helping will best serve the social work professional and, more important, will best serve his clients? The answer

4. See Bruck (1968), Carter & Stuart (1970), Morrow & Gochros (1970), and Franks (1969).

to that complex question is that the social treatment approach to interpersonal helping holds the most promise for the social work practitioner. With that in mind, let us turn now to an analysis of exactly what is meant by social treatment.

ADDITIONAL SOURCES

Alexander, L. B. Social work's Freudian deluge: Myth or reality? *Social Service Review* 46, no. 4 (1972):517–39.

Fischer, J. A framework for the analysis and comparison of clinical theories of induced change. *Social Service Review* 45, no. 4 (1971):440–55.

Miller, H. Social work in the black ghetto: The new colonialism. *Social Work* 14, no. 3 (1969):65–76.

Piliavin, I. Restructuring the provision of social services. *Social Work* 13, no. 1 (1968):34–42.

Richmond, M. *Social diagnosis.* New York: Russell Sage Foundation, 1917.

Scott, W. R. Professional employees in a bureaucratic structure: Social work. In *The semi-professions and their organization,* ed. A. Etzioni. New York: Free Press, Macmillan, 1969.

Shattuck, G., & Martin, J. New professional work roles and their integration into a social agency structure. *Social Work* 14, no. 4 (1969):13–21.

Sobey, F. *Implications for the seventies: The nonprofessional revolution in mental health.* New York: Columbia University Press, 1970.

Stuart, R. B. Research in social work: Social casework and social group work. In *Encyclopedia of social work* 2:1106–1122. New York: National Association of Social Workers, 1971.

Thurz, D. The arsenal of social action strategies: Options for social workers. *Social Work* 16, no. 1 (1971):27–35.

Van Til, J., & Van Til, S. B. Citizen participation in social policy: The end of the cycle? *Social Problems* 17, no. 3 (1970):313–23.

3

Social Treatment:
An Introduction

Social Work Practice: A Total View

Broadly speaking, social treatment includes all those remedial efforts directed at the resolution of individual problems. These include interpersonal and emotional difficulties as well as situational problems. Social treatment or remedial service covers all manner of direct treatment methods—individual and family counseling, group treatment—as well as collateral actions on behalf of clients.

To understand social treatment properly, one must understand its position in the broader field of social work practice. Traditionally the major divisions within social work practice have distinguished between change efforts directed at macro systems (organizations, communities, societies) and those directed at micro systems (individuals, families, small groups). Social planning, community organization, and community development exemplify macro or large-scale modes of intervention; individual casework, family treatment, and group treatment represent micro or small-scale modes of intervention. Administration and research are additional areas of social work practice.

The view of social treatment advanced here is based on the assumption that a distinction between macro and micro interventions is valid. While the two are not altogether mutually exclusive, one can distinguish between macro and micro intervention in the areas of client systems, goals, knowledge base, and strategies of change.

The client system for macro intervention may be a neighborhood, an organization (a county welfare department, for example), an entire community, or even a total society. The client system in micro intervention is always an individual, family, or small group.

Given these differences in client systems, it follows that the goals of macro and micro interventions will differ. The goals of macro intervention include changes within organizations, communities, and societies, while micro intervention aims at enhancing social functioning or alleviation of social problems for a particular individual, family, or small group.

There are also differences in the knowledge base for macro and micro interventions. Though there is clearly some overlap, macro intervention relies heavily on theories of "big system" change (formal organization theory, community theory) drawn from sociology, economics, and political science. Micro intervention tends to be based on theories of individual change drawn from psychology, small group sociology, and human development. As we shall see in Chapter 6, the social treatment practitioner is also interested in theories of organizational change, but for somewhat different reasons than the community organizer or organizational development specialist.

Finally, we can distinguish differences in the strategies of macro and micro interventions. Macro intervention uses social action strategies, lobbying, coordination of functions, and canvassing; micro intervention typically relies on more circumscribed strategies directed at individual change: direct counseling, individual advocacy actions, and crisis intervention. Figure 3.1 may help to illustrate the distinctions between macro and micro intervention.

	Macro Intervention	Micro Intervention
Client System	Neighborhood Formal organization Community Society	Individual Family Small group
Goals	Changes within organizations, communities, societies	Enhanced social functioning; alleviation of a social problems for an individual, family, or small group.
Knowledge Base	"Big system" change theories drawn from: Sociology Economics Political science Industrial relations	Personal change theories drawn from: Developmental psychology Human development

In Common:
Small Group Sociology
Communications Theory

Change Strategies	Community organizing Social action Lobbying Canvassing Coordination Community analysis	Direct counseling Crisis intervention Advocacy actions on behalf of individual clients

FIGURE 3.1 *Distinctions between macro and micro interventions.*

In essence, what is suggested is a two-track view of social work practice, consisting of macro intervention directed at changes within neighborhoods, formal organizations, communities, and societies and micro intervention directed at changes within individuals, families, and small groups. In actual practice, this division may be anything but precise. An individual professional may be charged with responsibilities in both areas, and social welfare agencies often combine macro and micro interventions within their purview. Social

treatment encompasses only that portion of social work
practice directed at changes within individuals, families,
and small groups. This said, it is well to keep in mind that
change efforts directed at larger systems (organizations,
communities, societies) are also needed for the effective remediation of social problems.

Interpersonal Helping in Social Work

Traditionally, social work practice with individuals, families, and small groups has been divided into social casework
and social group work. Social casework evolved from the individual family work of the friendly visitors in the charity
organizations. Its later development as a methodological specialization within the field of social work was characterized
by a movement from a sociological to a psychological orientation. The view of the client's problems and the strategies
and techniques of remediation increasingly became more
concerned with changes within the client than with changes
in his environment. Along with this trend went another toward the perfection of the means of treatment: diagnosis,
interviewing skills, problem-solving work, observation, and
process recording of client interviews. The result was the
creation of a strong social casework method both in social
work education and in practice. This method was not of a
single hue. Each of its chief theoreticians focused on specific
processes of helping with individuals and families, so that
while particular emphases of treatment or theoretical orientation changed from theoretician to theoretician, the idea of
a specific method of social casework nevertheless remained
constant.[1]

1. No attempt will be made here to identify the major theories of
social casework or social group work and their authors. See the *En-*

Social group work developed as a separate methodological specialization within social work; its roots were in the social settlement movement and its early focus was on the development of citizenship and small group participation. Later there was a decided shift among some social group workers toward a treatment or remedial orientation. Again, despite differences in orientation among group work theoreticians, in the main their efforts were directed at the development of a method of social group work.

Until relatively recently, there was little crossover between the methods of social casework and social group work. Schools of social welfare and social work usually required students to major in one or the other method, and even the professional's primary identification was in terms of his method's specialty: "social caseworker," "social group worker." A separate professional literature existed for each method, and until 1955 separate professional organizations existed for each.[2]

This trend toward separation was viewed by many within the field of social work as counterproductive, since it tended to isolate aspects of interpersonal helping which in reality constituted a unified whole. In working with families, for example, social caseworkers found that they needed to know more about group process for purposes of treatment. Similarly, social group workers needed to know much more about techniques of individual interviewing, since their interventions were not limited to group techniques. It was also, very simply, a matter of choice: few professionals wished to limit their practice exclusively to individuals and families or to small groups.

---

cyclopedia of Social Work for a summary of several models of social casework and social group work practice.

2. See Witte (1971).

In the last decade or so there has been considerable interest expressed in the social work generalist: one trained in both social casework and social group work. Consequently many professional schools of social work and social welfare now offer combined sequences in social casework and social group work. The trend would appear to be away from the use of method specialization in defining social work education and practice and toward integrating the best of both social casework and social group work into a single method framework. This framework is alternately called generic practice, combined practice, and social treatment.

Social Treatment

Siporin (1970) explores the origin of the social treatment approach within social work, calling it a "new-old helping method." He defines social treatment as a "general method for helping individuals and family groups cope with their social problems and improve their social functioning," and he traces the origin of the term in early social welfare practice and rightly points out its importance for a theoretician like Richmond, who saw it as the counterpart to social diagnosis. Siporin observes how the practitioners of social treatment "grew out of tune" with their more psychologically oriented colleagues. Social treatment was replaced by psychological treatment.

Today the emphasis on the psychological view of remedial practice is gradually giving way to a renewed emphasis on the social aspects of interpersonal helping. Human beings are viewed in the complex web of social relationships that surround them and the concept of treatment is once again broadened to include situational assistance. In effect, this emphasis would put the "social" back into social work practice. To accommodate to this trend, a new definition of social treatment is needed.

Definition of Social Treatment

Social treatment is an approach to interpersonal helping which utilizes direct and indirect strategies of intervention to aid individuals, families, and small groups in improving social functoning and coping with social problems.

What are the key elements in this definition?

"Approach": This definition views social treatment as an approach to interpersonal helping rather than as a particular method or mode of treatment. An "approach" provides a broad enough conceptual umbrella to cover any particular method of interpersonal helping or mode of treatment. The assumption is that the profession of social work, having expressed considerable dissatisfaction with one-method orientation (social casework, social group work), would be ill advised to replace it with another—that is, simply an integration of what was formerly called casework and group work. The great danger in using a particular method orientation to treatment is twofold:

1. It tends to lessen the possibility that new theories and technologies of helping will be utilized. In short, it tends to work against innovation in practice. The method becomes the practitioner's primary orientation and often defines his professional identity as well: social caseworker, social group worker. New approaches to interpersonal helping may be rejected without sufficient trial because it is determined *a priori* that they are "not social casework." Many in social work education and practice have pointed out the inadequacies of the present method orientation to practice; it would seem, therefore, to be folly to substitute another (albeit combined) method orientation for what is now felt to be inadequate. Social casework—a method of helping—has been the major force in social work practice over the last four dec-

ades. What is the record of this method vis-a-vis the incorpo-
ration of new change technologies and other innovations in
practice? If the answer is "not very good," what would lead
one to believe that more could be expected from another
method orientation to practice?

2. A primary allegiance to method makes it possible for
one to fall into the trap of fitting the client and his social
problem to the method of helping rather than vice versa. In
essence, if method is a given, then to a certain extent the
course of treatment for a given client is predetermined. The
approach to the client should begin with an analysis of the
problem *as he is experiencing it*. From this should flow the
treatment or plan of intervention.

In sum, social work practice would appear to be in need of
an approach to *all* of interpersonal helping: a conceptual
framework within which practitioners can develop intelligent criteria to allow for evaluation of the countless modes
of treatment and strategies of intervention for the purpose
of choosing the particular combination of help that best fits
the client's problem. The social treatment approach to interpersonal helping would appear to hold the most promise in
this regard.

"Interpersonal helping": Social treatment is concerned
with helping individuals, families, and small groups. Thus
its focus is distinct from community organization, social
planning, and other "big system" change approaches. Interpersonal helping is not restricted to psychotherapeutic help,
but includes the broad spectrum of activities that the worker
may undertake directly with, or indirectly on behalf of, his
client.

"Direct and indirect strategies of intervention": Social
treatment assumes that not all helping will transpire in a direct, face-to-face encounter between client and worker.
Direct intervention or helping, however, does constitute a
major portion of the worker's actual involvement with the cli-

ent. Meeting with a client in a counseling session, conducting a cottage meeting in a children's residential treatment center, interviewing a family—all these are examples of direct intervention.

Of equal importance is the whole range of helping activities that the worker undertakes indirectly on behalf of his client. Negotiating the maze of a welfare bureaucracy for a client in need of assistance, intervening with the school system on behalf of a family with a problem child, referring the client to other social agencies for specialized kinds of help— all these are indirect strategies of intervention.

"Social functioning and social problems": The social problem as related by the client is the starting point for social treatment. Problems are not narrowly considered as simply emotional, but as the result of the complex interplay between the individual and his environment. The *person* with all of his individual characteristics, the *social problem* with its particular ramifications, and the *social situation* with all of its complexities are considered to be in a constant state of interaction and interdependence.[3] The worker weighs all of these elements in assisting the client to arrive at a plan of intervention. Figure 3.2 illustrates the definition graphically.

The worker makes conscious use of himself in a relationship with the client (individual, family, small group) and exercises his professional judgment while recognizing his own personal values as well as those of the client in order to arrive at a plan of intervention based on the social problem as experienced by the client. His professional help may occur in a direct encounter with the client or indirectly on his behalf as the professional works through an informal organization, formal organization, or community to secure needed

3. Perlman (1957, 1971a) and Siporin (1970), among others, have described the interdependence of the person-problem-situation triad.

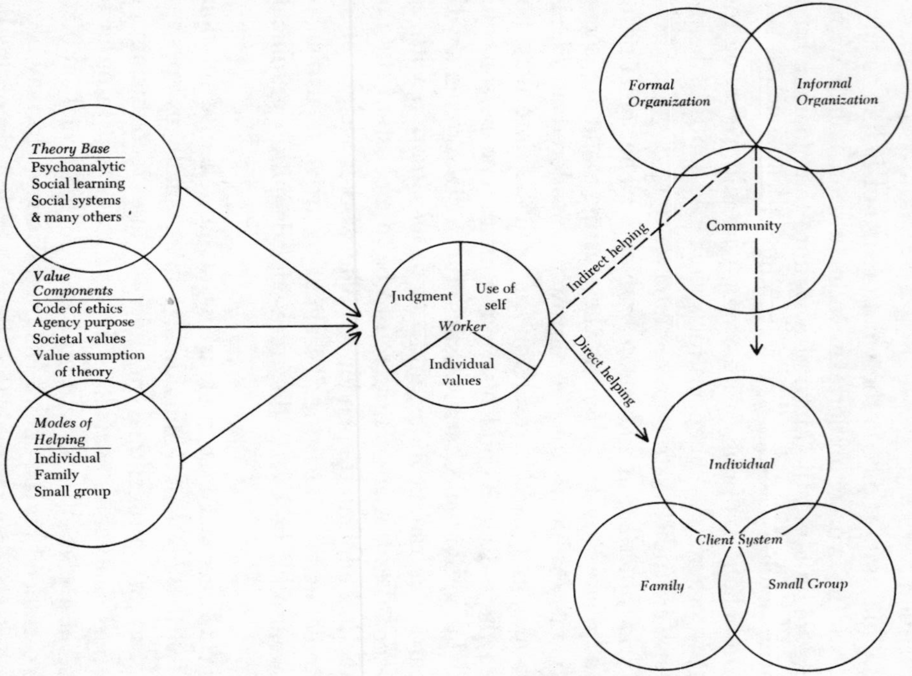
Theory Base
Psychoanalytic
Social learning
Social systems
& many others
Value Components
Code of ethics
Agency purpose
Societal values
Value assumption of theory
Modes of Helping
Individual
Family
Small group
Judgment
Use of self
Worker
Individual values
Indirect helping
Direct helping
Formal Organization
Informal Organization
Community
Individual
Client System
Family
Small Group

FIGURE 3.2 *Social treatment: a process view*

services for his client. The worker's arsenal of helping strategies is informed by a broadly eclectic theory base and may include any one of a number of modes of helping with individuals, families, and small groups. Finally, the worker's help is bounded by his allegiance to a professional code of ethics, by adherence to the purposes of the social agency that employs him, by the values of the larger society, and by the value assumptions of the theory that underlies this interventive strategy.

At each stage of the process of social treatment, worker and client are bound in a joint relationship, with the client bringing his strengths to the situation as well as the view of the social problem on which the intervention is going to be based. For his part, the worker brings his professional expertise and skill in relationship to the encounter; he may help to identify and clarify the problems experienced by the client, suggest a plan of treatment, engage the client in direct helping procedures, and undertake collateral helping of an indirect nature on the client's behalf. At no time does the worker seek to impose his view on the client (though he often makes known his view of what is wrong), and he continually seeks full and active engagement on the part of the client at all phases of the helping process.

Underlying this conception of social treatment is a view of the client freely seeking to engage in the helping relationship and the worker making contractual arrangements for his helping services. Hence the notion of an involuntary client would be incompatible with a social treatment relationship. The one exception might lie with the client in an involuntary setting (correctional facility or possibly mental hospital) who *freely chooses* to participate in the social treatment relationship, assuming all of the other conditions of the joint working relationship are met. Clearly there may be some exceptions to this general rule, as in the case of a severely disturbed child or an adult who is presently incapable of making a choice about entering into a joint working relationship for purposes of treatment. Few would consider depriving the autistic child or the severely regressed schizophrenic adult from needed help on the grounds that he had not formally requested it. On the other hand, the client's free commitment should be sought as soon as he is capable of giving it.

This, then, is a broad overview of the social treatment process. Each of the various parts, of course, requires much more detailed examination. First let us examine exactly what is meant by "professional helping" (as distinguished from any other kind of help) and identify some of the prominent roles that the professional plays in the social treatment approach.

Professional Helping

What is it that distinquishes professional helping from the over-the-back-fence variety of lay helping? Surely no one would suggest that interpersonal helping rendered by a professional is, in and of itself, superior to that offered by a lay person. But it is true that the client with a problem in social functioning should expect a certain quality to professional helping which includes a number of specific attributes.

First is an ability on the part of the professional helper to determine with the client exactly what the problem is. Often clients need real help in sorting out the strands of the web of social problems in which they are caught and establishing some hierarchy of need. This sort of help requires a thorough grounding in human growth and development and a high level of skill in the techniques of social diagnosis. The professional should know, for example, what facts to gather in a social history and how to relate those facts to the client's present life situation in such a way as to shed light on puzzling behavior. His practice skill should alert him to certain indicators in the client's behavior which yield valuable clues to the ultimate social diagnosis. While it is true that the beginning point for social treatment is the social problem as experienced by the client, it is equally true that many clients find it most difficult to specify their problems in terms that lend themselves to remediation. Finally, the professional is knowledgeable about the host of other resources that are available to him in identifying the problem.

The second distinguishing feature of professional helping is knowledge of the point at which the client's social problem should be engaged. At what system level should the worker direct his professional intervention? Often he will be operating on several different levels at the same time, through direct engagement of the client in a treatment relationship and by intervening indirectly on the client's behalf in an advocacy action. For example, should he focus on the individual child experiencing problems in school? On his teachers? On his family? Or on some combination of the them?

One problem the worker must resolve early is a decision as to who his client is. Often the worker and the client disagree about this. A family may view the cause of the trouble as a particular child, when in reality it is a family problem to which all members contribute; a spouse may see the problem in the marital relationship as stemming exclusively from his partner and refuse to enter into conjoint family treatment. These and related questions require special skills on the part of the worker to know exactly where to engage the problem early in the social treatment relationship.

Finally, it is assumed that the professional helping person has special knowledge and skill in determining how to attack the problem. What modes of intervention, what strategies and techniques of interpersonal helping will best fit the particular array of social problems experienced by the client? It is in this sense that the worker becomes a broker of services,

providing (through his own resources, as well as through referral) a variety of forms of help to clients with diverse
problems. A high level of quality and consistency in the
what, where, and how of social treatment distinquishes professional interpersonal helping from that offered by lay persons.

Worker Roles

In the course of the social treatment relationship with a particular client, the professional may operate within the
framework of a number of complementary roles, the most
prominent of which are the treatment agent, the advocate-
ombudsman, the teacher-counselor, and the broker of services and resources.

TREATMENT AGENT

Much of what the worker does may involve a direct treatment relationship with the client. Whatever the particular
mode of treatment (individual, family, or small group) or
the particular techniques employed (behavioral therapy,
psychotherapy, conjoint family therapy), the worker uses
his practice skill to influence those aspects of the client's social problem that will yield to direct treatment. Often the
worker uses supportive techniques to aid his client through a
particularly trying life situation. He may also use clarification and confrontation to home in on a particular form of
problem behavior.

The treatment agent role may be carried out in a treatment session in the worker's office or in the client's own life
milieu. The worker carrying on a family therapy session in a
client's home or meeting with a delinquent gang on the
street or talking with a troubled child on the school play-
ground is exercising his treatment agent role *in situ*.

Many have argued that social work professionals have become overly committed to the treatment agent role and have focused too much on the fifty-minute casework hour. This criticism is valid to some degree, and is partly explained by a rather widespread adherence to psychoanalytically oriented treatment, which emphasizes unconscious processes and the development of insight and more generally characterizes client problems as psychological rather than social in nature. Thus developed the stereotype of the psychiatric caseworker whose narrow clinical focus did not permit active intervention in the client's social environment and whose treatment arsenal consisted of psychoanalytically oriented supportive listening techniques.

Like most stereotypes, this one tends to break down upon close examination. If some practitioners have been narrowly clinically focused, others have taken full cognizance of the client's social milieu and developed strategies for operating within it. Perlman (1957), p. 62) speaks of the importance of knowing the resources available to a client in need and helping him to mobilize himself to make full use of them. Hollis (1964, pp. 76–78) stresses the importance of environmental work on behalf of clients and decries the fact that environmental intervention has come to assume a kind of left-handed or second-best quality. Similarly, in the area of social group work, Vinter (1967, pp. 110–23) has stressed the importance of using resources outside of the treatment group for the purpose of aiding individual clients. In the view of at least some of the primary theoreticians of social work practice, treatment is not something that occurs exclusively within the context of an office interview in a fifty-minute therapy session.

Once this has been acknowledged, however, it is probably fair to say that the treatment agent role has indeed been overemphasized in the last few decades, to the detriment of other worker functions, particularly client advocacy. Two things would appear to be needed to correct this situation.

First, equal prominence should be accorded the other roles fulfilled by social work practitioners and focus should be shifted from an exclusively clinical treatment orientation. Second, for that portion of the worker's time that he does fulfill his role as treatment agent, methods of treatment should be developed that are capable of lending themselves to comprehensive evaluation. In short, we need methods of treatment that are effective and can be proven so empirically.

ADVOCATE-OMBUDSMAN

The professional acts as the advocate or ombudsman for his client in championing his civil rights, or in helping him to negotiate the complex rules and regulations of a bureaucracy. Here the concept of advocate is broadened to include almost anything the worker does indirectly on behalf of his client. This might include helping him to obtain legal services when necessary; aiding him in seeking or holding employment; helping him to negotiate a social welfare bureaucracy such as the court system, the public school system, or the public welfare department; or initiating formal advocacy procedures on his behalf when his civil rights or civil liberties are endangered, as when he is subjected to dehumanizing practices.

The advocate-ombudsman role is co-equal in importance to the treatment agent role, and, as we have seen, is a traditional one for the social work practitioner. When many critics in the last decade or so were talking about "narrowly focused clinicians" and the need for more "socially conscious" treatment agents, it was the neglect of this role that they were referring to. In sum, the advocate-ombudsman role is integral to the practice of interpersonal helping in social work; it is not only sanctioned but required by the professional code of ethics and has its roots deep in the early traditions of social welfare.

TEACHER-COUNSELOR

The distinctions between this particular role and that of treatment agent are not always sharply defined. More and more, however, the social work practitioner acts in the role of teacher or educational counselor to his clients. The professional who offers a brief course for parents on parental competence, the worker who counsels his client about educational opportunities in the community, and the worker who offers a training seminar for paraprofessionals on techniques of crisis intervention with troubled families are all acting in the role of teacher-counselor. Overlap occurs with the treatment agent role when the worker models a desired behavior for the client or teaches him some alternate social behaviors to replace his maladaptive antisocial repertoire.

It is interesting to note the gradual blurring of these two roles at a point in time when the illness model of treatment is losing ground to a more learning-oriented approach to problems for which the remediation is educational. Thus the client becomes the student, the worker becomes the teacher, and the treatment encounter becomes an educational relationship. The growth in recent years of such educational approaches to human problems testifies to the popularity of this view of interpersonal helping (Patterson, 1971; Patterson & Gullion, 1968; Gordon, 1970).

It is conceivable that social work practitioners will be exercising this role much more frequently in the future. Even in terms of social acceptance, the teacher-student relationship would appear to have a much more positive valence than the therapist-patient or worker-client relationship. When this approach is used, the client becomes a customer who seeks to purchase a service in a particular area—parental effectiveness or improved marital relations or communication skills or social relationships—from a teacher (worker) who can offer expertise in that particular area. Thus parents who are experiencing disharmony in their marital relationship find themselves in a small class of individuals with similar difficulties who come together to learn better ways of relating to one another.

BROKER OF SERVICES AND RESOURCES

In this final role, the professional acts as a broker or dispenser of helping services ranging from direct treatment to advocacy procedures and teaching-counseling functions. Whether or not he actually offers the service himself, the worker becomes a kind of clearinghouse of information where the client may learn where the particular kind of interpersonal helping he requires may be found in the community. The worker must have a clear and up-to-date picture of the network of helping services that exist in the community, and he must know how to secure those services for his client when and if they are necessary. His function may be an indirect one and consist of a referral to another agency or professional, or the needed service may lie within his own repertoire of practice skill. Even when the needed service clearly falls outside of the worker's skill or the agency's purpose, he does everything possible to see that the client is linked up with the appropriate sources of aid.

Summary

Interpersonal helping has been viewed in the total context of social work practice and differences have been shown between macro and micro interventions with respect to client system, knowledge base, goals, and change strategies. The inadequacy of a method approach—social casework or social group work—as a conceptual framework for interpersonal helping in social work has been suggested. Social treatment has been offered as an alternate framework for interpersonal helping—a framework that stresses (*a*) an eclectic approach to theories and modes of interpersonal helping, *(b)* a focus on the social problem as experienced by the client as the beginning point of intervention (rather than a preconceived methodological approach), and *(c)* equal emphasis on what the professional does indirectly on behalf of his client and what he accomplishes with him directly.

Finally, professional helping has been distinguished from lay helping with respect to the professional's considerable expertise in determining what the problem is, deciding where to engage it, and how. Additionally, the worker roles of treatment agent, advocate-ombudsman, teacher-counselor, and broker of services and resources were identified. Having established this conceptual framework for interpersonal helping, let us now turn to some of the major bodies of theory that form the foundation for social treatment practice.

ADDITIONAL SOURCES

Berleman, W. C. Mary Richmond's *Social diagnosis* in retrospect. *Social Casework* 49, no. 7 (1968):395–403.

Gelfand, B. Emerging trends in social treatment. *Social Casework* 53, no. 3 (1972):156–63.

Gilbert, N. Neighborhood coordinator: Advocate or middleman? *Social Service Review* 43, no. 12 (1969):136–44.

McCormick, M. J. Social advocacy: A new dimension in social work. *Social Casework* 51, no. 1 (1970):3–11.

Meyer, C. H. Purposes and boundaries—Casework fifty years later. *Social Casework*. 54, no. 5, (1973), 268–276.

Renner, J., & Renner, V. Shall we be therapists or educators? *Canada's Mental Health* 21, no. 1 (1973):3–11.

Toward a new social service system. *Child Welfare* 50, no. 8 (1971):448–60.

4

Theoretical Bases of Social Treatment

It is essential for the practitioner of social treatment to have some understanding of the theories that underlie his practice. This is so not only because it is from theory that strategies of treatment are derived, but also because implicit in each theory is a value orientation and view of man which may have a profound effect on the nature of the helping service delivered by the professional. Some would ague that theories of human behavior are in themselves nonvaluative, and that it is only in their application that value questions arise. Therefore, the practitioner need only weigh the strategies of social treatment which the theory suggests against the ethical constraints of his profession and make a judgment as to their appropriateness.[1] Two things are wrong with this argument.

First, while it is certainly true that value questions arise in the application of theory, it is equally true that inherent

1. Thomas (1967, p. 18; 1968, pp. 25–26) and Briar (1968, p. 11) would appear to take the position that knowledge—in this instance from behavioral theory—is neutral and that only in its application do value questions arise.

in the theories themselves are value stances that influence the relationship between professional helper and client. Far from being value-free, theories of human behavior are replete with assumptions about the way human beings (individually and collectively) are constituted, how they grow and develop and change. When the psychoanalyst views the patient on the couch before him, not only does he have some notions of what psychoanalytic theory requires him to do in treatment, but his judgment is also influenced by a view of man implicit in that theory. Similarly, the behavioral therapist engaging his client in a therapeutic encounter is informed in his judgment not solely by the prescriptions of the learning theory, but also by certain assumptions about the nature of man and the preeminence of behavior which underlie the theory.

Clearly it is important that the practitioner of social treatment give at least cursory examination to the particular assumptions, value stances, and views of man inherent in the theories he is putting into practice.[2] Particularly at a point in time when professional helping is coming under attack from many quarters, it is all the more prudent for the helping professional to explore the assumptions on which his practice is based.

Second, it is unwise to lean too heavily on the professional code of ehics as the guarantor of ethical practice. Unfortunately, the present code can too easily become a blanket cover for any type of practice. Therefore, simply to say that one subscribes to the code of ethics does not in itself preclude unethical behavior. It is not enough simply to state that as social treatment practitioners we all hold the same code of ethics; we must specify just how that ethical code

2. A point made by Maier (1967, pp. 29–40).

serves to direct our practice stance. For if it does not serve to inform and mold our professional behavior, it runs the risk of becoming merely a collection of empty phrases.

A related point is that the code of ethics itself is general enough to provide for varying and sometimes contradictory interpretations of permissible behavior. Perhaps a better plan would be to abstract the value stance from the theory within which the practitioner is operating, rather than to assume *a priori* that his values are similar to those of others because they all subscribe to the same professional code of ethics. In short, tell me what you plan to do with the client and I'll tell you what value stance informs your relationship.

The theoretical underpinnings of a helping process as broadly conceived as social treatment would require considerably more space than can be allotted in a single chapter. The approach taken here is justifiable only by the fact that I make no pretense of saying everything there is to say about the knowledge base of social treatment, but rather examine the way in which a theoretical system (*any* theoretical system) tends to shape the view of the client held by the worker and imposes through its prescriptions a value set on the total helping relationship.

In choosing four substantive areas of knowledge for discussion—psychoanalytic theory, social learning theory, social systems theory, and humanistic-existential approaches —I am obviously leaving equally fruitful areas untouched and can barely scratch the surface of those areas I do examine. Nor do I imply that within these four areas lies all that a practitioner of social treatment needs to know about human behavior; that would presume a complete biopsychosocial picture of man which is far broader than the four areas I shall discuss. Here, then, is the barest of skeletal frameworks on which social treatment practice is structured.

Psychoanalytic Theory

Psychoanalytic theory is the direct result of the scientific and clinical endeavors of Sigmund Freud.[3] The theory, as propounded by Freud and by the countless theoreticians who further refined and expanded his original formulations, posits a view of the way man develops. From this psychoanalytic or psychodynamic theory of development flow several methods of treatment: psychoanalysis, psychotherapy, and psychoanalytically oriented casework. A brief examination of the psychoanalytic theory of development will clarify its implications for treatment.

MAJOR ASSUMPTIONS

Psychoanalytic theory, according to Langer:

> assumes that the organization with which the child is born constitutes the initial functional and structural basis of his development. Biologically rooted functions [drives] are the organizing forces that differentiate and relate inborn structures into increasingly complex organizations subject to the nature of the individual's particular history of interaction with his environment (1969, pp. 161–63).

Psychoanalytic theory stresses the importance of psychic energy, which "fuels the functioning of the individual's [personality] structures." This energy is assumed to be instinctually sexual and aggressive. "The instinctual activation of a bodily zone causes it to function. When the func-

3. Because of its sheer complexity and volume, psychoanalytic theory is extremely difficult to summarize in any of its dimensions. For an introduction, the reader is directed to the sources at the end of this chapter.

tioning of one zone is predominant, a stage of development is said to be constituted" (Langer, 1969, p. 162).

Psychoanalytic theory presumes that man develops through a series of phases, or stages, each corresponding to the instinctual activation of a particular bodily zone. Thus human development unfolds through the oral, anal, phallic, latency, and genital stages, with accompanying changes in the biological, psychological, and social spheres occurring in each. Psychoanalytic theory stresses the interaction of organism and environment and assumes that there are unconscious as well as conscious aspects to human functioning. It emphasizes the nonrational as well as the rational aspects of man and the existence of a developmental continuity between the nonconscious, prerational intentions of man and his conscious, rational processes (Langer, 1969, p. 14).

In sum, psychoanalytic theory conceives of the human being as essentially a dynamic energy system consisting of fundamental drives or instincts. This energy is invested in various bodily zones according to a predetermined schedule, resulting in phases or stages of individual development. Thus psychoanalytic theory assumes the existence of instinctual drives, psychic energy, stages of development, and unconscious as well as conscious processes, and underscores the crucial nature of early childhood experiences for later development.

VIEW OF MAN

Freud viewed man as a being whose essential psychological nature is desire rather than reason. The primary efficient cause of mental life is instinct. It is this irrational part of man that is later transformed through interaction with the environment into socialized, rational purposes. Thus man is seen as a purposeful animal from birth, though his intentionality need not be conscious and may stem from biological needs that predate consciousness or from other unconscious needs. "The thesis that man's essence is desire also led Freud to hypothesize developmental continuity between non-conscious prerational intentions and conscious rational processes. Both are energized by the same biological endowment, namely instincts" (Langer, 1969, pp. 13–14).

A group of neo-Freudians usually called "ego psychologists" posit that the child is born with rational as well as prerational instincts, which are presumed to energize some of the child's perceptions and thinking in his rational interaction with external reality (Langer, 1969, p. 15). The ego psychological theorists (and there is great variation within their thinking) have generally focused primarily on the development of the rational, conscious processes in personality.[4]

But whether one reads early Freud or those who later developed his original formulations (and both should be read if one is to get an accurate picture of psychoanalytic theory today), the view of man that unfolds is extremely complex. From the moment of birth, the individual is moved toward the satisfaction of basic drives and instincts. The resolution of these early strivings, the manner in which they are satisfied, modified, or channeled, will have a profound effect on the development of the adult personality. Further, human personality is presumed to consist of conscious, unconscious, and preconscious aspects and irrational as well as rational processes. Therefore, what is directly observable at any given time (conscious, rational processes or behavior) may be like the tip of an iceberg, which extends deep beneath the surface. Only through a careful exploration of its subterranean regions can one get an accurate picture of the whole personality.

4. See in Particular White (1960, 1963), Hartman (1958), Erikson (1959, pp. 18–164; 1963), A. Freud (1946), Baldwin (1968).

MAJOR TENETS

In summarizing Freud's final view of the structure of personality, Brenner[5] defines the famous triad of id-ego-superego: "The *id* comprises the psychic representatives of the drives, the *ego* consists of those functions which have to do with the individual's relation to his environment, and the *superego* comprises the moral precepts of our minds as well as our ideal aspirations" (1955, p. 45; italics added).

The ego has occasioned much in the way of later analysis, giving rise to what came to be known as psychoanalytic ego psychology. Commonly cited ego functions include motor control, perception, memory, affect, and thinking. The ego is also the locus of the mechanisms of defense, which help to maintain a basic stability in the total organization of personality by dealing with stress both from within (drives) and from without (external environment). Anna Freud has written the classic work on the mechanisms of defense (1946), and while there is some disagreement as to exactly what defenses make up the total armamentarium of the personality, those most commonly accepted are introjection, repression, denial, reaction formation, displacement, turning against the self, isolation, undoing, ritualization, intellectualization, rationalization, and sublimation (Cameron, 1963, p. 234).

The main function of the ego is to meet the behavioral management needs of the total organism. This distinguishes it sharply from the impulse system (id) and the morality system (superego). The basic function of the id is to seek impulse discharge, while that of the superego is to react to the moral appropriateness of the discharge-bound impulse and to flash danger signals when one of its standards is about to be violated. It becomes the job of the ego to deal

5. Brenner's text endures as a straightforward and easy-to-understand introduction to psychoanalytic theory.

with impulses (from the id) and morality signals (from the superego) in accordance with the best interest of the total person. The ego is constantly involved in reality testing: weighing alternative behaviors against the demands of the impulse system, the strictures of the morality system, and the realities of the physical and social environments.[6] The ego, then, acts as the executive of the total personality and is constantly involved in assessing, evaluating, and dealing with both the internal and the external environments.

As I mentioned earlier, psychoanalytic theory holds that an individual progresses through certain stages of development triggered by, though not limited to, activation of certain bodily zones. In his classic *Childhood and Society*, Erikson outlines what he refers to as the "eight ages of man," stages of development that are universal to all men. These stages are the result of the unfolding of the "ground plan" of personality, which is genetically transmitted. Associated with these stages are eight major crises that each person faces in the course of his lifetime. The person must adequately resolve each crisis in order to progress to the next stage of his development in an adaptive and healthy fashion. Here are Erikson's eight stages (1963, pp. 35–46):

1. *Basic trust versus basic mistrust*, in which the infant develops a sense of trust in the person upon whom he is most dependent for his very sustenance.
2. *Autonomy versus shame and doubt*, in which the child acquires a sense of autonomy and control over the basic bodily functions of elimination.
3. *Initiative versus guilt*, in which the child begins to intrude upon the environment and try on new roles in a much more sophisticated way than before.
4. *Industry versus inferiority*, in which the latency-age

6. Abridged from Wineman (1964).

child attempts to master all manner of physical, social, and cognitive skills.

5. *Identity versus role confusion,* in which the adolescent strives to attain a coherent and integrated sense of himself and his purpose.

6. *Intimacy versus isolation,* in which the young adult "loses and finds himself in another."

7. *Generativity versus stagnation,* in which the adult strives to "make be" and to "take care of" rather than being absorbed in himself. The primary personal aim is to establish a family and create a radius of external relations.

8. *Ego integrity versus despair,* in which the adult who has achieved gratification from creating and helping others to grow is equipped with the personal integrity necessary to face the final crisis of life, that of his own disintegration and death.[7]

Erikson's developmental schema is a good example of the kind of theoretical spinoff precipitated by Freudian psychoanalytic theory. Erikson has taken the original stage model of development (oral, anal, phallic, latency, genital) and given new emphasis to the interaction of the organism with its social-cultural environment, as well as extending the paradigm over the entire life cycle.

From a similar psychoanalytic base Robert W. White (1960, 1963) has explored the notion of competence and its acquisition in human development. White defines "competence" in its broad biological sense as "fitness or ability," and posits that the child is motivated to interact with his environment not merely by biological motives (hunger, thirst, sex), but also by an interest in exploring the world around him. White calls this other motive "effectance"—a kind of

7. In addition to Erikson, (1963), see also Maier (1969).

general motivational system that underlies the child's desire to master his environment. Thus when a child masters a simple task like closing a door, he is further motivated to try new and more complex tasks. White's notions of competence and effectance are rich with implications for the field of social treatment, as they shed new insight on the development of the concept of the self and provide an additional explanation of the individual's motivation to master his environment.[8]

IMPLICATIONS FOR SOCIAL TREATMENT

The treatment implications of psychoanalytic theory are numerous and far-reaching. In addition to psychoanalysis, a method of treatment developed by Freud himself, the theory has informed countless other therapies and methods of treatment. Inherent in the paradigm of the psychoanalytic structure of personality (id-ego-superego) are explanations of many emotional problems. As Brenner has said, "Cordial cooperation between ego and id is not what we are accustomed to in our ordinary clinical work . . . there we deal daily with severe conflicts between ego and id" (1955), p. 48).

At times this conflict between the ego and the id generates neuroses, which are the result of conflict between (a) the non-conscious or unconscious wishes for gratification or tensionlessness and (b) reason, that internal representation of reality or of social norms which produces tension through its conflict with id desires (Langer, 1969, p. 15).

The neurotic symptom develops in the following sequence: (1) increased tension or anxiety because of frustration, loss, threat, danger, or increased drive; (2) threat of ego disinte-

8. For an interesting perspective on the implications of White's model for the field of mental retardation, see Robinson & Robinson (1965, pp. 297–99).

gration; (3) partial regression to main levels of fixation; (4) reactivation of infantile conflicts and return of the repressed; (5) defensive transformation and secondary elaboration within the ego; (6) final emergence of the symptom (Cameron, 1663, p. 453).

This sketch of the development of neuroses illustrates the psychoanalytic approach to treatment. Therapy may well involve uncovering the conflicts between the warring parts of the personality, clarifying the nature of the conflict, exploring the relationship of the client's present condition to early developmental experiences and establishing linkages between past and present, helping the client achieve insight as to the reason he is feeling and/or acting the way he is, and helping him to resolve or work through the conflicts that beset him.

Psychoanalytically based treatment is thus extremely interested in the causality of behavior and often looks for some of the explanations in early childhood experiences. Helping the client develop insight is paramount, and often this involves getting behind the manifest content of a symptom, dream, or wish and exploring the latent meaning for the individual.

Other methods of treatment, while not classically psychoanalytic in nature, rely heavily on a psychoanalytic framework both for their view of human development and for many of the particular strategies and techniques they employ. Within the field of social work practice, for example, Perlman (1957, p. xi) describes herself as "psychoanalytically oriented" and acknowledges that she "can scarcely conceive of . . . being able not to think out of relation to these systems." Similarly, Hollis (1971), another leading theoretician of social casework, writes from a framework that is clearly psychoanalytically oriented.

The great legacy of psychoanalytic theory to the treatment field is not only the set of strategies and techniques for social treatment that it yields (and countless volumes have been written on these alone); through the developmental theories derived by Freud and later greatly expanded by Erikson and others, it has also provided a view of man progressing from the earliest of life experiences to the "final life crisis" of death.

LIMITATIONS

While psychoanalytic theory has made major contributions to our understanding of human development and has yielded numerous implications for treatment, it is not without limitations. Ironically, the very richness of psychoanalytic theory accounts for one of the difficulties in evaluating it: there are so many ways within psychoanalytic theory to explain behavior that it is difficult to conceive of any apparent contradiction that the theory would not explain. Terms like "ego," "id," "superego" are poorly defined, and the theory is notably lacking in operational definitions that would lend themselves to evaluative empirical research. To date little has been accomplished in the way of empirical validation of the theory.

Other limitations have been cited in the extension of psychoanalytic principles to the treatment encounter. Some have argued that psychoanalytically based treatment lays too much stress on changing individuals rather than their environments; it's the individual that is "sick," not the system. Also, the effectiveness of psychoanalytically based treatment is difficult to evaluate because of the lack of clarity of goals and the emphasis on altering inner personality states. Further, psychoanalytic treatment stresses insight over other forms of learning (such as imitation or reward and punishment), is relatively time-consuming and expensive (at least in the classic varieties of psychoanalysis and psychotherapy), and requires at least an average intelligence and ability to verbalize on the part of the client.

Despite these limitations, psychoanalytic theory is without peer in its contributions to the fields of social treatment and human development. Its continued existence and pervasiveness after so many years, as well as the kind of fruitful thought it has generated among both its staunchest advocates and its severest critics, are testimony to the genius of Freud.

Social Learning Theory

MAJOR ASSUMPTIONS

Social learning theory assumes that man's psychological nature *is* his behavior.[9] The child is born with certain reflex mechanisms that ensure that he will acquire and reflect the content inherent in the environmental agents that stimulate and shape his behavior. "Like a sculptor who shapes a lump of clay," according to B. F. Skinner (quoted in Langer, 1969, p. (159), the environment serves gradually to shape the behavior of the child, resulting in growth, which is a continuous process of learning behavior. Behavior (the directly observable and measurable actions of man) is assumed to be the sum and substance of personality; no "inner states" or elaborate "unconscious structures" here!

VIEW OF MAN

Langer describes the view of man held by social learning theory this way:

> The child is born empty of psychological content into a world of coherently organized content. Like a *mirror*, however, the child comes to reflect his environment; like an empty slate he

9. Social learning theory does not constitute all of what is generally considered to be learning theory. For a more complete view, see Langer (1969).

is written on by external stimuli; like a wax tablet he stores the impressions left by these stimuli; and like a machine he may be made to react in response to stimulating agents. . . . Insofar as the mechanical mirror theory has a model of mind, it is patterned after a mirror that reflects sensations from the environment [1969, p. 51; italics added].

The child, then, is born as a *tabula rasa* into an organized environment that becomes the source for all psychological phenomena. This environmentalistic assumption of social learning theory harks back to Locke's assumption in the seventeenth century that there is nothing in the mind that does not come from the senses.

Basically, the view of man held by social learning theory is far less complex than that of psychoanalytic theory. Man is a "mechanical mirror" of his environment and his behavior is the essence of his personality. Behavior is explained by environmental shaping and does not include reliance on concepts like "drives" or "inner states" for its explanation. Man is very much a product of his environment, and his behavior is the end result of many learning processes. Nurture rather than nature is the preeminent factor in later development.

MAJOR TENETS

The behavioristic movement in psychology began with the work of John B. Watson about 1910. Watson believed that only overt, observable behavioral concepts belonged in psychology; he discarded such concepts as "idea," "thought," "goal," "intention," and "will" as being nonbehavioristic (Watson, 1925). If behaviorists considered the concept "mind" at all, they conceived of it as a physiological complex that was manifested in a single observable response. Behavior was seen as something controlled by environmental events along with the operational response of the individual. The first recognition of "operant behavior" and its effects came from Thorndike, when he observed that cats that had some experience with a puzzle box could subsequently solve puzzles with greater ease than cats with no such experience. From this initial observation he formulated the "law of effect," which essentially stated that behavior was influenced by the effects of such behavior in the environment (Thorndike, 1911).

The locus of social learning theory in the 1930s was Yale University's Institute of Human Relations, founded by Clark Hull, who was intensely interested in the processes of socialization. Many studies emanated from the institute and many now-famous psychologists were at one time or another connected with it: John Dollard, Neil Miller, Robert Sears, O. Herbert Mowrer, E. R. Hilgard. A number of these men (Dollard *et al.*, 1939; Dollard & Miller, 1941) took the psychology of learning and applied it to some of the dimensional problems laid out by Freud in his general theory. This pattern was to be followed in numerous other studies, with the social learning theorists attempting to give substance and empirical validation to the dimensions laid out in classical psychoanalytic theory. Needless to say, this endeavor— whether undertaken to affirm or disprove psychoanalytic theory—is far from completed, and indeed is still in its infancy.

CLASSICAL CONDITIONING AND INSTRUMENTAL CONDITIONING

One of the basic tenets of social learning theory is that behavior is learned. Therefore, the essential question to be raised about any behavioral response is: "How was it learned?" Social learning theory not only emphasizes the view that all behavior is learned, but also stresses that learned behavior is the end result of many separate learning processes. The unit of behavior is a specific act and each act is independently acquired. This belief carries with it the tacit assumption that all behavior is almost infinitely malleable. Another presumption of social learning theory is that behavior is learned through external reinforcement. The theory does provide for acts that are "self-rewarding," and in some situations it is possible that the events that reinforce behavior do not appear to be rewards. The differences between classical or respondent conditioning and operant or instrumental conditioning can best be discerned by distinguishing between respondent and operant behavior:

Respondent behavior involves so-called reflex behavior, which consists of nonvoluntary responses mainly of the glands and smooth muscles. Examples of such nonvoluntary responses are eye blinks and tics, salivation, hunger contractions, and emotional reactions. The classical conditioning paradigm involves respondent behavior, in which an unconditioned stimulus (food) is paired with a previously neutral stimulus (bell) to produce a conditioned response (salivation). Thus Pavlov's dogs were taught to salivate at the sight of food when a bell sounded, after the bell and food had been paired over a number of trials. In one of the famous Pavlovian experiments, a bell was rung slightly before the food stimulus was presented. After this combination of bell and food had been repeated a number of times, the dog began to salivate whenever the bell was rung, even if on that particular trial no food was given.

Operant behavior, on the other hand, involves voluntary actions of the skeletal-muscular system. Here the muscles that are under the individual's control are involved in the conditioning process. The individual may modify his behavior in response to feedback from the environment; the feedback may or may not be reinforcing. The principles of operant and respondent conditioning are addressed to two basic and fundamental ways by which humans learn and perform in environments. The laws of respondent conditioning concern primarily the means by which previously neutral cues in the environment come to acquire a capacity to elicit responses involving the glands and smooth muscles. The propositions of operant conditioning treat primarily of the ways in which a freely behaving human is affected by the effect of his behavior in the environment (Thomas & Goodman, 1965, p. 12).

BASIC ELEMENTS[10]

A reinforcer is any stimulus that alters the strength of the response it follows. Reinforcers are determined empirically by observing any changes in response strength following their application. Certain stimuli—such as food, drink, sex, and shock—are thought to be innately reinforcing and thus are called primary reinforcers. Other types of reinforcers have acquired their reinforcing power through past pairing with primary reinforcers. These stimuli are not intrinsically reinforcing to the individual, but have acquired their ability to affect response strength. They are known as secondary reinforcers. Poker chips used in "token economies" would be examples of secondary reinforcers. When secondary reinforcers are paired with more than one primary reinforcer, they are called generalized secondary reinforcers. Money, approval, attention, affection, and submissiveness generally function as this type of reinforcer. A positive reinforcer is a stimulus that serves to increase the strength of the response it follows. One may also modify response strength through the removal of an aversive stimulus following a response; this is known as negative reinforcement. Punishment, by contrast, consists of the application of an aversive stimulus or the withholding of some positive reinforcement for the purpose of suppressing a particular response.

10. This section is based in large part on Thomas & Goodman (1965). See Bandura & Walters (1963), Dollard & Miller (1941, 1950), and Bandura (1969) for glossary purposes. See also "The world of behavior shapers" (1972).

"Shaping" consists of the selective use of some type of reinforcement to approximate successively a desired behavior that is not currently in the organism's behavioral repertoire. The shaping phenomenon is actually a complex stratagem involving extinction and differential reinforcement in a particular order. Skinner gives us the example of training dogs to touch their noses to a doorknob. Initially the experimenter paired a clicker with food, so that the clicker took on secondary reinforcing properties through respondent conditioning. Once the animal learned to perform for these clicks, their administration became highly selective. At first he would receive clicks if he walked in the direction of the door, and once these responses were established, the clicking reinforcement would be administered only if he raised his head while near the door. Through this procedure the animal would eventually learn the desired behavior of touching his nose to the doorknob. Numerous examples of the shaping can be found in the clinical literature.[11]

The shaping plan first calls for the selection of a reinforcer that may be easily applied or withheld and is adequate to sustain the behavior that occurs. The second part of the plan calls for stipulation of the initial, intermediate, and terminal behaviors. The initial behavior must have a relatively high probability of occurring freely. Murray Sidman (quoted in Thomas & Goodman, 1965, p. 22) has outlined some rules governing the shaping process:

1. Behavior must be reinforced immediately. A delay of even a few seconds may result in the inadvertent reinforcement of undesired behavior.

2. The shapers must not give too many reinforcements for approximations of the desired response. An excess of reinforcement at one of the intermediate levels may result in no further movement toward the final objective.

11. See Sherman and Baer (1969). See also: Browning and Stover (1971) pp. 134–139 and pp. 185–390.

3. The experimenter must not give too few reinforcements for approximations of the desired response. Each response level must be securely established before one proceeds to the following level, and this can be accomplished only through an adquate reinforcement period.

4. There must be careful specification of the response to be reinforced at each successive level.

PATTERNS OF REINFORCEMENT: SCHEDULING

Bandura and Walters (1963) point out the crucial significance of the scheduling of reinforcements for eliciting and/or maintaining behavior. Social learning theorists typically tend to speak of five reinforcement schedules:

In a *continuous reinforcement schedule,* each desirable response emitted by the subject is reinforced. This type of schedule is effective for eliciting a desired response, but is almost impossible to maintain outside of a laboratory situation.[12]

A *fixed-interval schedule* is one in which reinforcements are made available at fixed times, regardless of the rate of the desired response. Thomas points out that human subjects frequently figure out reinforcement intervals and respond only just prior to the next anticipated interval. One must take care to select an appropriate reinforcement interval: if the interval is too long, the desired behavior will not be securely linked to the reinforcers and will tend to disappear.

A *variable-interval schedule* is one in which the time interval for reinforcement varies instead of being fixed and predictable. Thomas gives the example of stock dividends to illustrate this type of schedule, which appears to be very common in everyday life. Subjects typically perform at a

12. For an example of the problems involved in maintaining a continuous reinforcement schedule, see Ayllon & Michael (1965).

rather moderate, stable, and uniform rate under this type of schedule.

A *fixed-ratio schedule* is one in which reinforcement is linked to a desired response rather than to a particular time period. Working at piecework rates, striving for grades in school, and saving trading stamps are examples of fixed-ratio schedules. There tends to be a very high rate of response under this schedule.

Finally, under a *variable-ratio schedule* a given response is reinforced at irregular emission intervals. This schedule is very effective in maintaining behavior and one finds the highest, most uniform, and most persistent rate of response when it is used. Examples include a salesman working on commission, a gambler, a scholar, and an artist working for prestige and acclaim. Thomas and Goodman (1965) point out that in many ways this schedule is most pertinent to the field of social work, since therapeutic rewards are frequently irregular and the social worker may have to go for long intervals without receiving much satisfaction in the form of client improvement. Despite the intermittent and unreliable quality of this kind of reinforcement, his professional behavior is generally maintained. In most real-life situations, social reinforcements are delivered according to this type of schedule.[13]

IMITATION

Imitation may be defined as the matching of behavior to that displayed by actual or symbolized models. Thomas and Goodman (1965) hold that, by definition, imitation is behavioral and observable. It typically includes motor responses, attitudes, thought processes, and indeed all aspects of human

13. See Stevenson (1965) for a review of the literature on the effects of social reinforcements on children's behavior.

behavior that may be observed directly or reliably inferred from overt responses. Bandura and Walters (1963) point out that since the eliciting and maintaining of imitative behaviors are highly dependent upon the response consequences to the model, an adequate social learning theory must also take account of the concept of *vicarious reinforcement*, through which the behavior of an observer is modified as a result of the reinforcement administered to a model. There is some question as to what actually constitutes true vicarious reinforcement. For example, when we see a child in an experimental situation match the behavior of an aggressive model, is this a truly reinforcing event? In most studies, researchers have been unable to make this assumption. It may be that in the prior socialization of the child he has already learned (through discrimination) that it is better to imitate models who are rewarded for their behavior and not to imitate those who are punished. If this is the case, then prior discrimination learning would account for the imitation and it could not truly be called a reinforcing event. Many feel that vicarious reinforcement involves more than the mere contiguity of model and subject; the subject must have undergone some prior experiences that provide a cognitive linkage between what is happening to another and what is going to happen to him. Maccoby (1959) has looked at imitation in the broader context of "role taking" in children and its implications for social learning.[14]

Bandura and Walters propose three possible effects of model presentation (1963, p. 60):

1. A *modeling effect*, which occurs when the imitation involves novel responses that were not previously a part of the subject's behavioral repertoire.

---

14. For a more complete discussion of imitation, identification, and modeling, see Mussen (1971).

2. An *inhibiting or disinhibiting effect,* which involves an increase or decrease in the frequency, latency, or intensity of previously acquired responses, following exposure to model.

3. An *eliciting effect,* which involves the releasing of previously acquired noninhibited responses of an observer.

Finally, it should be noted that there is currently a good deal of interest in the question of "first imitations" of a social nature. Some have suggested that contiguity of infant and model is not sufficient to explain such behaviors, and they point to something like the existence of a social drive.

EXTINCTION

Baldwin (1968, pp. 399–400) points out that conditioning, whether of the classical or instrumental type, can be undone. In the classical conditioning experiment, after the dog had learned to salivate in response to the sound of the bell, the conditioning could be destroyed by presenting the bell over and over again without ever reinforcing its connection to salivation by presenting food. Similarly, a response acquired through operant learning can be extinguished by repeatedly failing to reinforce it.

However, the withholding of reinforcement may be frustrating and produce some emotional reactions, just as punishment does. The process of extinction may also involve stimulus satiation—the reinforcer is presented so frequently and in such abundance that it loses its reinforcing qualities. For example, Ayllon and Michael (1965) describe how a mental patient was cured of his compulsion to steal towels from the ward bathroom: every time he secreted one under his bed, the attendants would bring in two additional towels, until his room was literally filled with them, at which point he angrily demanded that they be removed and ceased his stealing.

PUNISHMENT

Punishment consists of the application of an aversive stimulus or the withholding of a positive reinforcer for the purpose of suppressing a particular response. Punishment is not an extinction procedure, however, since the responses are presumably still part of the individual's behavioral repertoire and may reemerge in the future when punishment is no longer used. We now know that punishment does not necessarily affect the strength of the response tendency, though it may well account for the disappearance of a response, if only temporarily through its suppression. Walters and Parke (1966; Parke and Walters, 1967) explore the influence of punishment and related disciplinary techniques on the social behavior of children. Their basic findings are that in real-life situations, the suppressive effect of punishment is usually of value only if alternative social responses are elicited and strengthened while the undersirable behavior is held in check. Such factors as timing, intensity, and frequency of aversive stimulation can greatly influence their effectiveness as disciplinary procedures. The manner in which a disciplinary technique is applied may be more important than the form it takes. Most studies tend to show a high correlation between the effectiveness of the punishment and the subject's personal relationship to the punishing agent.[15]

Punishment may be accompanied by certain side effects that should be kept in mind (Thomas & Goodman, 1965):

1. The individual may resort to *escape behavior*, in which he acts to reduce directly the aversiveness of the stimulus after it has been applied; for example, the child who runs from the punishing adult.

2. *Avoidance behavior* occurs when one avoids the punish-

15. For a further discussion of this most complex subject, see Aronfreed and Rever (1965), Solomon (1964), and Becker (1966).

ment by not exposing himself at all to the aversive situation. Avoidance is very difficult to counteract, since the individual creates a situation in which he will not expose himself to the stimulus so as to learn that it may no longer be aversive. For example, the child brutalized by a punitive father may thereafter avoid all contact with men.

3. Finally, *emotional reactions* may occur; anxiety, panic, fear, or fury may be triggered by the aversive stimulus employed. These emotional reactions become conditioned, through respondent conditioning, to the otherwise neutral cues attending the punishment situation. The punishing behavior, or even the mere presence of the punishing agent, may instigate other behaviors over which the person doing the punishing has little or no control. These side effects may persist long after the acts of punishment have occurred.

Finally, Aronfreed and Rever (1965) point out that the really crucial question regarding punishment is whether or not the individual is acquiring self-critical responses in the process of attaining self-control. Aversive stimulation, if well timed, consistent, and sufficiently intense, may create conditions that accelerate the socialization process, provided that the socialization agents also make available information concerning alternative prosocial behavior and positively reinforce any such behavior when it occurs. The general trend of the research in this area seems to suggest that we should not rule out the use of punishment despite its possible harmful side effects, and that we should attempt to learn a great deal more than we currently know about the factors that influence the effectiveness of punishment, the importance of the punishing agents, and the significance of the circumstances attending the punishment situation. For example, there is some evidence to suggest that the effectiveness of punishment may be enhanced when its termination is made contingent upon a child's complying with the demands of the socialization agent. Finally, an extremely interesting

paper on the conditions necessary for an effective punishment situation from the point of view of ego psychology is
offered by Fritz Redl (1967).

IMPLICATIONS FOR SOCIAL TREATMENT

The implications of social learning theory for social treatment are numerous. If behavior is the sum total of man's
personality, then behavioral change through a program of
behavior modification will be the treatment of choice for the
individual who exhibits socially unacceptable or maladaptive
behaviors. Thus, for the delinquent to stop stealing cars and
fighting is to cease being a delinquent; for the emotionally
disturbed child to relate well to his peers and attend classes
regularly is to cease being emotionally disturbed; and for
the psychotic adult to stop "talking crazy," to refrain from
bizarre behavior, and to be able to hold down a job is to
cease being psychotic. The definition of the problem and its
remediation takes on behaviorally specific meaning.

The worker helps the client to identify and specify the
problem behavior. The desired end state (or goal) is determined with equal emphasis on behavioral specificity. A
schedule for learning is set up, utilizing reinforcers determined to be appropriate for the client. The worker guides
the learning process and may selectively administer reinforcement for client behavior which successively approximates the desired end state, until that state is reached.

Though social learning theory has been around for quite a
while, its practical counterpart, behavior modification, is a
relative newcomer to the treatment field. Often beginning
with groups of clients for which traditional methods have
failed—such as regressed psychotic adult mental patients—
behavioral techniques have enjoyed a recent surge of popularity with a variety of client problems in outpatient and
community as well as institutional settings.

In essence, social learning theory holds a rather optimistic view of man's ability to change his behavior. Since all behavior is malleable, and if the conditions maintaining behavior can be controlled and the proper reinforcers found, then change is possible. This is an important distinction between social learning theory and psychoanalytic theory, which lays a good deal more emphasis on the primacy of early experiences in determining later development and which often stresses the resolution of inner conflicts as a necessary prerequisite to behavioral change.

Since behavioral modification emphasizes behaviorally specific goals, its results are much more easily measured than those of treatment modalities that employ more diffuse goals relating to changes in inner states of personality. While results are still sketchy, early research shows promising results in work with children and effectiveness with particular psychological manifestations such as phobias and problems of sexual deviance.

LIMITATIONS

If one could criticize psychoanalytic theory for an overemphasis on man's inner nature, a like criticism could be extended to social learning theory for an overemphasis on environmental nurture. Can we really assume, for example, that man is simply a *tabula rasa* or mechanical mirror of his environment? Are we content to say that behavior constitutes the essence of an individual's personality? In its parsimonious approach to theory building, social learning theory has contributed much in the way of sound empirical data about the processes of human learning. In including only those data that are quantifiable and objectively verifiable, social learning theorists have tended to assume that the mention of any term not so rigorously defined is tantamount to mysticism. Baldwin provides us with a good observation on this point (1968, pp. 476–77):

There is a place for rigor and for tolerance in building a science. A formal theory must be rigorous and a statement of empirical fact dependable. If a scientist reports a result of his research, he must be able to verify it, and in this verification rigor and objectivity are essential. Stimulus-response theory has perhaps been too rigid in assuming that all contributions to science must be factual. Theoretical speculation, even if it is not clean and rigorous, is not necessarily useless. Explanatory studies, observational reports, case studies and other naturalistic observations have a place in scientific literature, even though they are based on too few cases to be statistically significant, have no control group, or in some way fail to meet the requirements for rigorous testing of the truth of an empirical statement. The mere fact that social learning theory has fed on Freud's observations for twenty-five years is evidence of the value of other strategies.

Since man is not strictly a product of either his nature or his nurture, it is clear that all manner of data should be examined in what will ultimately be a unified theory of human development.

On another level, the application of social learning theory principles to social treatment has come under fire from some quarters as being manipulative, mechanistic, and generally out of harmony with the professional code of ethics. Finally, some would argue that the evidence supporting behavior modification practice is still too sketchy to justify the claims made by some of its proponents.

The degree to which behavior modification is necessarily manipulative is readily disputed, especially when one sees the extent to which the client is involved in shaping the goals for his treatment;[16] whatever degree of manipulation is inherent in the behavioral approach is clearly not limited

16. See Gambrill, Thomas, & Carter (1971) and Morrow & Gochros (1970).

to that approach, but is a problem with all methods of treatment. Claims of mechanism perhaps confuse the fact that social learning theory is indeed a theory about the mechanics of the way people acquire behavior. It does not necessarily follow that its application need be mechanical. Finally, it is true that the research underlying behavioral practice is limited, but the research underlying other modalities of treatment whose practice is of longer standing and is more widespread is more limited still.

In sum, the promise of social learning theory for the treatment field appears to be great. What we need most now is adequate research to answer the questions of *where* and *how*.

Social Systems Theory

MAJOR ASSUMPTIONS

Social systems theory deals with the way in which various social systems such as families, small groups, organizations, communities, and societies are created and the numerous processes by which they are maintained and/or changed. Basically, systems theory assumes an interaction and an interdependency between social systems, as well as a high degree of organization within each system. It follows, then, that if change occurs in one part of a social system, its effect will be felt in all other parts of the system. For example, if one member of a family is stricken with a serious illness, the effects of that illness, both direct and indirect, will be experienced by all family members. Similarly, because of the interdependency of social systems, changes that occur in one system are likely to have effects in other contiguous systems. The seriously ill family member may precipitate special helping from the informal network of relatives and friends that surrounds the immediate nuclear family (extended family and friendship system) and in addition require financial and other assistance from local social service agencies (social welfare system). Finally, enough sick individuals in enough families might constitute a need great enough to occasion change in the national policy toward family health (societal system). The central point here—and a basic assumption of social systems theory—is that change in one part of a social system may exert a ripple effect of change throughout that system and on into other systems as well.

VIEW OF MAN

From the social systems perspective, man is viewed not as an isolated entity, but as a participant in a number of interacting and interdependent dynamic social systems. This view of man is extremely important to the process of social treatment, as it tends to define problems more in terms of systems than in terms of individuals. Thus, for the family therapist, the problem is not one of "sick" individuals, but of a maladaptive family process. Problems are woven into the very web of family relationships and the family itself is seen as the client. Similarly, the worker operating from a social systems framework may spend a good deal of time mediating between his client's immediate system and the other social systems that have an impact upon it. The worker helping his cottage group in an institution for delinquents to negotiate for privileges from the administration would be fulfilling this function. In the view of one theoretician, the task of the social work practitioner is "one of mediating the often troubled transactions between people and the various systems through which they carry on their relationships with society—the family, peer group, social agency, neighborhood, school, job and others" (Schwartz, 1971, p. 1258). Man and the social systems with which he interacts are viewed as having a symbiotic relationship, each needing the other for its own life growth.

MAJOR TENETS

Social systems are defined as "the patterns of action of people and culture. They may involve one or many persons, together with cultural phenomena such as words, ideas, artifacts, rules, beliefs and emotions . . . a system is as big as the actions and things it includes; they define its boundaries" (Monane, 1967, p. 1).

Social systems involve the sending and receiving of energy/information; these occur both within the system and between the system and its environments. A system's environment is anything external to it, to which it sends or from which it receives.

Monane views most social systems as composed of

(1) components (people, artifacts, ideas, emotion) of varying manipulative power in regular non-random patterns of action with one another. This involves the (2) sending and receiving of energy/information among components of the system. The system is simultaneously involved in the (3) sending and receiving of energy/information with its (4) environments, including other systems. Its patterns of action within and with its environments constitute (5) modal norms providing it with a distinctive identity. Its (6) power units, internally and in their actions with the system's environments, seek (7) positive feedback implementing their direction of system action and resist (8) negative feedback impeding their action. (9) Change . . . that is perceived by a system's power units as providing positive feedback is encouraged, while (10) change that is perceived as providing negative feedback is resisted internally through patterns of (11) expulsion, confinement, or conversion; externally such change is resisted by withdrawal, a tightening of gateways, or a joining with it so as to remove its danger. (12) Change that succeeds in creating negative feedback produces varying degrees of system disintegration. This, however, is rarely final. New systems spring up from the ashes of the old through (13) resystematization [1967, pp. 3–5].

If this represents a skeletal view of the way human systems work, Chin (1961, pp. 201–214) has provided us with definitions of some of the key components of social systems.

System presupposes organization, interaction, interdependency, and integration of parts and elements. Chin helps us to visualize a system by

> drawing a large circle. We place elements, parts, variables, inside the circle as components and draw lines through the components. The lines may be thought of as rubber bands . . . which stretch on contact as the forces increase or decrease. Outside the circle is the environment, where we place all other factors which impinge upon the system [1961, p. 203].

System boundary is operationally defined as the line forcing a closed circle around selected variables where there is less interchange of energy/communication across the line than within the delimiting circle. Tension, stress, strain, and conflict are central processes in all systems; they may result from pressure within the system or from without. *Equilibrium* and *steady states* refer to the tendency of systems to achieve a balance among the various forces operating within and upon it. *Feedback* refers to the process by which information is fed back into the system as the result of its attempt to affect its environments. This information is used by the system as input to guide its future operations. Feedback may be positive or negative. Systems may be relatively open or closed to feedback, change, or information, and often systems are linked together in an intersystem framework.

The social systems literature draws from sociology, social psychology, human relations, engineering, and the natural sciences. The original work of social systems scholars such as Talcott Parsons, Robert K. Merton, George C. Homans, P. A. Sorokin, C. P. Loomis, Warren G. Bennis, R. O. Lippitt, and others has been expanded and refined by numerous other theoreticians.

IMPLICATIONS FOR SOCIAL TREATMENT

Hearn views the systems approach as particularly well suited to the profession of social work for several reasons (1969, p. 2):

> It [systems approach] is based on the assumption that matter, in all of its forms, living and nonliving, can be regarded as systems and that systems, as systems, have certain discrete properties that are capable of being studied. Individuals, small groups . . . families, organizations . . . neighborhoods, and communities—in short, the entities with which social work is usually involved—can be regarded as systems with certain common properties.

Others[17] have suggested that social systems theory could provide a mode of conceptualizing which "would bring phenomena and events into dynamic relation to each other, taking time span into account and encompassing the steady inflow of life." This view holds that general systems theory is not in itself a body of knowledge, but a "way of thinking and analysis" which will help us to understand the relational determinants of behavior in the person-in-situation configuration (Janchill, 1969, p. 77). Another asset of the systems approach is that it replaces a linear approach to causation and emphasizes an understanding of cause by the observation and interpretation of functional consequences, both manifest and latent. The practitioner is directed to see that the reason for behavior may lie in another system, rather than in the system of origin (Janchill, 1969, p. 81). Thus systems theory would provide a "richer understanding of symptomatology" by viewing a symptom in terms of function for and across systems. Finally, systems theory "presents the challenge of identification and selection" of appropriate points

17. See Janchill (1969, pp. 74–83).

for intervention, while leaving unsettled the choice of strategy or technique of helping. This is viewed as an alternative approach to the profession's current tendency to dwell exclusively on process and technique and to confuse these with the goals they were meant to serve (Janchill, 1969, p. 82).

Lippitt, Watson, and Westley (1958, pp. 5–9) have outlined the role of the practitioner operating from a social systems framework. The change agent (for our purposes, social work practitioner) typically intervenes on behalf of the client system (specific person or group that is being helped) in one or several of the following systems:

1. Individual personality system.
2. Face-to-face group system.
3. Organizational system.
4. Community system.

The client system is viewed not as an isolated unit, but as a part of a dynamic system that in turn is related to other systems. The change agent works with the client system to change its structure or way of functioning in order to cope more effectively with its changing environment. The role of the change agent will typically include (1958, pp. 104–111):

1. Diagnostic clarification of the problem.
2. Assessment of the client system's motivation and capacity to change.
3. Assessment of the change agent's motivation ("Why is he there in the first place?") and available resources.
4. Aiding the client system in selecting change objectives.
5. Choosing an appropriate helping role:
    (*a*) Mediating and stimulating new connections within the client system.
    (*b*) Presenting expert knowledge on procedures.
    (*c*) Providing strength from within (change agent joins client system as an autonomous subpart).

(d) Creating special environment.

In addition to this somewhat general framework for the social systems–oriented practioner, other attempts have been made to utilize systems concepts in the process of interpersonal helping.

Schwartz (1971) has developed a theory of practice called the interactional model, which views the individual not as an isolated entity, but as existing in a symbiotic relationship with his nurturing group.[18] Polsky, Claster, and Goldberg (Polsky, 1962; Polsky, Claster, & Goldberg, 1968, 1970) have utilized a social systems approach in analyzing change processes within residential settings for delinquent youth.

LIMITATIONS

A major problem for change agents has been the systems approach's primary emphasis on processes of integration and stability within social systems and only secondary interest in processes of change. "A 'system' model emphasizes primarily the details of how stability is achieved and only derivatively how change evolves out of the incompatibilities and conflicts in the system" (Chin, 1961, p. 212).

Historically, this has had to do with the different perspectives of the social scientist and the change agent. The social scientist has generally preferred not to change the system, but to study they way it works. The change agent has been much more interested in a theory of changing a system. Part of the problem, then, lies in the distinction between knowledge for the sake of knowledge and knowledge to inform action. Later developments in systems theory have emphasized change processes to a greater degree and have offered models that assume constant change and development and the decay of systems over time.

18. See Schwartz & Zalba (1971) and Shulman (1968).

Another problem with the systems approach has to do with the closeness with which the theoretical model fits the realities of the practice situation. How translatable are systems concepts to the actual practice of social treatment? Consider the dilemma of the practitioner who is called upon to act, but is confronted with a variety of theoretical models that do not readily yield directions for intervention. What Chin describes as an "intellectual challenge" of great import (1961, p. 214) awaits the scientist-scholar who can bridge the gap between systems theory and practice.

Finally, the role of the change agent in the systems model is still somewhat ambiguous. Does he remain outside of the client system or become an autonomous part of it? By what sanction and under what legitimation does he enter into a relationship with the client system, and what is to be his role in the development of objectives of change? These and other questions await the further conceptualization of the systems approach to planned change. Despite these and other limitations, the fact remains that the utility of the systems model for social work practice—either in the application of specific concepts or in the provision of an overall conceptual framework for practice—has only barely been explored.

Humanistic-Existential Approaches

Existentialism, while less a formal theory of human behavior than a philosophy of man's relationship to himself and others and the cosmos, has nonetheless had an impact on the field of social treatment. The approaches I categorize as humanistic-existential contain a greater range of variation than, for example, behavioral approaches to treatment. Nonetheless, there does appear to be a common core, particularly in regard to the view of man, which transcends the various other approaches discussed here. It should be noted that the common bedfellows I create might not, if given the option, choose to see themselves in similar company.

MAJOR ASSUMPTIONS

Krill (1966, p. 291) has provided a working definition of existentialism: "meaningful living through self encounter in the situation at hand despite a world of apparent futility."

According to Krill, meaningful living is not necessarily equated with happiness or pleasure; self-encounter is essentially awareness of one's own personal freedom of choice and the responsibility one bears for his actions as he responds to others and to the world of possibilities available to him. The world of apparent futility is an awareness that one can act despite the lack of a guarantee of reward for one's behavior.

Existential philosophy and specifically existentially based treatment operate on the following assumptions: (1) that man has the potential freedom to make choices in a responsible manner, though this freedom may be impaired by inner conflicts or blockages in development; (2) that man can be helped to find meaning in life through the liberation of his inner strengths; (3) that dignity is inherent in the human condition; (4) that man is a being in the process of becoming; and (5) that with help man may move to a higher level of authenticity (Sinsheimer, 1969, p. 68). The assumptions reflect Camus's (1961) comment about the source of man's greatness: "It lies in his decision to be stronger than his condition."

VIEW OF MAN

The existentialists view modern man as beset by the twin problems of alienation and anomie (Krill, 1969, p. 36):

> There is a sense of aimless drifting, or at times being helplessly driven, both of which relate to one's sense of impotence and personal insignificance. One considers oneself as being fixed in place either by tradition, heredity, social position, or psychological and social determinisms. One has been formed, or perhaps victimized, by the powers that be or by those that were before.

Paradoxically, along with this missing sense of personal freedom and hence diminished responsibility, there is an increased expectation that one's surrounding environment should change in such a way as to bring one increased comfort, protection and happiness. The experience of suffering is therefore felt to be unfair, and bitterness as well as envy arises toward others in more fortunate circumstances. Quick and easy solutions are sought to manipulate the environment in order to reduce any personal pain and bring about a state of pleasure or comfort. The variety of efforts is vast and extends from pills and television to infidelity and alcoholism.

By contrast, the existentialist man is a free agent who achieves his meaning through responsible choice and through the stance he takes toward life's pain and suffering (Sinsheimer, 1969, p. 68). Man hungers for a unity both within himself and with the rest of the universe. "Man's most human and passionate need is for a fullness, an expressiveness of the self that can bestow upon every single behavioral act a unifying sense of meaning" (Krill, 1966, p. 292). It is the assertion of man's freedom to act, no matter how grim the circumstances, that allows him freedom and affirms what is unique about him as a human being. Krill cites Camus, who spoke of the authentic man as "one in permanent revolt" (1956), and quotes Kazantzakis (1959) through Zorba on the subject: "You know, they say that age kills the fire inside of a man—that he hears death coming. He opens the door and says come in, give me rest. That is a pack of lies! I have enough fight in me to devour the world—and so, I fight!"

Krill provides a good summary of the existential view of man (1966, p. 293):

To conceptualize this experience of [man's] freedom, we may look at it in two ways. First, one's awareness that no man can manipulate the world so as to create a guaranteed sense of security and happiness means that he need not bow to any authority that promises it. . . . Second, if one is sensitive to the vitality that yet remains within himself, and is true to it as the essence of his human being, he has experienced the fact of freedom within himself. He is aware that knowledge of a frustrating world does not defeat him. . . . The unifying action between himself, others and the world is something he decides to create and be responsible for himself, as a man, and he bases his whole sense of direction upon his vitality that refuses and revolts against the frustrating limits the world presents. He asserts his human longing for unity over and against the indifference of the universe.

The assertion of his freedom is meaningful in and of itself and is not dependent upon the outcome of his action, which is often determined by an unpredictable and at times absurd world. Humanness is not viewed as a fixed state of being, but as a constant process of becoming, unfolding, and venturing forth. Existentialism argues against the fragmentation of man and seeks to view him in his sense of wholeness, rejecting a deterministic view of life.

MAJOR TENETS

Existentialism is less a theory than a school of thought concerned with issues of choice, freedom, and responsibility. Its roots are deep in the thinking of Pascal, Kierkegaard, Heidegger, Nietzsche, and Buber, and its tenets have been popularized in the recent philosophical, literary, and artistic creations of Sartre, Camus, Hesse, Ionesco, Kazantzakes, and Bergman. Practitioners and theoreticians of the helping professions—Gordon Allport, Rollo May, Erich Fromm, Victor Frankl, Donald Krill, Karen Horney, Carl Rogers, Fritz Perls, O. H. Mowrer, William Glasser, Ludwig Binswanger, Erwin Straus—while not necessarily all existential therapists, have extrapolated helping principles from existentialist thought to the treatment encounter.

The essence of existentialist thought is perhaps best captured in Kierkegaard's use of the word "existence" to mean "man's possibility of being himself by realizing his potentialities to the full" (quoted in Sinsheimer, 1969, p. 67). Man, faced with an absurd and unpredictable world and burdened with doubt and anxiety, chooses nonetheless to act in a way that is responsible to his innermost being and in so doing authenticates his existence, is saved from total despair, and gains his freedom.

IMPLICATIONS FOR SOCIAL TREATMENT

Existential treatment is based on the union of human behavioral and existential concepts within the treatment relationship. The goal of therapy is the client's achievement of a firm sense of wholeness and a fuller experiencing of freedom and autonomy. Psychopathology is viewed as an arrest in man's ability to unfold his inner potentialities (Sinsheimer, 1969, p. 68). Central to existentially based treatment is the fact that the therapist views the client as a "whole man" and tries to grasp him in his present reality. Any fragmented view of man (narrow view of symptomatic behavior) is rejected in favor of a total conception of the person in his life state. Both therapist and client become "humanized"; that is, the therapist *feels with* and *is with* a part of his client's experience as it connects with part of his own humanity (Tropp, 1969, p. 21E). The worker attempts to establish an "I-thou" rather than an "I-it" relationship with his client.[19] The helping stance is viewed as an encounter in which one human being shares his humanity with another. The humanist credo may be stated as follows:

> I see in him [the client] what I am too—mortal, fallible, subject to pains, misfortune and crisis, strong and weak. . . . Today, he . . . is ridden by things that are in the saddle—tomorrow it

19. See Buber (1958, p. 3).

may be me. How, then, can I play a god, if I am as one human being to another? . . . I can only help, as sometimes I too may need help from a fellow man . . . (Tropp, 1969, pp. 20–21E).

Thus, as one human being to another, do helper and helped come together in the therapeutic encounter.

Krill outlines five goals of existential treatment (1969, pp. 38–49): (1) aiding the process of disillusionment, in which the goal is to reveal to the client the reality that the very way he goes about thinking of himself and relating to others defeats his purpose of seeking peace and harmony; (2) confronting freedom, in which the client becomes aware that he does have a choice in action different from the one prompted by childhood strivings and past history; (3) discovering meaning in suffering, in which the client learns that suffering is an inherent part of life and one's growth as a person is dependent on acceptance of and willingness to grapple with this suffering; (4) realizing the necessity of dialogue—creaive growth and change are seldom intellectual decisions activated by will power alone, but require the sharing of humanity with one's fellow man; (5) accepting the way of commitment—being loyal to those realities of the human condition one has discovered to be true and meaningful for oneself.

Gestalt therapy (Perls, 1969) bears many resemblances to existential therapy in its view of the totality of the person in his life situation and its emphasis on sharing of the human experience. Glasser's (1965) "reality therapy" and some of the work of Mowrer (1961) appear to have a base in existential thought. Within the field of social work, in addition to Krill, Tropp (1969, 1971) has developed a humanistic-existential approach to working with groups. Countless other modalities of social treatment, too numerous to detail here, owe at least part of their heritage to existentialist thought.

LIMITATIONS

It is difficult to criticize existentialism in relation to its potential for social treatment, since it is first and foremost a philosophy—a way of living—rather than a theory of behavior. It is precisely this fact that makes for a perplexing problem: Does the client need to accept the philosophy in order to get help? Take the died-in-the-wool materialist (or anyone else, for that matter) who is experiencing problems in his marriage or elsewhere in his personal life; what if he simply cannot come to grips with Krill's first stage? The end result of existential treatment is that professional and client share the same existentialist view of life, at least insofar as it requires being honest and responsible to their inner beings. This entails quite a commitment on the part of the client (as Krill's last step suggests), so what of clients unwilling or unable, for whatever reason, to make such a commitment? In no way does this problem negate the value of existential thought for social treatment; rather it underscores the key difference between this and other approaches. When one enters existentially based treatment, one encounters not simply a technology of helping, but a philosophy of life as well.

Another limitation of the application of existential thought to social treatment is the dearth of literature on the subject, particularly in social work. We need a great deal more clarification of just what it is that an existentially oriented helping professional actually does in the therapeutic encounter. One hopes that what is now a mere trickle in the literature will increase considerably in the near future.

Summary

In sum, three bodies of theory and one philosophical system constituting some of the major underpinnings of social treatment have been examined. This examination yields the following theory profile:

THEORETICAL BASES OF SOCIAL TREATMENT

Major Assumptions

Psychoanalytic Theory

1. Basic personality organization with which child is born constitutes the structural and functional basis for later development.
2. Phases of development rooted in biological drives.
3. Personality consists of unconscious and preconscious as well as conscious processes.
4. Critical importance of early childhood experiences.

Social learning Theory

1. Man's psychological nature is his behavior.
2. Directly observable and measurable actions of man constitute the sum and substance of his personality.
3. Behavior (personality) molded by environment: nurture more important than nature.

Social systems theory

1. Systems theory assumes an interaction and interdependency between systems and a high degree of organization within each system.
2. Change in one part of a system will have implications for all other parts of the system and may have effects in contiguous systems as well; e.g., ripple effect.

Humanistic and existential approaches

1. Man has potential freedom to make choices.
2. Man can be helped to find meaning in

life through the liberation of inner
strengths.
3. Dignity is inherent in the human condition.
4. Man is in the process of becoming: "Man's
greatness lies in his decision to be stronger than his condition" (Camus).

View of Man

Psychoanalytic
theory

1. Man's essential nature is desire rather
than reason.
2. Man is a "purposeful animal" from birth,
though his intentionality need not be
conscious.
3. Man is an extremely complex being consisting of conscious and unconscious, rational and irrational processes.
4. Overt, observable behavior is only the
tip of the iceberg of man's personality.

Social learning
theory

1. Man is born a *tabula rasa*, a mechanical
mirror of his environment.
2. Man's personality is largely a product of
his environment and his behavior is the
end result of many separate learning
processes.
3. Behavior is largely explicable by environment, not by drives or inner states.

Social systems
theory

1. Man is viewed not as an isolated entity,
but as a participant in a number of interacting and interdependent dynamic social
systems.

Humanistic and
existential
approaches

1. The existentialist man is a free agent who
achieves his meaning through responsible
choice and through the stance he adopts
toward life's pain and suffering.

2. Humanness is not a fixed state of being, but a constant process of becoming unfolding and venturing forth.
3. Man is viewed in his wholeness, in the totality of his humanness.

Major Tenets

Psychoanalytic theory

1. Psychoanalytic theory of development and psychoanalytic treatment; psychoanalytic ego psychology.
2. Basic structure of personality: id-ego-superego.
3. Stages of development: oral, anal, phallic, latency, genital.
4. Defense mechanisms; ego functions; psychic energy.
5. Erikson's "eight ages of man"; White's "competence."

Social learning theory

1. Respondent and operant behavior.
2. Reinforcement, extinction, shaping, schedules of learning, successive approximation, imitation, modeling effect, punishment, extinction.
3. A single behavior is the end result of many separate learning processes.

Social systems theory

1. Social systems; "the patterns of action of people and culture" (Monane).
2. Systems, environment, feedback (positive and negative), ripple effect of change, interaction, interdependence of systems, system boundary, equilibrium, closed system, intersystem framework.

Humanistic and existential approaches

1. Less theory than philosophy.
2. Man, faced with an absurd and unpredictable world and burdened with doubt

and anxiety, nonetheless chooses to act in a way that is responsible to his innermost being and in doing so authenticates his existence, is saved from total despair, and gains his freedom.
3. "I-thou."

Implications for Treatment

Psychoanalytic theory

1. Psychoanalysis, psychotherapy, psychoanalytically oriented casework.
2. Importance of uncovering conflicts, "working through" problems, developing insight.
3. Diagnostic implications of developmental theory.

Social learning theory

1. If behavior is the sum total of personality, then behavioral modification is the treatment of choice for the individual with social or emotional problems.
2. Behaviorally specific treatment goals.
3. The "problem" (delinquency, mental illness) is defined in equally behaviorally specific terms.

Social systems theory

1. Offers a conceptual framework for all of social work practice; micro and marco intervention. Social systems theory offers strategies for indirect as well as direct intervention.
2. Emphasizes person-problem-situation complex.

Humanistic and existential approaches

1. Existential therapy; Gestalt approaches.
2. Therapist rejects any fragmented view of man and attempts to grasp him in his wholeness. He *feels with* and *is with*

the client's experience as it connects with his own humanity.

3. The helping stance is viewed as an encounter in which one human being shares his humanity with another.

Limitations

Psychoanalytic theory

1. "Richness' of theory leads to contradictory explanations.
2. Poorly defined terminology.
3. Difficult to evaluate; terms like "ego," "id" do not yield readily to operational definition.
4. Too much focus on the individual, not enough on his environment.
5. Deterministic.

Social learning theory

1. Overemphasis on environment.
2. Limited view of man. Is behavior really the sum and substance of personality?
3. Not always possible to control the conditions of learning.
4. Difficulty in specifying complex problems.

Social systems theory

1. Problem of closeness with which social systems model fits with real world.
2. Problem of changing systems.
3. Role of change agent needs further clarification.
4. Lack of many specific strategies and techniques for action.

Humanistic and existential approaches

1. Lack of specificity about exactly what it is that an existentially oriented therapist actually does.
2. Does one necessarily have to accept the existentialist point of view in order to be helped?

In an admittedly limited examination of some of the major bodies of theory that underlie social treatment, a number of points have been underscored. First among these is the idea that any theoretical orientation not only yields strategies and techniques for the practice of social treatment, but also contains within it a certain value orientation and view of man which may have a profound effect upon the nature of the helping relationship. Second, major bodies of theory pertaining to human growth and development are often based on very different assumptions about the nature of man, the importance of early life experiences, the degree to which behavior is determined, and the relative importance in developmental terms of man's inborn nature, versus the nurture he receives from his physical and social environments. One thing that should be clear from both of these points is that the choice of theoretical orientation has a great deal to do with shaping the atmosphere of the therapeutic encounter between client and worker. Because of some of the potential problems inherent in that relationship (as outlined in earlier chapters) and in line with the conception of social treatment offered in the preceding chapter, it would behoove the practitioner of social treatment to examine closely the particular theoretical stance(s) within which he is operating, to see how they influence the social treatment relationship.

It should also be apparent that there is little that falls under the heading of "right" or "wrong" when one discusses theoretical orientation. There simply does not yet exist good empirical evidence suggesting that one theoretical orientation is superior in every respect to all others in the implications it yields for social treatment practice. The aim of the practitioner should be to disavow an either/or approach to theory and attempt to make use of as many theoretical models as possible in order to ensure a broad range of interventive strategies to fit the particular problem of the client. This approach to theory is systematically eclectic and not simply an amalgam of theoretical models. One's choice of theory to inform practice is made with an eye toward purposeful professional activity: the worker has a reason for doing what he does, based not merely on a value orientation but on an evidence orientation as well.

Finally, the criteria for choosing a particular orientation will be twofold: (1) Does the theory and its practice implications fit with the value requirements of the social treatment helping relationship? (2) Does the theory work? Is the effectiveness of the particular techniques suggested by the theory sufficiently evident to warrant adoption?

I hope this chapter has provided a pathway toward the examination of theory for the practitioner. Neither dazzled by the brilliance of the concepts nor put off by the level of abstraction, the practitioner goes right to the heart of the theory in asking: What are the basic assumptions on which this theory rests? What are the inherent value orientation and view of man implicit in the theory? What are the major tenets of the theory and what implications do they yield for practice? What limitations appear evident in the theory or in its application? What is the empirical evidence that supports this theory? Finally, how does this theory fit with the value constraints that should inform the professional helping relationship? To execute such an analysis of practice theory, difficult as it might be in some respects, is to go a long way toward clarifying the foundation of social treatment.

ADDITIONAL SOURCES

Anderson, R. E., & Carter, I. *Human behavior in the social environment*. Chicago: Aldine, 1974.

Freud, S. *Complete introductory lectures on psychoanalysis*. New York: Norton, 1966.

May, R., ed. *Existential psychology*. New York: Random House, 1961.

Skinner, B. F. *Contingencies of reinforcement*. New York: Appleton, 1969.

Von Bertalanffy, L. *General systems theory: Essays on its foundation and development*. New York: Braziller, 1969.

5

The Social Treatment Sequence I: Direct Helping in the Beginning, Intermediate, and Ending Phases

The discussion of social treatment thus far has gradually narrowed its focus from broad ecological and social concerns to issues related to the total field of social work practice to a conceptual framework for interpersonal helping with individuals, families, and small groups, and finally to a brief overview of some of the theoretical foundations of social treatment. In this and the following chapter, the focus will sharpen even further as we examine what the social treatment practitioner actually does in the helping relationship.

The particular emphases and activities of the beginning, intermediate, and ending phases of the social treatment sequence will be examined in the light of four major elements in the helping process:

1. *Basic objectives.* What is the essential purpose of each phase in the social treatment sequence?
2. *Worker activities.* What are the major tasks of the worker in the beginning, middle, and ending phases of social treatment?
3. *Client perspectives.* What is the consumer view of the various phases of the social treatment sequence? What expectations are placed on the client? What demands

are made of him? What are his special needs?

4. *Resources.* What resources are available to client and worker to aid them in implementing the social treatment sequence?

This chapter will stress direct helping—what the worker does directly with the client in their face-to-face encounter. Indirect helping, or what the worker does on behalf of his client, will be covered in the following chapter. Taken together, direct and indirect helping constitute the process of social treatment. In reality, direct and indirect helping are integrated into a unified process that extends from the beginning to the ending phases of the social treatment sequence. It is only for purposes of explication and elaboration that they are treated separately here.

Phases of the Social Treatment Sequence

There are eight identifiable phases in the social treatment sequence:

Beginning phases:	1. Intake
	2. Assessment and social diagnosis
	3. Determination of goals
	4. Selection of social treatment plan
	5. Establishment of working agreement
Intermediate phases:	6. Sustaining social treatment
Ending phases:	7. Evaluation
	8. Termination and Aftercare

Two general points may be made about the eight phases: they are *sequentially related* (one flowing from the other) and *nonmutually exclusive*. It is important, therefore, to

conceive of the social treatment sequence not as a series of
rigidly fixed steps to be followed, but rather as a continuum
of distinct but free-flowing phases, each assuming a greater
or lesser degree of prominence at given points along the continuum. For example, assessment culminating in a social diagnosis is identified as the primary activity in the second
phase of the social treatment sequence. Given a fairly typical
case of a couple seeking help in dealing with the behavioral
problems of one of their children, the early activity of the
worker will consist largely of assembling all of the relevant
biopsychosocial and cultural information about the family
and assessing its relation to the problem. This early assessment will raise a number of basic questions (for example,
who is the client—the child? the family?) and will doubtless
make use of many different formats for obtaining helpful information (diagnostic psychological testing, school reports,
observations of the family process in natural surroundings).
The results of these efforts will be a social diagnosis (a redef-
inition of the problem constellation) followed in turn by a
determination of change goals and a plan of action. But the
derivation of a working hypothesis of what is wrong and
what might be done about it does not signal the termination
of assessment activities. On the contrary, the worker constantly reassesses the problem, tests his early hunches, seeks
new information, and rechecks old. In brief, while assessment activities assume a high degree of prominence early in
the social treatment sequence, they continue to a lesser degree throughout all of the phases. A similar point could be
made regarding other components of the social treatment sequence, particularly social diagnosis, goal determination,
and selection of a social treatment (or case) plan.

The major point is that the social treatment sequence is
anything but a lock-step process involving completely separate and unrelated phases. From the first moment of contact
with the client, the worker is (or should be) offering help

and support, building the relationship, beginning the process of assessment, and formulating with the client tentative hunches as to the nature of the problem. What the various phases offer, then, is a kind of road map to help guide the worker's activity, rather than a single track consisting of mutually exclusive steps leading to a particular course of action. Finally, it should be emphasized that the various phases are sequentially related. This is important particularly in light of some of the potential problems with the narrow method approach to practice described in Chapter 3. For example, the sequence suggested here would have the social treatment plan flow directly from a statement of client goals, which in turn are based on an assessment of the social problem as experienced by the client. This sequence diminishes the chance of molding the client to the method of helping rather than vice versa.

Activities of worker and client will of course vary depending on the method of social treatment used. Method-specific techniques (for example, from behavior modification, individual psychotherapy, or transactional analysis) will not be discussed here; my goal is to provide some awareness of the basic steps taken by the worker to engage the client in a helping relationship.[1] In this sense, procedures will be discussed at a level applicable to many different methods of social treatment.

What the worker can offer the client (at least initially) is less dependent upon his mastery of any particular method of treatment than on his ability to convey to the client a sysematic approach to problem solving. Finally, I do not agree with the view that helping clients is synonymous with the application of a particular method of treatment. People in trouble need someone to listen to their problems attentively,

1. For a brief description and bibliography of specific methods of social treatment, see the Appendix.

support their decision to seek help, and offer a systematic
way of proceeding to assess and cope with their difficulties.

Objectives. The basic purpose of this initial phase of the
social treatment sequence is to determine whether help is
needed and, if so, where in the network of community services it may be found. There are three possible outcomes
when a client makes contact with a social agency to request
help or information: (1) a decision that service is not required at this particular time, (2) a decision to refer the
client to another social agency for the appropriate help, and
(3) a decision to accept the client for service.

The first alternative applies to those situations in which a
client desires only some preliminary information (as in the
case of a prospective adoptive parent), has already initiated
a service contact with another agency and is merely cross-
checking to see that the appropriate contact has been made,
or has decided in the interim between the initial contact and
the first appointment that service is not required.

The second alternative (referral) is commonly used in social agency practice and underscores an important point regarding the intake process: responsibility to clients in the
intake phase extends beyond the pool of client applicants for
whom the agency's services are deemed appropriate. The
reasons for referral are many, but perhaps the two most important are demand for services that the agency does not
provide (the client seeking genetic counseling from the family service agency) and appropriate requests for services
that cannot be met because of prior commitments (as in the
case of an emotionally disturbed child unable to be placed in
residential treatment because the service has reached its capacity). In these instances, the function of the intake worker is to try to arrange for alternative helping services at

appropriate agencies—perhaps a university hospital for the client seeking genetic counseling and outpatient treatment for the emotionally disturbed child.

The third alternative—the decision to offer service—signifies that the client has entered the service system of the agency and begun the process of social treatment. The decision to offer service may be altered at some later point in the treatment sequence—for example, after a full assessment and social diagnosis have revealed new information requiring a referral for services outside the scope of the agency—or may continue through to termination of service.

Worker Activities. The central activity in this initial phase of social treatment involves helping the client to specify the problem that caused him to seek help and deciding whether to accept the client for service. Though the method of intake varies considerably from agency to agency, certain worker activities remain fairly consistent. From the first moment of contact, the worker attempts to convey to the client a concern and respect for him and his problem. He or she doesn't try to allay completely the client's anxieties and doubts, but attempts to use them to help the client mobilize himself to tell about his problem. The worker begins with gathering the basic facts of identifying information—name, age, sex, place of residence, occupation, and the like—and even in this fairly perfunctory activity begins to convey to the client a planful approach to the problem. Client doubts about seeking help are addressed directly, but the worker avoids falling into the trap of making promises ("Everything will be all right") that cannot be guaranteed. One of the most important things the worker does at this stage is to listen attentively, not only to what the client is saying, but also to the way it is said. The affect of the client, the order in which spouses and children speak (in a family interview), and such things as physical posturing and nonverbal communication may provide important clues to the worker later in the assessment phase. Effective listening is an acquired skill and is an active rather than passive technique. Mastery of it helps the worker to avoid the tendency to fill up the air with words in order to overcome his own anxiety.

Other worker activities in the intake phase might well include exploring with the client the kinds of help that the agency offers, including the form it might take (personal counseling, family therapy, group sessions), what the cost might be, what kind of commitment would be required from the client, and finally a discussion of the professional staff and their qualifications and areas of expertise. The client is advised as to what he might reasonably expect in the way of process—continued assessment, goal setting, treatment planning—and may be urged in the initial session to commit himself to exploring the presenting problem further in several diagnostic sessions. The worker avoids accepting ready-made diagnoses of the problem (as when a parent sees the problem as being exclusively the child's) as well as "quick fix" solutions offered by the client seeking legitimacy for a predetermined course of action: "If you could only talk to my husband about his drinking . . . The children and I are afraid to bring this up with him." Here the worker would accept the presenting problem (the husband's drinking and its effects on the family) as experienced by the client, at least as the beginning point for social treatment, but would avoid accepting the ready-made solution of the client of talking "to my husband about his drinking." Undoubtedly the worker will want to talk with the father as a spouse and family member, but not under the preconception that he is the *cause* of the problem.

One useful technique in the initial session is to summarize briefly with the client: what brought you together in the first place (the presenting problem); where you are now in the initial process of assessment; where you would like to proceed in the immediate future: referral or continued assessment. In effect, this summary indicates to the client:

1. A systematic approach to problem-solving as distinct from friendly advice-giving.
2. A concern for the client as a person: *he* is important
3. Some sense of the kind of help available from the agency.
4. Some indication of what the client's involvement in and commitment to the social treatment process are expected to be.

Client Perspectives. Landy (1965) has delineated some of the problems faced by a person seeking help in our culture. Among them are:

1. The probability that his problem will become known to relevant others, who may in turn question his role and achievement capacity.
2. The likelihood that the client will have to admit to the help-giver that he has failed in his attempts to conquer the problem on his own, as the culture demands.
3. The fact that he will probably have to surrender some autonomy in relying on the expertise and judgment of the helper.
4. The possibility that existing relationships may be threatened or changed as a result of the remedial process.

Small wonder, then, that many clients experience fear of self-examination and change, anxiety over the possible consequences of seeking help (for example, negative influences on employment), and ambivalence about entering into a helping relationship that will, of necessity, involve a certain degree of dependence upon a professional person. Along with this uncertainty there is often a compelling need to know what the professional view of the problem is and what should be done about it. Thus the client will often use the initial intake session to push for answers to questions that will require a much longer period of assessment, and which even then may not be completely resolved. For example, the parents of a child with emotional and behavioral problems who want desperately to know how serious their child's difficulties are and what part they played in their development; the depressed middle-aged person who wonders, "Am I going crazy?"; the young couple experiencing sexual problems in their marriage who wonder (separately), "Is something wrong with me?"—all are hoping for some reassurance that they are not the cause of the problem, or crazy, or abnormal. Having mustered the courage to seek help (after some soul-searching and doubt, one can almost always assume) there is a need for early resolution: "What is the matter?"; "What can be done to help?"; "How long will it take?"—questions that by and large the professional will be unable to answer with certainty in an initial session.

These questions being largely unanswerable (at least initially), the client often desires to hear some reaffirmation of the decision to seek help, as well as some specific steps to be taken to initiate the remedial process. If, after all the indecision and difficulty in initiating the help-seeking process, the client has come to the initial session, then it is a fair assumption that he has developed a motivation to do something about his problem—a motivation on which the worker can capitalize to engage the client in the assessment process.

Resources. Perhaps the greatest single resource available to the professional in the intake phase is a thorough knowledge of community facilities and services. Clients in need do not always make the correct choice among the places where one can go for help, and referral for service elsewhere after an initial screening interview is typical. What is crucial here is that the worker build the bridge to the needed service and help the client cross it. Plagued by doubts concerning the need for help and frightened of the consequences of change, the client may interpret the referral as a sign that his problem is "really not that serious" and remove himself from the help-seeking process. One way to avoid this is to personalize the referral process, by referring the client to a specific professional with whom the intake worker has a relationship. Follow-up may be needed to ensure that the contact is made —a phone call for an appointment, arrangement for transportation, a later check to make sure that the client made contact with the appropriate person. What is important is that help can be rendered—not only in the mainstream of the agency service, but in the interface between agencies as well. Acting in the role of broker of services, the intake worker may provide the crucial link in the chain of helping even though his own contact with the client is minimal.

The proper fulfillment of this broker role requires the professional to have a knowledge of community services extending beyond a directory of social agencies. This should include specific information about who is offering the needed services and an up-to-date fact sheet on the kinds of clients sought by particular agencies.

ASSESSMENT AND SOCIAL DIAGNOSIS

Objectives. Richmond (1917, p. 39) describes assessment and social diagnosis as consisting of "those items, which, however trifling or apparently irrelevant when viewed as isolated facts may when taken together throw light upon the question: What course of procedure will place this client in his right relationship to society?" This view stresses the linkage between fact-gathering (assessment), description of the problem (social diagnosis), and goal-setting and treatment-planning. Hamilton (1951), p. 214) distinguished between diagnosis (understanding the client's psychosocial problem) and evaluation (understanding the total functioning of the person with respect to his problem). Later, Perlman (1957, p. 171) described diagnosis as a "kind of cross sectional view of the forces interacting in the client's problem situation," and Hollis (1964, p. 178) defined diagnosis simply as an undertaking to answer the question, "How can this person be helped?" Finally, Sarri, Galinsky, et al. (1967, p. 39–72) distinguish between diagnosis as a process (of fact-gathering and assessment) and as a product (a diagnostic statement of the client's problem).

Common to each of these descriptions of diagnosis is the notion of a joint process of fact-gathering toward the end of developing a statement of the problem that will lend itself to the development of specific change goals. For present purposes, assessment and social diagnosis may be described as a joint process through which worker and client explore and assess the physical, psychological, and social conditions as they impinge upon the client and then attempt to relate their findings to the range of social problems experienced by the client in a manner that yields objectives for change as well as a plan of action.

This latter point is important to underscore: *The development of a diagnostic statement of the client's problem should not be viewed as an end in itself, but as a means of producing concrete change goals and a plan of intervention.* Thus the result of the diagnostic process should not be the attachment of the proper label to the client's problem, but rather should provide a working statement of the problem which will yield specific objectives for social treatment.

Worker Activities. The primary objective of the worker in this phase of the social treatment sequence is to collect and assess all of the relevant information concerning the client and his problem, toward the end of arriving with the client at a statement of his difficulty which will yield specific objectives for change. To do this effectively, the worker must have some knowledge of the client's total functioning as a person. In essence, the worker views the client and his presenting problem through four different lenses: physical functioning, psychological functioning, social functioning, and environmental context. Within each category there are several kinds of information that the worker will need to know in order to arrive at a social diagnosis. These areas of information are briefly summarized below. It may be well to note here that "client" may refer equally to an individual, a family, or a small group. In any event, the kinds of information the worker needs to know about the individual remain essentially the same.

Physical Functioning. In addition to the basic identifying information—age, sex, race, physical dimensions—the worker attempts to develop a picture of the general medical history of the client, including physical impairments or abnormalities, present physical condition, neurological impairments, prominent diseases, and medications currently being taken. The purpose of all this is not to arrive at a medical diagnosis—though a medical examination may be suggested as part of the assessment process—but to get as complete a picture as possible of the way the client's physical condition effects his psychological and social functioning.

For example, the knowledge that the husband of a middle-aged couple seeking counseling for sexual problems had a history of coronary difficulties might well prove to be crucial to the social diagnosis and subsequent treatment plan for the pair. Similarly, the fact that an eight-year-old child referred by his parents for behavior problems at home and in school had a younger sibling afflicted with leukemia could have a direct bearing on the presenting problem. On a more general level, it would be well to remember that soma cannot be completely separated from psyche, and that physical well-being (or the absence of it) influences emotional well-being and vice versa.

Thus, things like a person's general physical appearance, including such elements as gait and posture, may yield important clues to the worker. The father who cheerfully tells the worker that his is a "normal, happy family" with no real problems is at least partially contradicted by the look of deep concern on his face; the slouched and dejected posture of the delinquent may say more about his real feelings about himself than contradictory verbal messages; the young child of recently divorced parents who contributes little verbally to an initial interview may reveal a great deal of his feelings of sadness and loss through his husky voice and clinging to a favorite stuffed animal.

In sum, adequate knowledge of the client's physical functioning should be considered requisite to social diagnosis, and even the most fleeting of physical clues given in the early sessions should be noted, as they may shed light later on in the assessment process.

Psychological Functioning. One typically thinks of psychological evaluation in terms of a battery of psychological tests administered by a professional psychologist. Batteries may include any of a number of intelligence tests, tests of general ability or level of development, vocational preference tests, or projective tests designed to give a picture of an individual's personality characteristics. Such a battery of tests is often requested by the worker early in the assessment process to enable him to get a reasonably complete picture of the individual's psychological functioning. Particularly in the case of children referred for behavioral and/or learning difficulties, an accurate account of intelligence, developmental level, perceptual ability, and language development will be crucial to the social diagnosis. Suffice it to say that the special expertise and skill in testing of the psychologist are often drawn on heavily by the social treatment practitioner in the assessment phase.

Perhaps more important for our present purpose, however, is the range of psychological information the worker can obtain directly from the client through the interview process and as a result of direct observation. Critical to the social diagnosis and later treatment plan is a thorough knowledge of the kinds of coping mechanisms that the client characteristically employs in problem situations. Of interest here are the client's typical manner of handling external difficulties—for example, interpersonal conflict, financial difficulties, job pressures—as well as internal emotional states, such as stress, anxiety, fear, sadness, anger, pain, elation. Thus the child who typically handles fear of failure in the classroom by throwing his books on the floor, the office worker who deals with job pressures by excessive drinking, and the submissive wife who harbors deep resentment toward her husband and who handles it by becoming even more docile and outwardly sweet—all provide useful information to the worker for the later task of planning with the client for alternative way of dealing with problem situations.

Also important is the client's self-concept. Does he consider himself worthless, bad, powerless, capable? Another factor is his "learning profile." Whether or not a behavior modification approach will eventually be used, it is important to have some idea of the formats that are most conducive to client growth and learning. For example, is this a person who would respond well to peer pressure and would do well in the context of a group situation, or is the client highly self-motivated, well disciplined, and able to act on the basis of insight and carry out change assignments with only the support and encouragement of the worker? A good indicator of the client's preferred format for learning is his past success or failure in other change situations: self-help groups, adult education, one-to-one counseling.

In sum, what the worker needs to know is some very practical information about the individual's characteristic coping patterns, self-concept, and learning profile—all of which information will be brought directly to bear in subsequent phases of the social treatment sequence.

Social Functioning. The starting point for social treatment was previously defined as the social problem as experienced by the client—indicating a need for some knowledge of the client's functioning with relevant others in his life web. For example, what is the nature of the client's role performance? What multiple roles does the client fulfill (husband, father, mother, breadwinner) and how well does he or she perform in each of these roles? Often clients experience strain between some of the multiple roles they must fulfill (for example, breadwinner and father) and in many instances role expectations may not be clearly spelled out.

Communication is another important area of social information to be explored by the worker. In the troubled family, for example, what are the patterns of communication? Who talks to whom? How do the important messages of family life get communicated? Directly? Nonverbally? Not at all?

Similarly, when the client is a family it is useful to get some measure of total family functioning. Families, like individuals, function as organic wholes and may be assessed in the light of their ability to cope with stress to solve problems, or simply to deal with the exigencies of family life.

The worker will also want to know something of an individual client's peer group relations. Does he have close friends? How does he view them? What are his work group relationships? Even more important to assess is the individual's relationship skills. How capable is he of forming close relationships with other people? How easily does he meet other people? Is he comfortable or uneasy in social relationships? Often the worker may discover poorly developed relationship skills in clients for whom the presenting problem is something different. For example, the child who has difficulty carrying out assignments in the classroom and who is prone to temper tantrums may also prove to be relatively "empty" of marketable peer relating skills, and as a consequence have few if any friends.[2]

Environmental Context. Environmental context, as used here, includes the sociocultural matrix of which the client is a part, as well as any help-giving organizations or institutions with which he is currently involved. Important variables to examine include social class, race, cultural heritage, religious affiliation, and major reference groups. The white, middle-class bias of much of social work practice has been recounted in detail elsewhere, and there is a growing body of literature designed to inform the practitioner of the culture and heritage of various minority populations, as well as numerous articles on social work practice with clients from differing class and ethnic backgrounds.[3]

One very important area of information is the preferred pattern of helping in a particular group or subculture. To whom, for example, does an individual turn initially for help with problems: family? friends? religious leader? What kind of help is he likely to find when he gets there? friendly advice? admonition? ritualistic prescription? Similarly, how does a particular culture or class view interpersonal problems (for example, marital problems)? Are they to be discussed openly, or borne stoically? What subjects, if any, are taboo?

Often the worker may find the client linked to another source of help—the parish priest or minister, the physician, the family friend, the relative. The worker should at least be

2. For a further elaboration of relationship in social learning terms, see Brendtro (1969).

3. See, for example, selected bibliographies prepared by the Council on Social Work Education on the Asian, black and chicano, and Indian communities in America (1971).

aware of any such source to avoid working at cross-purpos-
es. To be sensitive to such alternative channels of helping, as
well as to the client's particular sociocultural heritage, signifies an attempt to individualize the person seeking help and
to understand him and his or her situation to the fullest extent possible.

In this respect, it would be remiss to close a discussion of
sociocultural factors without some mention of women's issues and their particular relation to social work practice. In
recent years the women's movement has raised the general
level of consciousness with respect to the special problems of
women in modern society. Sex discrimination, occupational
channeling, and sex role stereotyping are but a few of the
abuses frequently cited. In light of the fact that a majority
of clients seen by social treatment practitioners are women,
it is hoped that the trickle of articles and books on the subject currently in the social work literature will soon become
a torrent.

Working Diagnostic Statement. When the relevant biopsychosociocultural information has been collected, the worker
is ready to prepare a working diagnostic statement. The
purpose of this statement is to order and evaluate all of the
appropriate information in such a way that it can intelli-
gently inform the worker's recommendations to the client.
Typically, a working diagnostic statement would include the
following information: (1) the presenting problem (as experienced by the client); (2) summaries of relevant physical, psychological, social, and environmental data; (3) diagnostic summary (the worker's restatement of the problem in
light of the relevant information); and (4) tentative recommendations.

The worker, as full and equal partner in the helping process, does everything in his power to bring his professional

expertise in problem-solving to bear in the service of the client. This does *not* mean passing on a package of diagnosis, treatment goals, and plan of action to the client as a *fait accompli*. The final selection of specific objectives for change and the selection of a method of social treatment await the joint decision of client and worker in subsequent phases of the social treatment sequence. It *does* mean that the worker does everything in his power to ensure that his recommendations and role in the process of decision-making are informed by the best professional judgment he can muster.

Often he will request a case consultation or staffing, where his working diagnostic statement is reviewed and analyzed by other members of the professional staff. New insights, alternative recommendations, or a need for additional information may emerge from such a conference, which in addition serves the useful function of placing the worker's judgment and fact-finding abilities under the scrutiny of his peers—a scrutiny that helps to ensure high-quality service to clients. Skill in diagnosis comes only after considerable practice, and the level of expertise needed to weave seemingly unrelated facts gathered in assessment into a tentative relation to the client's presenting problem gives added credence to the notion of a case conference where expertise may be shared.

With the completion of the working diagnostic statement —possibly revised or amended through peer consultation— the worker has completed the early task of assessment and evaluation and is ready to engage the client in the major activities of goal-setting and case-planning. Perhaps it is wise to reiterate here what was stressed earlier: the completion of the working diagnostic statement does not signal the end of assessment activities. On the contrary, the worker's tentative diagnostic summary and recommendations, as well as the change goals and case plan selected by client and worker,

will be continually reviewed, revised in accordance with new
information and circumstances, and evaluated during the
entire course of the social treatment sequence.

Client Perspectives. "I am in need of help, but afraid of
self-exposure and commitment to change." This might express the feelings of the client in the second phase of the social treatment sequence. Finding out about the problem will
undoubtedly mean talking about painful things: the marriage that's not working, the child who is increasingly difficult to live with, past failures in making friends and establishing lasting relationships—all this to a stranger who may
or may not prove to be helpful. Small wonder that many
clients fear exposure of their problems, which may lead (in
their view) to moral judgments on the part of the worker or
of the larger society. Particularly for the client with emotional or interpersonal difficulties, the growing fear that he
is abnormal or incomplete as a person may work against an
open examination of problem areas in the assessment phase.

Other clients may doubt the wisdom or necessity of going
into seemingly unrelated, often highly sensitive areas when
to them the problem is clear. Confidentiality of material may
be an issue ("To whom will this information be made available?") and, in the case of married couples or families, the
worker's seemingly innocent question about role relationships or patterns of communication may strike a sensitive
area never openly discussed before.

Counterbalancing the client's reservations about the assessment process will (we hope) be his continued motivation
to seek relief from his problem. As in the intake phase, the
wish for a ready-made and clear-cut solution to his difficulties may cloud over the rationale for a thorough assessment
of functioning. Important in this respect is the client's perception of the early sessions; help cannot be postponed until

a complete social diagnosis is available, and the sessions must offer something in the way of tangible rewards to the client if he is to continue. This early helping can take many forms—having an interested person actually listen to one's concerns, being able to think through more clearly a systematic approach to problem resolution, as well as more concrete forms of assistance such as financial aid, action on one's behalf with the courts, schools, or other agencies, or the provision of some supportive services (a homemaker, visiting nurse, child care).

Again, it is important for the client to know at the end of each session where he and the worker stand in the process of assessment. What kinds of additional information will be necessary and what is expected of him before the next interview? In addition, clients need continued reassurance that they have made the right decision to seek help and praise and encouragement for dealing with areas that are sensitive and often painful to discuss. In sum, the client wishes to feel that he is providing information not to a computer, but to another human being who is sensitive to his needs, respectful of his concern for privacy, and supportive of his desire for change.

Resources. The resources available to worker and client during this second phase of the social treatment sequence are as varied as the kinds of information needed. Some of the typical formats for obtaining information are these:

1. Direct interviews. These may include the client alone and/or his spouse and other family members.
2. *Home visits.* The worker may elect to see the family in its natural life pattern and surroundings.
3. *Diagnostic groups.* Here the client becomes a member of a short-term group for the express purpose of en-

abling the worker to observe his behavior in a peer group. This particular format is often used with children referred for behavioral difficulties for whom few data exist on their functioning in group situations.

4. *Psychiatric, psychological, or physical examination.* Many times the worker calls on the expertise of another professional to shed light on a particular aspect of the individual's functioning.

5. *Collateral contacts.* The worker may initiate contact with relevant others in the individual's social network (in each instance with the permission of the client) to obtain material on role performance and social relationships.

6. *Direct observation.* Finally, the worker may wish to observe the client directly in any number of real-life situations—in the classroom, in a work situation, with spouse and family—to get a more accurate picture of the way the client comes across in a social situation, or, in the case of a family, to get some sense of the family process, a slice of the family life in action.

Supervisors and colleagues provide another useful resource to the practitioner attempting to get some clues to the client's problem in a very short time. Often an initial interview session will yield new insight or avenues of exploration on second examination with a supervisor or colleague one step removed from the process. Many workers make use of video or audio tape recordings to help them remember salient points in an interview, and practitioners working as a team have the advantage of two sets of eyes and ears recording each diagnostic session. Highly successful practioners develop a keen sense of their own diagnostic strengths and weaknesses and know immediately where to turn in the agency or community network to find the necessary skills in assessment to complement their own.

DETERMINATION OF CHANGE GOALS

Objectives. The purpose of this third stage in the social treatment sequence is to identify specific targets for change from the presenting problem as related by the client and elaborated in the working diagnosis. In this phase the client takes the lead in determining the range and order of specific problems to be worked with. Behavioral therapists more than any other single group have delineated the necessary steps in the formulation of specific change objectives (Gambrill, Thomas & Carter, 1971; Bandura, 1969, pp. 70–113; Rose, 1972, pp. 61–72). Typically, the process involves several steps, including client identification of problem areas, establishment of problem hierarchy, and specification of change objectives. Vinter (1967, pp. 13–15), writing from a group work frame of reference, suggests criteria for the formulation of goals, several of which have general applicability to social treatment practice. Goals should (1) be directly related to the client's presenting problem, (2) be formulated in such a way that they seek to reduce stress or difficulty as experienced by the client, and (3) refer to a state of improved functioning outside of the helping encounter. i.e., carry over to the client's real-life situation. Additionally, goals should attempt to be behaviorally specific and capable of lending themselves to subsequent evaluation.

One of the major difficulties with social treatment practice in the past was its failure to identify specific objectives for changes in client functioning. Consequently, improvement often meant presumed changes in inner states ("improved self-image," "better ego integration"), or referred to end states that were overly general and nonspecific ("The client exhibited fewer aggressive and acting-out tendencies"). In fairness, it is not always an easy task to identify behaviorally specific targets for change in the complex web of problems which typically surrounds clients in need of professional help. It is also unfair to say that because specific goals are not identified in a given case, clients do not receive valuable assistance.

The major point here is neither to beat the dead horse of some segment of social treatment practice which underemphasized specific, measurable outcomes nor to seize on the behaviorist approach as the only answer for social treatment. Rather I mean to stress the importance of attempting to identify measurable outcomes in social treatment for two basic reasons: (1) Accountability to individual clients would seem to demand that social treatment practitioners make every attempt to specify clearly what the client can reasonably hope to gain in the treatment encounter. Similarly, the emphasis on specificity and client-problem relatedness provides a check against the imposition of change goals from worker to client. (2) In a more general sense, if we are ever to arrive at a point where we can speak with some degree of certitude about the effectiveness of a given method of social treatment, then criteria for individual client improvement cannot be determined *a posteriori* and must be capable of lending themselves to comprehensive evaluation.

Worker Activities. The worker's central task in this phase of the social treatment sequence requires a delicate balance between enabling the client to identify specific objectives for change and helping him to formulate and order those objectives, while taking care not to subsume the task of goal-setting. In brief, the worker's activities could be summarized as follows:

1. Reiteration of the presenting problem: what the client initially related as the problem that caused him to seek help.
2. Helping the client to delineate other areas of difficulty that have emerged in the subsequent assessment phase:

what is the problem constellation that surrounds this client?

3. Assisting the client in developing some priorities for problem resolution: these particular areas are of most concern to me now.

4. Finally, aiding the client in specifying desired end states for the problem areas to be worked on initially: successful resolution of this difficulty would mean the following. . . .

Let us examine the process by means of an illustration.

Client. Family: mother, father, three children.

Presenting problem. Oldest child (age nine) referred by parents for temper tantrums, fighting, refusal to follow directions and help out around the house.

Problem constellation. Poor communication within family. Role conflict: both parents working and away from home for considerable periods of time. Favoritism toward the "baby" in the family (problem expressed by the oldest child). Lack of clear-cut role expectations for parents or children.

Priorities. Everyone in the family agrees that an end to fighting among the children and the spelling out of mutual expectations, as well as the establishment of a format for communication, should be first on the list of priorities.

Desired end states.

1. Every family member, allowing for differences in development, should have a clear idea of what is expected of him by the other members of the family, and in turn what he or she may reasonably expect from them.

2. Ways other than fighting will be used to settle disputes between children.

3. The family will develop a format for a weekly meeting to deal with family issues and problems.

Having once established this hierarchy with the family, the worker can then bring to bear his considerable expertise in problem-solving and the knowledge he gained in the assessment phase to suggest a method of helping which best fits the family's problem. Goals may be further specified and elaborated to include more proximate objectives ("What could we reasonably hope to accomplish in the next few weeks?") and new goals added or old ones revised as the family grows and changes.

Perhaps it is wise to state here that the linear relationship between assessment, goal-setting, case-planning, and implementation described thus far may prove to be more the exception than the rule. In real life, workers may be forced to intervene *before* all of the relevant information has been collected and assessed. Perlman (1971b, p. 110) says, "Assessment is often the product of intervention, not its precedent." Of course, the worker does not hold the client in abeyance while he waits to collate the necessary social data, nor does help always wait upon a clear statement of goals. It is advisable, however, for the worker to adhere as closely as possible to the sequence suggested in order to avoid the twin pitfalls of intervention based solely on intuition instead of adequate assessment and defining treatment goals for the client instead of aiding him to formulate his own. As stated earlier, the task of assessment, goal-setting, and case-planning will be a continuing one as the interaction of client and worker brings new information to light and as the client grows and develops, conquering old problems and encountering new ones.

Client Perspectives. To a client who may feel trapped in a web of problems, the task of selecting particular areas to work on first may appear as difficult as the ultimate solutions themselves. The client feels pain and desires relief. Unlike the worker, he does not have the benefit of viewing his problems from a distance, nor does he sort them out in a way that clearly identifies targets for change. To him, family difficulties, interpersonal problems, and work-related problems are woven together in a single tapestry that appears to have neither beginning nor end. His skill at problem specification is not highly developed and he has never really thought very much about what he would like to change first. Finally, he still has doubts about the wisdom of seeking professional help and wonders if he couldn't simply work it out on his own or with the help of family and friends, as he had before.

In truth, however, he knows that he will need some help getting things straightened out, and at some point he wishes that someone—perhaps the worker—would simply tell him what it is he ought to do. Thus, vacillating between a desire for independence on the one hand ("I'll just have to work this out for myself") and dependence on the other ("Tell me what to do"), he finds it difficult to find the middle ground on which he must choose where he would like to go and then engage with the worker in figuring out how to get there.

Resources. Perhaps the most important resource available to the worker in the process of goal formulation is the material he gathered in the preceding phase of assessment. This information should serve to aid the client in the process of selecting specific objectives for change by presenting him with the total picture of functioning assembled in the assessment phase. The worker may help the client to summarize the results of the assessment sessions: "I've heard you speak now on several occasions about three major areas of difficulty . . ." or "From our previous discussions, these same issues appear to come up again and again. . . ."

Sometimes, as in the case of the family previously cited, the worker may wish to elicit a direct statement of the problem from a member of the client group: "You [mother and father] have indicated several areas in which you would like to see Tim [oldest child] make some changes. I remember from an earlier meeting that Tim talked about some things that *he'd* like to see happen differently in this family, and I wonder if he could remember some of these now." Thus the worker acts to avoid what might be a one-sided view of the family problem and seeks to reintroduce into the interview material discussed at some earlier point in the assessment phase. Of course the worker must guard against imposing his own set of priorities upon the family, and the constant reference back to the assessment phase helps to keep his contribution in line with the total range of problems expressed by the family.

SELECTION OF SOCIAL TREATMENT PLAN

Objectives. The purpose of this fourth phase of the social treatment sequence is the selection of a social treatment or case plan, including the following:

1. Method of social treatment to be employed (behavioral modification, family treatment, group approach, insight-focused counseling, other).
2. Indirect helping procedures to be employed (client advocacy, ombudsman services, collateral contacts on behalf of client).[4]
3. Ancillary or supportive helping services to be employed (educational/vocational counseling, homemaker services, other supportive services).

Thus the case plan should represent the total range of help to be provided and should be formulated as closely as possible on the set of objectives developed by the client and worker. Having helped the client specify the nature of his problem, the worker now must determine how to intervene with maximum effectiveness. His experience with many different

4. Indirect helping procedures will be covered in Chapter 6.

methods of social treatment, along with his knowledge of community resources, will enable him to make the best match between the client's problem and the method of helping.

Worker Activities. The formulation of the case plan begins with the selection of a method of social treatment. In making this decision, the worker takes into account three factors: (1) Who is the client? (2) What is the nature of the client's problem and what are the objectives for change? (3) What is the client's learning profile?

The determination of who the client is is not always an easy task. Problems with a particular child, for example, may precipitate a referral for service and only later in the assessment phase will it become apparent that the difficulty is really a problem with total family functioning requiring a family treatment approach. Similarly, one marital partner may initiate a contact with a social agency and later examination will reveal that both spouses should be considered for counseling. Or an adolescent may be referred by his school counselor and teachers for behavior problems in the classroom and only later will it become clear that this child is only the most visible member of a predelinquent subgroup that properly should be considered as the "client." In each instance, the decision as to who the client is will have a marked effect on the preferred method of social treatment.

Of course, there is no assurance that the worker's determination of who the client is will be acceptable. Parents may object that the problem is the child's, not theirs; the other spouse may be unwilling to seek help; the other members of the adolescent's subgroup may be unavailable for participation in group sessions. Consequently, the worker may be forced to settle for a less desirable alternative: working singly with the problem child, counseling the spouse on a one-to-one basis, providing some crisis intervention for the adolescent to keep him in school while trying to reach the peer group informally.

Second, the worker considers the nature of the client's problem and the objectives for change. A client who expresses a desire to improve relationship skills, achieve a higher degree of comfort in social situations, and become more outgoing might profit considerably from a small group experience that focused on social skills. The previously cited family with problems in communication, role relationships, and mutual expectations would appear to indicate a family treatment approach that included all family members and focused on the family as the problem-solving unit. Other specific problems might lend themselves more easily to a one-to-one approach: providing supportive help to the person engaged in preparing himself for death from a terminal illness (Kubler-Ross, 1969), helping the client with a phobic reaction (Bandura, 1969, pp. 424–92), helping the child of recently divorced parents work through feelings of separation and loss.

Many client problems would not necessarily indicate a specific method of social treatment, but might be amenable to several different approaches. In part, the decision as to the choice of helping method will be based on the nature of the change goals developed by the client. For example, the client with a low self-image, poorly developed interpersonal skills, and periods of depression may set "feeling better about himself," "getting and holding a job," and "initiating some social contact" as proximate goals for the helping encounter; in which case, a one-to-one format employing a behavioral approach would probably be sufficient. If, later on, the client desired to gain more insight about himself, to learn more about the way he was perceived by others in social situations, and to work on his relationship difficulties, a group format might prove more effective. Similarly, many clients who are seen initially in a situation in which the immediate objective is the resolution of some crisis—a suicide attempt, a bad experience with drugs or alcohol, or a mental breakdown—may later choose to move on to address more basic personal and social difficulties requiring different formats for help.

A third factor considered by the worker in his choice of helping method is the client's learning profile. Almost always this is a matter of worker judgment of the client's preferred format(s) for learning. Questions to be answered here include: What other change formats have worked well for the client—educational approaches? personal counseling? self-help groups? How has the client made use of the helping relationship thus far? Does he respond well to suggestions? Is he well organized enough to carry out behavioral assignments on his own? Does he appear to develop insights readily and (most important) does he act on the basis of his insight? Does he respond well to peer group pressure? Does he appear ready to function in a group situation? The basis for the worker's judgment will be the client's own preference, his behavior as observed during the assessment phase, and his record in past behavior change situations.

On the basis of these three factors—the client's problem, change goals, and learning profile—the worker is ready to make a decision about the preferred method of helping. As mentioned earlier, the choice will seldom be clear-cut and will be further complicated by at least two other factors: the worker's own skill and competence and the resources of the agency. For example, the preferred method of helping for a predelinquent adolescent may be a group approach, but the worker may be unskilled in group work technique or the agency may not be in a position to provide group work services. Thus a one-to-one approach must suffice unless other arrangements can be made. Few practitioners have competence in all methods of helping or in working with many different types of problems, and few agencies can provide the full range of helping services needed to match all client problems. In addition, there are compelling arguments for many different methods of helping, given the same type of problem constellation and differing client characteristics. Worker preference will enter in here, and this in turn should be based in large measure on what the research or the worker's evaluation of his own practice indicates is most effective with a particular problem.

Client Perspectives. If in the previous phase of goal-setting the client exercised leadership in decision-making, here his judgment gives way to that of the worker in selecting the proper method of social treatment. This is, after all, the reason he sought help in the first place: to find someone who *knew* how to help with his problem. As earlier, he may wish for a "quick fix" solution to his difficulties. The thought of a longer term encounter, in conjoint family therapy or in group treatment, may be threatening to him. He needs assurance that this is what is needed to realize his goals and added encouragement to commit himself to the helping process. He may legitimately be wondering when he and the worker will be getting down to business and working directly on his difficulties, and, as before, he may question his decision to seek professional help.

Often clients will be unaware of some of the progress they have made since the initial encounter with the worker and may need to hear this repeated. Similarly, the presenting problem may have abated somewhat and things may again look normal: the problem child has a good week, the depressed person feels a little better about himself, an acute family crisis is averted. This seeming return to normality may lessen considerably the client's motivation to work on his problem, and he may need to be reminded that problems of long standing are likely to recur and that temporary quiescence should not be mistaken for cure. Finally, the client may have to be reminded again of his vital role in the helping process. The worker cannot solve his problem for him and he must be encouraged to view the helping process as truly a joint endeavor.

Resources. As in earlier phases, one of the most important resources available to the worker here is his knowledge of professional services. Assuming that no single practitioner can cover either in skill or in knowledge the entire field of interpersonal helping, he needs to know where in the network of community services help of the appropriate nature may be found. That means not only where individual, family, and group services may be found to supplement the capabilities of the individual practitioner and the services of his agency, but also which practitioners have the most highly developed skills in working with particular kinds of clients or problem situations: the adolescent in need of group counseling, the autistic child, the depressed client, the couple experiencing severe sexual difficulties in their marriage.

The practitioner attempts to keep abreast of new developments in the helping field and furthers his knowledge by keeping up with the professional literature, attending professional conferences and symposia, and making use of the continuing education programs offered by professional schools and institutes, as well as through in-service training.

ESTABLISHMENT OF WORKING AGREEMENT

Objectives. The working agreement is a statement of intention by worker and client to work toward the realization of the agreed-upon goals in accordance with the case plan. Included in the working agreement are a statement of mutual expectations as well as a recording of the time, place, nature, and frequency of the therapeutic encounter. What are the reasons for this formal statement of intent?

First, the working agreement provides a focus and direction for worker-client activities. It crystallizes the results of the earlier phases of the helping sequence and puts into perspective what needs to be done. Second, it helps to reduce discrepancies between the expectations of the client and those of the worker. Clients, as consumers, have a right to know what they may reasonably expect from the professional helper, and in turn what they will be required to give. Since the helping process is a joint endeavor, it is imperative that the client see himself as an active participant in the therapeutic encounter, rather than as the passive recipient of service. The working agreement provides a documentation of the client's intent—to attend weekly counseling sessions, attend meetings of a self-help group, carry out behavioral assignments, or any other activities specified in the case plan. The worker can refer to this record later on if the client is falling short on his end of the agreement. Finally, the working agreement provides a basis for evaluation. At given intervals, worker and client can step back from the process of helping and measure their progress toward the change goals. For some clients, particularly children, a visual record of progress—for example, a wall chart or graph —is an important aid to professional help and can supply added motivation as well. At the very least, such a periodic evaluation helps to orient the client who may at times wonder, "Have I made any progress at all?"

Worker Activities. The worker's function during this phase of the social treatment sequence is simple and straightforward: to draw up a working agreement as previously described, discuss it in full with the client, and obtain his commitment to work toward its stated objectives. Of course, with some clients, especially those who are well organized and highly motivated to change, this accounting of objectives will be brief and the working agreement merely a written statement of clearly mutual expectations. For others, in particular those who lack any real systematic approach to problem-solving, the working agreement will become more of an anchoring point for the social treatment sessions to follow.

For still other clients—for example, families in which there may be considerable differences in maturity and understanding—the formulation of the working agreement may afford the worker an excellent opportunity to go back and raise basic questions: Why have we come together? What does each of us hope to realize in our subsequent sessions? This recapitulation of basic family goals, stated so that even the youngest child has some appreciation of their meaning, will provide the foundation for the family sessions to follow. Finally, with younger clients—for example, with a group of latency-age children or adolescents—the worker may use the occasion of the formalization of the working agreement to discuss again the basic purposes of the group and their implications for each of the members. In this instance, the group may formulate a set of objectives of its own in addition to the individual "contracts" of the members.

In sum, the worker may use the discussion of the working agreement with clients to recapitulate basic objectives of the helping encounter, reaffirm client commitment to work toward the realization of change goals, give added emphasis to the client's role in the process of helping, and provide some timetable for evaluation.

Client Perspectives. For many clients, the presentation of the working agreement may, more than anything previously, signal the beginning of active and full participation in the helping process. As earlier, the client may feel, "Do I really want to go through with this?" The working agreement serves to demystify the therapeutic encounter and points out to the client just what his part in the helping process will

entail. Perhaps the acute problem that prompted the client's
search for help has abated somewhat, or he sees that change
is going to come about only as a result of hard work on his
part, or his situation has changed so that other problems—
financial difficulties, employment problems—now command
the major share of his attention. The couple with marital
problems may feel that the air has been cleared and they can
now work things out on their own; the parents with a difficult child may decide that he will probably grow out of it
soon. To a certain extent, the worker may take client hesi-
tance to enter into the working agreement as a sign that he
has done his initial work well: the client possesses no illu-
sions about a magical solution to his problem and he now
sees that the worker cannot do it all for him.

It is well to remember here that change will probably involve a fair degree of discomfort and pain for the client, will
not be easily accomplished, and may require the client to lay
aside old coping patterns that, while they cause him difficulty, have become part of his personality. If change is to be accomplished, he will not only have to do some things differently, but also think about himself in a different way. To a
client who has always considered himself incompetent, weak,
bad, or unattractive, the thought of a new self-concept may
be as threatening as the actual work of behavioral change
which lies ahead. The wish that things will get better on
their own or that the child will grow out of his problems is
usually just that: a wish. The worker can make the point
that problems severe enough to prompt the client to seek
help will seldom just go away, and that even if they do, they
are likely to be replaced by new ones. Thus, what the client
can hope to gain from the helping process is not just relief
from present difficulties, but a more productive way of meeting new problems when and where they occur. The client
needs the worker's support for his decision to enter actively

into the helping process and understanding of the difficult path that lies ahead.

Resources. Rose (1972, pp. 95–105) has written in detail on the formulation of behavioral contracts with children in groups, and Browning and Stover (1971, pp. 35–38) describe a contract between agency and family. Beyond these and a few other scattered references, materials on the subject of working agreements are scarce. Two factors that partially explain this scarcity are the lack of emphasis on behaviorally specific goals in much of social treatment practice and the recent rise of consumerism among client groups. With this new client awareness, reflected in some recent publications on "how to" choose a psychotherapist, and with the increasing emphasis on accountability and goal-directed worker activity in many social agencies, the use of contracts or working agreements will probably become more widespread. At present, the best resource for formulating such a contract lies within the social agency staff, which can draw up a general worker-client contract that fits both the particular characteristics of the client populations served—children, families, adolescents—and the general purposes of the agency.

SUSTAINING SOCIAL TREATMENT

Objectives. This phase of the social treatment sequence could perhaps more accurately be described as a series of intermediate stages during which the case plan is implemented. The work of social treatment may include family treatment, individual counseling, group treatment, family life education, self-help groups, and any of a number of other helping approaches. It is difficult to ascribe a particular period of time to the implementation of the case plan, since this will vary considerably in accordance with the nature of the client's problem and the method of social treatment employed.

Crisis intervention with a family may take place in several sessions, while group treatment of adolescent delinquents may take upwards of a year or longer. The pros and cons of time-limited and open-ended approaches to social treatment are numerous (Smalley, 1971), but the trend toward increased emphasis on behaviorally specific change goals, as well as some evaluative research on long-term and short-term intervention (Reid and Shyne, 1969), seems to signal a shift toward more time-limited social treatment. Whatever the duration of the helping encounter, the primary purpose of this phase of social treatment is the realization of the client's change goals.

Worker Activities. The worker's activities during this period of social treatment are many and varied. He may lead group meetings, conduct conjoint family treatment sessions, provide individual counseling, and teach family life or parent education classes. In his role as a broker of services, the worker may also secure needed help for the client outside of the agency. Finally, the worker will probably undertake a number of collateral contacts on the client's behalf to help ensure the progress realized in the direct social treatment relationship. These contacts may include working with teachers, employers, other family members, or friends on the client's behalf.

The worker monitors the client's progress and continually reassesses the situation to uncover new information that may alter the client's change objectives or the method of helping. For example, in working with children one assumes that, in addition to the presenting problem and those uncovered in the assessment phase, the child will, as a function of growth, face new developmental challenges that may lead in turn to other difficulties. Similarly, families or individual adult clients do not exist in a vacuum and may be expected to encounter new problems during the course of social treatment.

Indeed, the helping process itself may precipitate problems for the client, and these should be anticipated by the worker. For example, the child who is difficult to manage may actually become more difficult (in fact, this is to be expected) during the early phases of a behavioral program designed to extinguish temper tantrums and provocative behavior around the home. Similarly, the shy, retiring child may suddenly appear outspoken and aggressive, making for some difficulties in adjustment for parents and teachers. Finally, the initiation of assertive behavior in an adolescent group's scapegoat may signal the rise of more general name-calling and ranking as the group searches for a new target for its negative feelings. The worker tries to anticipate such difficulties with the client, who may feel that the helping relationship is producing negative results.

Families, too, may experience difficulties as the result of entering into family treatment. A new emphasis on openness in family communication may mean that certain issues previously swept under the rug now come to the fore, or previously docile family members now begin to assert themselves in and out of the family treatment session. Perhaps for the first time, parents are hearing how their children really view them, or spouses see themselves through each other's eyes as never before. The major point the worker makes is that change—even productive change directed at agreed-upon goals—will make a certain amount of difficulty for the client. The worker knows that this change is quite likely to be perceived as threatening to the client or those around him, and he attempts to provide a safe context—in the group meeting or family session or individual interview —where difficulties can be resolved and feelings worked through.

The worker continually refers back to the social diagnosis and working agreement to orient his activities. All of his interventions with the client are directed at the realization of the previously agreed-upon goals, or at new objectives that develop in the course of social treatment. As noted earlier, adequate assessment of client difficulties may come only after considerable worker-client interaction, and the worker must be flexible enough to switch social treatment plans in midstream if they do not match the new view of the problem. For example, the worker may begin work with one family member—a child referred by his parents for behavioral problems—only to discover later that the real difficulty is one of total family functioning requiring total family involvement.

Finally, despite the best intentions of clients expressed in the working agreement, some will remove themselves from the helping process before the real work of behavioral change begins. Problems in communication between worker and client (for a variety of emotional, social, and cultural reasons), situational difficulties (such as the absence of transportation), or feelings that change is simply not worth the effort or is too threatening may prompt the client to drop out. Special attempts may be made to engage the client who is hard to reach—aggressive, outreaching social treatment and multiple impact approaches—and the worker should make every attempt to follow up and find out why the client chose not to continue. In the final analysis, frustrating and difficult as the worker may find the client who chooses not to continue, one basic fact is reaffirmed: the decision to enter social treatment is a voluntary one, and without a joint commitment on the part of client and worker there exists no helping relationship. So whatever the reason for the client's failure to continue, and despite the worker's best efforts to reach his client, sometimes the very real limitations on what the worker can do to help will be made abundantly clear to him.

Client Perspectives. "Where have I come from and where am I going?" might be the refrain of a client in this intermediate phase of social treatment. Having resolved his early indecision and committed himself to a joint working relationship, the client now finds himself in the very middle of the helping process. He may feel alternately that he has made great progress or none at all; his self-concept may be enhanced or still somewhat shaky in light of what he now sees as the tasks that lie ahead of him; and while old difficulties may be resolved, new life situations have arisen which tax to the limit his newly acquired problemsolving abilities. His view of the social treatment process is different than it was in the beginning. He sees that there are no magical solutions or easy answers here. While he feels the worker has been a great help to him on many occasions, at other times he feels impatient and wishes the worker would make more direct suggestions regarding what he should do. He generally views the relationship as beneficial, though he is sometimes hard put to specify exactly how he has changed. Getting to weekly counseling sessions, group meetings, or family interviews is difficult, though he is generally glad he came once he gets there. Dealing with personal things (feelings, thoughts, emotions) is still difficult for him, though he is sometimes amazed at how readily he discusses these things with the worker. More than anything else, the social treatment sessions have become part of his routine, like going to work, and he looks forward to his "special time" to discuss problems. In fact, he now uses the sessions to think things through and generally feels that he reflects a good deal more on what he's doing than he did before. Finally, he feels at times as if maybe he'd like to terminate the relationship, though in a way he's gotten rather used to it and would miss it if he did.

It is important for him to hear from the worker how *he* feels things have gone, what progress has been made, what tasks remain. The worker's judgment is valued, though at times the client feels he has been off base in some of his impressions of the way the client is feeling or the reasons he acted in a certain way. Whoever the client is, he begins to feel that the worker and the helping context—individual session, family interview, group meeting—is somehow different from any situation he has been in before. The latency-age child feels his "club" is really special and looks forward to the weekly meetings; the depressed middle-aged client views her weekly session as most rewarding and different from other situations in which friends have offered advice; the elderly client feels a real bond between himself and the other members of his group, as well as a special relationship to the worker. In sum, it is during this phase of the social treatment sequence that the therapeutic encounter may assume a prominence and a reality all its own.

Resources. In addition to considerable knowledge and skill in the methods of direct helping, the worker intervenes indirectly on behalf of the client to help ensure that gains realized in the helping process are carried over to the client's total life situation. The worker's own efforts may be supplemented by additional services that he procures: tutoring for the child with learning difficulties, family management classes for the homemaker, medical care for the elderly single adult, vocational education for the delinquent adolescent. In addition, other significant people in the client's life web—parents, teachers, probation officers, peers, employers—may be involved in implementing certain segments of the case plan. Even now the worker is considering what community services and resources will help the client maintain his progress, once the social treatment relationship has been terminated.

EVALUATION

Objectives. The purpose of this phase of the social treatment sequence is the measurement of the extent to which client change goals have been realized. It comes as no surprise that the behavioral therapists (Bandura, 1969, Browning & Stover, 1971, pp. 42–75; Rose, 1972, pp. 46–61; Stuart, 1971) have the most to say on the subject of measurement. The behaviorists' emphasis on specificity of goals and establishment of a base line of problem behavior prior to intervention make the later task of measurement considerably easier. As noted earlier, one of the major problems facing social treatment practitioners is the difficulty of measuring diffuse client goals. How, for example, does one go about measuring such things as "improved ego functioning" or "enhanced self-image"? The client's self-evaluation is of course helpful, particularly in the assessment of changes in affect ("I feel better about myself"). But if the social treatment goal is an improved state of client functioning in the interpersonal arena, then more objective measures will be required. In this respect, client self-evaluation of progress may bear little relation to actual achievement (Berleman, Seaberg, & Steinburn, 1972).

Measurement of progress does not necessarily wait until the ending phase of the social treatment sequence, but is carried out at intervals along the way. This may include weekly charting of client progress or several periodic evaluations in the course of social treatment. Such sessions are useful in that they say to the client, "Here's how far we've come and here's where we need to go." For some clients, particularly younger children, a visual representation of progress (chart, graph) may supply added social reinforcement to continue in the helping process.

Worker Activities. Part of the worker's task in the evaluation phase consists of the tabulation and measurement of
behavioral change. Whatever the agreed-upon goals, the
worker goes over with the client his record of progress: for the
parents with the difficult child, "Johnny hasn't had a temper
tantrum in over two months"; for the delinquent adolescent,
"You've managed to avoid contact with the police and to attend trade school for a whole semester"; for the regressed
schizophrenic, "During the last three months you've made
more than two hundred contacts with other patients, attend-
ed weekly dancing lessons, and helped out with the orientation program for new patients"; for the couple with marital
problems, "Every week now for the last month you've been
able to tell me how you have both used your weekly meeting
to work out a problem, and you also report several social occasions recently where you've really enjoyed each other's
company."

In addition to simply tabulating behavioral progress, the
worker can use the evaluation sessions to explore with the
client feelings about his personal changes. These may be as
important to the client as the actual changes themselves. Often the feeling of competence that comes from successfully
mastering a difficult situation gives the client a new and
broadened view of his own capabilities and may provide added encouragement to confront new problems. The skillful
worker uses these times to reinforce the client's newly acquired problem-solving abilities with an eye toward the time
when he will be approaching difficult situations on his own,
without the support of the worker.

Client Perspectives. "I can't believe I've actually come this
far" might be one feeling of the client in this phase of social
treatment. Remembering, with the worker's help, what
things were like earlier in contrast to the way they are now

may tend to bolster the client's sense of his ability to face problem situations in the future. Conversely, some clients may feel discouraged at the rate of progress and need added support to renew their commitment to the process of helping.

The client feels a strong relationship to the worker and needs to hear that he is still accepted as a person, whatever his success or failure in behavior change. To some clients for whom a long-standing difficulty has shown little measurable progress—for example, a child who exhibits behavior problems at home and in school and has learning difficulties as well—the "quick fix" solution (changing schools or teachers) again looks attractive. The client may need to hear again from the worker that problem situations that took years to develop will not go away in a few months. One of the most difficult tasks for worker and client is to build into social treatment opportunities for small successes along the way, so that all success is not tied to one variable (the child's successful completion of a school year). For the client who has been motivated from the beginning to participate actively in the helping process, this is the phase in which he can most easily become involved, since he and the worker will be discussing his gains as well as those areas of difficulty still needing attention. At this stage workers should not hesitate to give praise for client accomplishment. Changing behavior involves much hard work, and to hear from the worker, whose opinions are highly valued, that he has done well is an important reinforcement to the client.

Resources. As noted earlier, the behavioral literature on the subject of measurement provides much useful information on establishing base-line behaviors, monitoring progress, and measuring case outcomes (Stuart, 1971; Bandura, 1969, pp. 242–44). Crawford (1971) indicates many helpful uses of visual materials in assessment and evaluation which have implications for the client-worker relationship. Similarly, video and audio tapes can be highly effective in pinpointing behavioral progress over time. Other evaluative techniques include the use of the client's own story (before and after) and, in the case of groups, a group evaluation of the progress of individual members.

TERMINATION AND AFTERCARE

Objectives. The purpose of this final phase of the social treatment sequence is to ensure the client's smooth transition from the helping relationship to other sources of aid and support. Termination means that the client has realized the goals specified in the working agreement and is ready to sever his relationship with the worker and operate independently. Problems will be faced with newly acquired skills, and should the burden again become too great, the client knows where he can turn for assistance. Termination of the formal helping relationship does not mean the end of the client's difficulties; rather it signifies that worker and client have ceached a certain plateau of achievement and have mutually agreed to end the helping process. The aftercare plan may involve the client in any of a number of helping services in the community, or may involve periodic checks with the worker to report on progress.

Worker Activities. Long before the actual point of termination, the worker attempts to foster independent activity in the client and is alert to community resources that may help to cushion the end of the formal helping relationship. Termination is a gradual process that extends far back into the early phases of social treatment, with emphasis on developing change goals that carry over into the client's natural life situation.

Some times termination may signal more than simply the end of the relationship between client and worker. The mental patient leaving the hospital, the child returning home from the residential treatment center, and the child being placed in a foster home will all require special help in adjusting to their new situations. In each instance the worker searches for helping services in the community to ease the transition from one life situation to another. These might include a halfway house and membership in a self-help group for the former mental patient; a pretermination group experience for the child leaving residential treatment, perhaps in the community to which he will return; and an activity group membership in a local boys' club, YMCA, or YMHA for the foster child about to be placed in a new community.

The worker draws on his extensive knowledge of community resources to meet the client's special posttermination needs. Toward the end of the formal helping process he may make increasing demands on the client for independent activity and more and more give over his function to others in the client's life orbit. Thus the child with learning and emotional problems is directed toward a more substantial relationship with a school counselor; foster parents are introduced into a parent self-help group; the elderly medical patient is linked up to a senior citizen's center; the former delinquent is introduced to the services of the volunteer crisis clinic. As in the initial phase of intake, the worker views his responsibility to the client as extending beyond the context of their direct helping relationship and does everything in his power to ensure that the progress achieved in social treatment will be maintained. He is sensitive to what may be the client's concern about going it alone once the formal helping relationship has been terminated, and attempts both to reinforce the client's own strengths in problem-solving and to help him identify alternative sources of support in the community.

Not all terminations take place smoothly, however, and many times the ending of the helping process may be abrupt.

The client may be faced with a situational difficulty—a move to another city or loss of employment—which precipitates a sudden termination of the relationship. Sometimes clients may terminate the helping process when they feel they have received all the help they need, and other problems—such as a change of workers or a prolonged illness of either client or worker—may force a premature ending of social treatment. In view of the many unforeseen events that can alter the course of social treatment, it is good practice to begin the process of termination gradually and to be constantly aware of alternative helping services and other community resources of which the client can make use when the formal relationship with the worker is ended.

Client Perspectives. "I know how far I've come and I know I can work out my problems a lot better now, but I still get nervous when I think of having to cope with everything on my own." These might be the thoughts of a client at the point of termination. He knows the progress he's made, has a much better grasp of his own abilities to solve future difficulties, but feels unsure of his future and fearful of terminating a relationship that has been extremely helpful to him. This ambivalence about formal termination may be translated in a variety of ways. The latency-age group regresses to earlier levels of problem behavior, as if telling the worker, "We still need the group" (Garland, Jones, & Kolodny, 1965, p. 42); the adult client begins to make increasing demands of the worker as the point of termination approaches; the adolescent criticizes the worker and devalues their relationship ("We never did anything but talk") as a way of handling his sense of impending loss. Indeed, anger, either openly or covertly expressed, is a fairly predictable response to termination. To the client who may now realize just how much he has come to depend on his relationship with the worker and how much he will miss their sessions, some hostility toward the worker—perhaps for some things the client feels he hasn't done—may somewhat lessen the sadness the client feels and make the actual termination easier for him.

Many clients feel a need at this time to put the whole experience in some sort of context: to recapitulate their basic reasons for seeking social treatment, to recount the progress they have made thus far, and to identify those areas they will work on in the immediate future. This reconstruction of the helping process can be a very meaningful way for the client to experience again some aspects of the relationship —the low points as well as the major accomplishments—and to use that reexperience as a bridge to the immediate future. When a client feels a number of things simultaneously—some hostility toward the worker, fear of the future, doubt about his own gains—the worker would do well not to try to tie up all the loose ends of his problem, or spend a great deal of energy trying to make him feel good about the parting. The client's ability to deal with a sense of loss and still face his life situation may constitute an important learning experience for him. The worker may have a greater need than the client to have things end on a high note.

Resources. At this phase more than any other, the worker draws on his extensive knowledge of community resources to provide support for the client once their formal relationship is ended. This may mean a variety of things: knowing the medical services in a community; being aware of service club activities for the client who may need transportation or tutoring or home visits; knowing where the client could turn for help in a moment of crisis (clergyman, crisis clinic, self-help group). As during the intake phase, the greater the degree to which the worker can personalize the referral, the greater the chance for its success. Clients are not problems, but people with problems, and consequently should not be referred to "programs" or "agencies" for help, but to another person who represents the needed service. It is also a good idea for the worker, knowing how easy it is for the client to fall between the cracks, to follow up and make sure that the contact has been made and the aftercare plan implemented. Finally, the worker looks to the client himself for knowledge of supports that will maintain his progress. Family members, friends, and employers all may be enlisted by the worker to aid in the process of helping.

Summary

There are eight identifiable phases in the social treatment sequence: intake, assessment and social diagnosis, determination of goals, selection of social treatment plan, establishment of working agreement, sustaining social treatment, evaluation, and termination. Taken together, these phases form a continuum of helping based on the joint participation of worker and client, and include activities undertaken by the worker directly with the client and indirectly on his behalf. The major components of the social treatment sequence may be summarized as follows:

PHASES OF THE SOCIAL TREATMENT SEQUENCE

Phase 1: Intake

Objectives

1. Determination of client need for service.
   (a) Client accepted for service.
   (b) Client referred for service elsewhere.
   (c) Service not necessary at this time.

Worker activities

1. Identification of presenting problem.
2. Determination of need for services.
3. Location of needed services.
4. Reinforcement of client's decision to seek help.
5. Describing nature of service available.

6. Outlining client's role in helping process.
7. Provision of crisis service if needed.

Client perspectives

1. "I need to know what's wrong with me."
2. Problems faced by person seeking help in our culture (Landy 1965).
3. Fear of self-examination and change.
4. Anxiety and ambivalence about seeking help.

Resources

1. Thorough knowledge of community resources.
2. Personal contacts in alternative helping services.

Phase 2: Assessment and Social Diagnosis

Objectives

1. Social diagnosis is a joint process through which worker and client explore and assess the physical, psychological, and social conditions as the impinge upon the client and then attempt to relate their findings to the range of social problems experienced by the client in a manner that yields objectives for change as well as a plan of action.

Worker activities

1. Collection and assessment of relevant information.
   (a) Physical functioning.
   (b) Psychological functioning.
   (c) Social functioning.
   (d) Environmental context.
2. Preparation of diagnostic statement.
   (a) Presenting problem.
   (b) Summary of biopsychosociocultural information.
   (c) Diagnostic summary.

(d) Tentative recommendations.

3. Case consultation or staffing.

Client
perspectives

1. "I know I need help, but I'm afraid to let any one know it and to really try to change."

2. Fear of entering into helping relationship.

3. Recurrent doubts about necessity of seeking professional help.

4. Wish for a ready-made solution.

Resources

1. Formats for obtaining information.

(a) Direct interviews.

(b) Home visits.

(c) Diagnostic groups.

(d) Psychiatric, psychological, physical examinations.

(e) Collateral contacts with relevant others.

(f) Direct observation.

Phase 3: Determination of Change Goals

Objectives

1. Identification of specific targets for change.

(a) Directly related to presenting problem.

(b) Designed to reduce stress as experienced by client.

(c) Refer to state of improvement outside helping relationship.

(d) Behaviorally specific.

(e) Capable of being evaluated.

Worker
activities

1. Reiteration of presenting problem.

2. Determination of total problem constellation.

3. Development of problem hierarchy.
4. Specification of desired end states.

Client
perspectives

1. "I feel trapped in a web of problems that has neither beginning nor end."
2. Difficulty in specifying problem hierarchy.
3. Conflicting desire between "working this out on my own" and obtaining a quick-fix solution from the worker.

Resources

1. The information gathered in the prior phase of assessment.

Phase 4: Selection of Social Treatment Plan

Objectives

1. Development of case plan.
   (a) Method of social treatment to be employed.
   (b) Indirect helping procedures to be used.
   (c) Ancillary services.

Worker
Activities

1. Determining who the client is.
2. Determining nature of problem and objectives for change.
3. Determining client's learning profile.

Client
perspectives

1. "I want direction for working on my problems."
2. Vacillation over making commitment to helping process.
3. Things look normal again.

Resources

1. Knowledge of alternative helping services.
2. Knowledge of latest developments in helping methods.

Phase 5: Establishment of Working Agreement

Objectives
1. Statement of client/worker intentions.
2. Focus for helping.
3. Basis for later evaluation.

Worker activities
1. Formulate working agreement, including change goals, method of helping, expectations of client, expectations of worker, time, place.
2. Discussion with client, obtaining his commitment.
3. Recapitulation of basic objectives.

Client perspectives
1. "Do I really want to go through with this?"
2. Demystification of helping process.
3. Hope that maybe things will just straighten themselves out.

Resources
1. Behavioral literature on contracts.
2. Worker's creativity.

Phase 6: Sustaining Social Treatment

Objectives
1. Implementation of cases plan.
2. Realization of change goals.
3. The work of social treatment: individual sessions, group meetings, family interviews.

Worker Activities
1. Direct helping procedures: leading the group, conducting conjoint family treatment sessions, doing individual counseling.

2. Undertaking collateral contacts on client's behalf.
3. Monitoring client progress.
4. Reassessing new information and helping client to manage life crises.

Client perspectives

1. "Where have I come from? Where am I going?"
2. Conflicting feelings: "I've made progress"; "I'm still in the same place."
3. Wish that the worker would do more.
4. Client feels that he really uses social treatment sessions well.

Resources

1. Ancillary helping services.
2. Sources of support in the client's own life web.

Phase 7: Evaluation

Objectives

1. Measurement of client change goals.

Worker activities

1. Tabulation and measurement of behavioral change.
2. Exploration of client's feelings about behavior change.
3. Assessment of total helping process.

Client perspectives

1. "I can't believe I've actually come this far."
2. Elation at progress, discouragement about work still to be done.
3. Need for continued acceptance as person, regardless of success-failure rate.

Resources

1. Behavioral literature on measurement and evaluation.

Phase 8: Termination and Aftercare

Objectives

1. To ensure the client's smooth transition from the helping relationship with the worker to other sources of community support.

Worker activities

1. Identification of possible supportive services in the community.
2. Formulation of aftercare plan.
3. Reconstruction of helping relationship: beginning, middle, and end.
4. Support for the client's ability to "make it" without direct help of the worker.

Client perspectives

1. "I know how far I've come, but I still feel frightened at the thought of terminating the relationship."
2. Fear of future.
3. Anger/closeness toward worker.
4. Feelings of being abandoned.
5. Need to place the helping experience in some perspective.

Resources

1. Community services: Medical, social, recreational.
2. The client himself.

After this overview of the social treatment sequence, it may be well to end here with the observation that real problems do not fit neatly into sequences or stages. What the worker does with any client should be guided primarily not by prescription or technique, but by an appreciation of the client as another human being with a problem: pressured by real difficulties, fearful of self-exposure and change and desirous of help, but unsure of his decision to seek professional assistance. Perhaps the most important tool the worker brings to the therapeutic process is the conscious use of himself to relate to the client as a fellow human being in search of help.

ADDITIONAL SOURCES

Fox, E. F.; Nelson, M. A.; & Bolman, W. M. The termination process: A neglected dimension in social work. *Social Work* 14, no. 4 (1969):53–63.

Hollis, F. A profile of early interviews in marital counseling. *Social Casework* 49, no. 1 (1968):35–43.

Kanfer, F., & Sanslow, G. Behavioral diagnosis. In *Behavior therapy: Appraisal and status,* ed. C. Franks, pp. 417–43. New York: McGraw-Hill, 1969.

Lieberman, R. Behavioral approaches to family and couple therapy. *American Journal of Orthopsychiatry* 40, no. 1 (1970):106–118.

Mayer, J. E., & Timms, N. Clash in perspective between worker and client. *Social Casework* 50, no. 1 (1969):32–40.

Meyer, J. B.; Srowig, W.; & Hosford, R. E. Behavioral-reinforcement counseling with rural high school youth. *Journal of Counseling Psychology* 17, no. 2 (1970):127–32.

Mullen, E. J. The relation between diagnosis and treatment in casework. *Social Casework* 50, no. 4 (1969):218–26.

Reid, W. J., & Epstein, L. *Task centered casework.* New York: Columbia University Press, 1972.

Silverman, P. R. A re-examination of the intake procedure. *Social Casework* 51, no. 10 (1970):625–34.

Siporin, M. Situational assessment and intervention. *Social Casework* 53, no. 2 (1972):91–110.

Sporakowski, M. J., & Mills, P. R., Jr. What is it all about? An overview of family therapy. *Family Coordinator* 18, no. 1 (1969):61–69.

Whittaker, J. K. Observing and recording children's behavior. In A.E. Trieschman, J. K. Whittaker, & L. K. Brendtro, *The other 23 hours: Child care work in a therapeutic milieu,* pp. 198–219. Chicago:Aldine, 1969.

The Social Treatment Sequence II: Indirect Intervention on Behalf of Clients

Not all helping takes place in a direct encounter with the client. Equally important is the whole range of helping activities which the worker performs indirectly on the client's behalf. For present purposes, *indirect helping* refers to all activities that the worker undertakes on behalf of the client to further the mutually agreed-upon goals of the helping relationship. These may flow from a number of roles—advocate-ombudsman, broker of services and resources—and include a variety of functions. These functions encompass a number of specific interventions directed at any of the various social systems in which the client participates—family, peer groups, organization, community—for the purpose of enhancing individual change efforts. As stated earlier, change strategies directed at organizations or communities are not within the purview of this discussion. I am focusing here on systems intervention undertaken on behalf of specific clients in the context of the social treatment relationship. Finally, many of the other roles that social treatment practitioners sometimes fulfill—administrator, supervisor, consultant, team leader—will not be discussed here.[1]

Indirect helping in the context of social treatment might

1. See Meyer (1970, pp. 186–221, Miller (1971), Sarri (1971), and Glidewell (1969).

accurately be described as an attempt to put the "social" back into social work practice. Indeed, if one refers to the earliest literature of social work practice (Richmond, 1899), one sees what working on the client's behalf once entailed: advising a wage earner on the dangers of buying on the installment plan, knowing what kind of fuel burned best over the long winter and what food represented the most value for a limited budget. Though many of these problems and their solutions appear quaint by today's standards, clients continue to seek out personal help while enmeshed in a web of situational difficulties: financial problems, legal problems, health problems, religious problems. While the social worker is neither doctor, lawyer, nor financial analyst, he should at least be able to direct the client to appropriate sources of help where his problems might be addressed. This is consistent with a view of the client as a total person with multiple life problems, not merely as someone with an "emotional difficulty." Few people have neatly defined and well-encapsulated problems, but to the client in distress, his financial, emotional, and physical difficulties may be *felt* as a single weight. One task of the social work practitioner is first to relate to the client as a person with multiple difficulties and then begin to factor out the pieces of the problem that can be addressed directly in the helping relationship and those that should be redirected to other sources of aid. Such an orientation clearly presupposes a practitioner who is both knowledgeable about community services and actively involved in intervening on behalf of his client to ensure that the appropriate services are made available.

Another factor that underscores the importance of indirect helping is that interpersonal or emotional gains made in the social treatment encounter will endure only to the extent that they are supported in the client's natural life milieu. This often requires an active involvement with relevant others in the client's life web—family, friends, teachers, employers—to ensure that hard-won gains are maintained and enhanced. To undertake such intervention on behalf of individual clients effectively, the worker must have some knowledge of the various social systems in which his client participates, and in addition must know something about influencing each of those systems on the client's behalf.

Bases of Power

Indirect helping is predicated on the assumption that the practitioner has at his disposal various sources of influence with which to effect change on his client's behalf. Whatever specifics are involved—working with the convict's family to prepare for his return to the community, intervening with a teacher to help a school dropout reenter the educational system, negotiating with a health care bureaucracy on behalf of a family in need—each system intervention undertaken by the worker draws to some extent on the sources of power available to him. What are these bases of power? French and Raven (1968) identify five of them:

1. Reward power, akin to positive reinforcement.
2. Coercive power, roughly equivalent to punishment or negative reinforcement.
3. Legitimate power, derived from cultural values, the social structure, and the legitimizing agency.
4. Referent power, derived from a desire to be like someone else.
5. Expert power, derived from possession of special knowledge or information.

Patti and Resnick (1972) use the foregoing list to analyze sources of power available to organizational change agents and it is clear that the bases of power bear some relation to social treatment practice as well. French and Raven's analysis seems to suggest that the practitioner would do well to think about a range of interventions based on various sources of influence to effect change on behalf of his client. For example, the school social worker attempting to mediate between the disruptive child and his teacher may gain considerable leverage if he can demonstrate to the teacher his expertise in managing children's behavior, perhaps by offering some specific suggestions for managing the child's behavior in the classroom. The juvenile corrections worker may place heavy emphasis on the fact that his legitimate authority derives from the court when calling together a family resistant to the idea of examining the behavior of a predelinquent child. The community service worker may use threats of legal action to help ensure that his client receives adequate redress in a case of consumer fraud. The aftercare worker makes certain that community businessmen and labor leaders receive public commendation and recognition for their efforts to find jobs for ex-convicts.

In brief, the worker exercises a variety of options and uses a number of influence techniques to "work the system" on behalf of his client. These may be based on his legitimate authority as representative of a community agency, or on his ability to reward or sanction, or on his professional expertise in dealing with problems.

Locus and Focus of Intervention

The worker's major focus for change is on the client system, which may be an individual, a family, or a small group. One way of viewing the client system is to think of it as interacting with other social systems that affect it and upon which it in turn has an effect. It is reasonable to assume, then, that changes in the client system brought about in the context of social treatment will have effect over the other systems in which the client participates, and changes in any of these systems will in turn have some effect on the client system; in particular, they may result in the enhancement or diminution of changes accomplished in the treatment encounter. For this reason the worker tries at least to be aware of what is happening in the major areas of the client's life and often intervenes in one or more of the systems that affect him. The practitioner may be working indirectly on his client's behalf on several system levels and simultaneously carrying on a direct treatment relationship. What are the major systems in which the client participates?

FAMILY SYSTEM

Even when the family is not itself the client, it can be an important source of support for individual gains. Conversely, a family may thwart individual change goals by being unwilling or unready to accept the individual family member who desires to alter his behavior. The literature on family dynamics is voluminous and will not be summarized here.[2] Rather, let us develop several examples of the way a worker might intervene with the family system on behalf of his client.

For the child returning home for the holidays from a residential treatment center, one issue that needs to be faced is: How ready is his family to accept what may be fairly substantial behavioral changes? For example, the formerly shy, withdrawn youngster may suddenly appear more demanding and challenging of parental authority. The impulsive child may appear a good deal more mature and capable of managing his own behavior. Even if no significant change has taken place either in the child or in his family, the family as a system has still had to adjust to the fact that one member is missing and will have to readjust to his return, even if only for a short while.

Under the best of conditions, the total family unit would

2. For an introduction, see Satir (1964, 1972), Ackerman (1966), Leader (1969), Stein (1969), and Handel (1967).

be seen as the client and actively involved from the outset in family treatment. But, for a variety of reasons, family involvement is not always possible. In such instances the worker undertakes some active intervention with the family prior to the holiday visit to ensure that he, the family, and the child share a common view of the progress the child has made, the issues that may come up over the vacation (for example, the whole question of the child's readjustment to a different set of routines, activities, and expectations), and some ways of easing the transition from treatment center to home and back again.

In another area of practice, the social worker in the coronary care unit of a large hospital might work very closely with all members of a patient's family to help them readjust to a routine of daily living. Finally, social workers in the field of aging often do considerable intervention with family members on behalf of an aging parent. This may entail helping the elderly person and his family work through the ramifications of this new dependency.

PEER GROUP SYSTEM

One important client reference group is the peer group, and the worker often intervenes with a client's peers to help bring about some individual change. For example, the school social worker who is working with a dropout who desires to reenter school may attempt to link his client up with a group of students who have successfully mastered the transition back to school. Such a group could provide some important emotional support, as well as some valuable information to the new student.

Similarly, an invitation to a ward activity club would aid the mental patient preparing himself for a return to the community. The group provides a valuable laboratory for trying out new social skills and developing self-awareness, as well as the opportunity for a successful recreational experience.

ORGANIZATIONAL AND COMMUNITY SYSTEMS

Each client belongs to a number of larger social systems: place of employment, church group, health care system, court system, welfare department, or voluntary associations such as lodges or social clubs. The worker, focusing on specific tasks, may intervene in any of these systems on the client's behalf. For example, the juvenile worker may intervene with the court to try to avert an institutional placement for his client, and offer instead a plan for community treatment. The family worker may bring together creditors and legal counsel to help his client avoid having his wages garnisheed. The medical social worker may prod the hospital into providing special visiting arrangements for the family of a patient with a terminal illness.

Specifically, what indirect helping roles is the worker fulfilling when he takes action on his client's behalf?

Indirect Helping Roles

In an earlier discussion of social treatment, two major indirect helping roles were identified: advocate-ombudsman and broker of services and resources.

ADVOCATE-OMBUDSMAN

Since much of the debate surrounding client advocacy has been introduced in Chapter 2, it will not be elaborated here. Rather I shall focus on what the worker actually does in his role as client advocate.

Earlier, advocacy was defined to include any action undertaken by the worker on the client's behalf. Advocacy actions include those taken to alleviate some form of dehumanizing practice that violates the client's sense of dignity as well as the professional code of ethics[3] and steps taken to ensure

3. See Wineman and James (1969).

that a client receives equitable treatment from a public or private agency. An ombudsman is defined by Webster as "one appointed to receive and investigate complaints by individuals against abuses or capricious acts of public officials." Some countries—Sweden, for example—have institutionalized the functions of the advocate in the person of an ombudsman. Similar functions are often performed by public interest groups (such as the Consumer's Union) or through citizen action lines maintained by the media. Let us examine some examples of social workers performing in their role as advocates.

The Smiths, a low-income family from Appalachia, moved north in search of employment several years ago. Their middle son, Lyle, has had the most difficult time adjusting to urban life. He has done poorly in school, has made few friends, and has been picked up by the police several times for curfew violation and truancy. Recently he was taken to detention after a loaded shotgun was found in his possession. Lyle maintained he had only planned to go hunting. A school social worker who has worked with the family as the result of Lyle's truancy makes contact with the juvenile judge to request permission to attend Lyle's hearing. Prior to that, she will meet with the family and the court intake worker to see if some plan can be worked out for Lyle that will avoid court placement.

Mrs. Y. is eighty-five years old, partially blind, and lives alone in a third-floor walk-up apartment. She would very much like to move to lower cost housing designed specifically for older people, but is confused about how to proceed with her application. She fears, among other things, that if her landlord finds out, she will be asked to leave and may find herself without a place to stay. A community service social worker helps Mrs. Y. fill out her application, then goes with her to the housing authority to see that she gets to the proper officials. The worker also checks with the community legal aid office to see exactly what Mrs. Y.'s rights and responsibilities are in relation to her landlord.

Judi Miller is a social worker at a community mental health center. Over time, she notices that many walk-in clients simply do not return for follow-up treatment. Fear of stigmatization seems to play a significant part in the process. Clients are fearful of being labeled "mental cases." Judi approaches the mental health center staff with a proposal for a more aggressive outreach program, particularly designed for those clients who do not return to the center, and in addition suggests a new brochure to explain in detail the kind of services the agency offers.

John, a social worker with the juvenile court, is shocked to learn that the juvenile detention facility has no clear-cut policy on the use of solitary confinement. Certain staff members seem to use it rather freely, and recently one child spent a week there for a rather minor rule violation. John's efforts to clarify the situation with the staff have met with resistance and he has been told, in effect, to mind his own business. John assembles all of the facts he can muster on the present situation in detention and goes to see the juvenile judge with a request that a clearly defined policy on confinement be drawn up and adhered to by all staff members.

Mr. and Mrs. Martin have been summoned to elementary school several times because of their son's disruptive behavior in the classroom. The Martins feel that part of the problem is the teacher, whose expectations they have never really understood. The parents are fearful of broaching this subject with the teacher or the principal, and generally are intimidated by the notion of being called to a conference at the school. A family service worker who has been seeing the Martins for counseling calls the school—with the parents' permission—and sets up a meeting with everyone concerned. The family worker does not side with either the Martins or the school at this meeting. Rather she attempts to mediate between the school and the Martins, with the goal of determining just what the problem is.

In many cases the worker performs an advocacy function by bridging the gap between existing services. This is particularly true with a multiproblem family, which may need to initiate contact with a number of social agencies and will require the services of an advocate to negotiate successfully all of the various entry requirements and expectations. In any event, this type of advocacy, or another designed to alleviate some punitive practice to which the client is exposed, makes up a good deal of what social workers actually do in the context of social treatment.

BROKER OF SERVICES AND RESOURCES

It is perhaps more the exception than the rule when an individual worker or agency can provide all of the services required by clients. This is particularly true for agencies with relatively open intake policies—courts, schools, mental health centers, hospitals, welfare departments—and is reflective of two factors: (1) clients often come to social agencies with multiple problems requiring a variety of solutions, and (2) the range of helping technologies has grown to the point where no individual worker or social agency can be expected to offer all of the help necessary. In many instances the worker acts as a kind of clearinghouse for services, making information about needed services available to clients and then seeing that they get linked up with the appropriate sources of aid.

For example, Joan has been in treatment for several months at the mental health clinic. One problem area that she has identified is a morbid fear of flying, which causes all sorts of complications in her new job, which requires a good deal of travel. Joan's social worker, unskilled in behavior therapy, refers her to another therapist at a local clinic who has had good success in treating phobic patients through systematic desensitization. Joan continues her visits with the original worker, who in turn keeps in close touch with the behavior therapist.

Jill Owen's case load of welfare clients includes a number of homemakers who want more information on budgeting, food buying, and menu planning. Jill arranges for reduced tuition, transportation allowance, and child care for those who wish to attend a home management course offered at a local community college.

Traditionally, many practitioners have functioned informally as resource brokers, referring clients to the appropriate sources of help or collaborating with other professionals to offer the needed service. Some social agencies are now moving in the direction of a more formalized social broker role, in which the worker in effect becomes a case manager who oversees the delivery of all services. Under such an arrangement, the agency may not offer any services itself, but purchases them through contractual arrangements. The social broker, then, is responsible for an initial assessment and then delivers and monitors the appropriate service package to meet the client's needs. Such a model leaves the worker free to perform other vital functions, such as client advocacy, and frees the agency from heavy investment in limited service programs. This model of service delivery can be very responsive to changing consumer needs and expands greatly the range of helping services offered by a central agency. From the client's point of view, it means that he does not have to search out where in the labyrinth of community social services his needs will best be met and then negotiate with a number of agencies to obtain service. It is likely that there will be a greater development of the social broker role as both human problems and the array of services designed to meet them become more complex.

Even in the absence of a formal social broker, however, individual practitioners need to know something of the network of helping services in a given community—where they are located, what kinds of help they offer, and what their entry requirements are.

Community Social Services. Generally, a helpful guide to the social agencies in a community is the directory of agencies provided by the local United Fund organization.

Medical Services. Even if his specialization is not in the field of health, every practitioner should know something of the community's health care system. Many clients or their families are in need of medical services and have little or no knowledge about where to obtain them. Especially for clients with limited incomes—though the problem of financing health care extends through the middle class as well—it is helpful to know where in the community medical care is available at reduced rates. Some clinics, particularly in teaching hospitals, seek certain types of patients and offer reduced charges. Countless physicians donate a portion of their time to patients with limited ability to pay. Negotiating the health care system in any community is a formidable task for the most informed and self-sufficient individual; for a person with some special social or emotional burden, the problem is compounded. Social work practitioners should know—or know where to find out about—the intricacies of health care financing: what are the advantages and disadvantages of private insurance plans and what services are provided by public programs?

Dental Services. Dental services are a major expense for many families and are often covered inadequately, if at all, by private insurance plans. Like medical practitioners, many dentists donate their time in clinics and community dental programs of all kinds. Local dental societies are often a good source of information on these services.

Legal Services. Numerous clients come to social agencies enmeshed not only in social and emotional problems, but in legal difficulties as well. These may range from domestic relations problems to criminal violations to landlord-tenant difficulties. Community legal services, often free, are available in many areas, and local bar associations often have lawyer referral services for clients who do not know an attorney in the community.

Consumer Protection and Financial Services. Closely linked with community legal services are agencies and organizations designed to help the person who has been the victim of consumer fraud. Many clients are embroiled in extremely complex situations involving credit purchases which threaten to push them over the brink. In many states the attorney general's office maintains a division of consumer protection. Other voluntary consumer groups may provide valuable information and assistance. To the client in financial distress, an attorney and/or a certified public accountant may offer some alternatives to the spiraling costs of private loan companies. The local society of C.P.A.s may be of assistance in locating sources of help in this area.

Employment Counseling Services. Many services are offered through the various state employment agencies. In addition, practitioners should have some knowledge of the advantages and disadvantages of private employment agencies and be aware of current regulations regarding unemployment compensation.

Educational Services. Particularly for the adult client with special learning needs—the returning veteran, the person who wishes to change his career, the former dropout—the worker needs to know something of the range of educational programs available in the community: vocational-technical programs, evening classes, community college programs, adult education, work-study programs, university programs. One tends to think stereotypically of the unemployed welfare client, but many others may be in equal need of special educational programs: the middle-aged, middle-class professional who suddenly finds himself out of work, the mother who decides to launch a new career, the parents who desire some family life education.

Religious Services. The importance of having sufficient knowledge in this area cannot be overestimated. Many clients will confide more to a clergyman than they ever would to a professional social worker. Often clergymen and helping professionals can work hand in hand with a troubled family. Many religious centers offer a host of other services besides worship and pastoral counseling, including adult education, child care, consumer co-ops, youth programs, and recreational programs.

Child Care Services. For many clients the problem of quality child care is crucial. Working parents—particularly single parents—depend on reliable child care services during working hours. Other families have a less pressing need for daily child care services, but need alternative care on occasion. Some families have special child care needs—an emotionally disturbed, mentally retarded, or physically handicapped child—while others simply need time away from their children to pursue their own interests and maintain a sense of mental balance. Anyone who knows how closely guarded is the name of a reliable child care person knows the seriousness of this problem. Practitioners should know about the range of public and private child care facilities in the community, and in addition be able to advise parents about what to look for in a child care setting.

Crisis Services. Clients do not have problems between the hours of nine and five exclusively. Many find themselves in some sort of crisis—legal, physical, emotional—at times when their social worker may be unavailable. Practitioners should know about the crisis services that exist in a community: crisis clinics, walk-in drug programs, alcohol counseling programs, suicide prevention programs, and teenage "hot lines," to name a few. The worker's knowledge of these programs should include familiarity with their hours, the services they offer, and means of getting in touch with them.

Summary

The fifty-minute treatment hour, group meeting, or family therapy session is simply not sufficient to meet the multiple life problems that clients bring with them to social agencies. In addition to the direct helping encounter, the practitioner of social treatment may undertake considerable intervention on the client's behalf in working with family, peer group, work group, organization, or community agency to seek aid for his client. The practitioner is aware not only of the community's social services, but of the range of alternative helping services as well. The client is viewed as a total person who has multiple life problems requiring intervention on many levels.

Additional Sources

Agnew, P. C., & Hsu, F. L. K. Introducing change in a mental hospital. In *Social system perspectives in residential institutions,* ed. H. Polsky, D. S. Claster, & C. Goldberg, pp. 151–61. East Lansing: Michigan State University Press, 1970.
Litwak, E., & Meyer, H. A balance theory of coordination between organizations and community primary groups. *Administrative Science Quarterly* 11, no. 1 (1966):31–58.

Marmor, J. Social action and the mental health professional. *American Journal of Orthopsychiatry* 40, no. 3 (1970):373–74.

Sarri, R. C., & Vinter, R. D. Organizational requisites for a socio-behavioral technology. In *The socio-behavioral approach and applications to social work*, ed. E. J. Thomas, pp. 87–99. New York: Council on Social Work Education, 1967.

Smith, A. D. The social worker in the legal aid setting. *Social Service Review* 44, no. 2 (1970):155–69.

Sunley, R. Family advocacy: From case to cause. *Social Casework* 51, no. 6 (1970):347–57.

Thompson, J. D., & Tuden, A. Strategies, structures, and processes of organizational decision. In *Comparative studies in administration*, ed J. D. Thompson et al., pp. 195–216. Pittsburgh: University of Pittsburgh Press, 1959.

Townsend, R. *Up the organization.* New York: Knopf, 1970.

Wax, J. Developing social work power in a medical organization. *Social Work* 13, no. 4 (1968):62–71.

Zander, A. Resistance to change: Its analysis and prevention. In *The planning of change*, ed. W. G. Bennis et al., 2nd ed., pp. 543–47. New York: Holt, Rinehart & Winston, 1969.

7

The Future for Social
Treatment

The future for social treatment must properly be viewed in
relation to the future for the entire remedial field: the organizations, social agencies, policies, and programs designed to
alleviate human problems. When posed in that context, the
initial question becomes, as in Chapter 1: Will there be a future for social treatment as we now know it? Whatever else
may be said, it does seem clear that in social treatment and
the larger remedial field things are not likely to remain un-
changed. What will the future shape of the remedial field be,
then, and more particularly, what problems and issues will
confront the social treatment practitioner of the future? To
begin with, two questions: What exactly is the remedial
field? What is the nature of its present crisis?

Attempts to define the remedial field often lose more than
they gain in elaboration. Once stripped of categories ("mental health," "corrections," "retardation"), unencumbered by
labels ("multiproblem family," "emotionally disturbed
child," "juvenile offender"), and liberated from technical

This chapter is adapted from an earlier version: Problems of effective functioning in *A Century of concern*, ed. C. A. Chambers
(New York: National Conference on Social Welfare, 1973, 21–31).

jargon ("psychosocial diagnosis," "therapeutic intervention"), the remedial field may be seen in its essence, which is, quite simply, people helping people.

It is of course true that we now know a great deal more about the kinds of problems people have and, we hope, more about ways to be of help to them. But quite apart from the techniques, at the heart of every true remedial effort lies a personal encounter between two people who attempt to share in each other's humanity, with the ultimate goal, in the words of Jane Addams (1910), of "raising life to its highest value." This concern for the worth of individual life, from Mary Richmond's exhortations to respect the dignity of clients to present efforts directed at humanizing social work practice, emerges as a central point in the last century's history of remedial efforts in the field of social welfare.

At present, the problems facing the remedial field are legion: internecine quarrels over which technology of helping works best, and when and how it should be delivered; problems of financial support, particularly among the voluntary agencies; mounting volumes of research that question the efficacy of present methods of social treatment; and larger issues raised by the social actionists and the environmentalists, who at times question the wisdom of financing any ameliorative efforts when massive programs of prevention and protection are so clearly needed. Of course, there have always been strains within the helping professions and pressures from without, but at almost no other time were they as divisive and intense as at present. In all quarters of the remedial field and in the seats of state and federal government one may hear the rumblings of dissension and view the bitter fruits of an effort plagued always with too few resources and often launched too late to provide anything but the most superficial care.

While the number of dependent children in institutions

has dropped sharply over the last fifty years, the number needing some form of help with emotional problems has risen to the point where the President's Joint Commission on the Mental Health of Children estimates that we are currently providing care for roughly one-third of the children in need. The inadequacy of our institutions to deal with the problems of juvenile offenders—indeed, the inadequacy of our system of juvenile justice, which still places in detention young children whose only "crime" is that they are victims of crisis or neglect—is still evident despite numerous attempts at reform. Programs in such specialized problem areas as juvenile drug abuse are still far from adequate, and conditions in some institutions for mentally retarded children give the lie to the belief that this nation subscribes to Dewey's dictum: "What the best and wisest parent wants for his own child, that must the community want for all of its children."

In the field of corrections the inability of present programs and resources to meet current problems is as visible as an open wound. The rare adult offender who does survive his period of incarceration unscathed is likely to be released to a community suspicious of his presence and offering few of the supports he needs to readjust to the demands of productive social life.

The crisis in health care touches virtually everyone in the society. Beyond the obvious and acute manifestations of physical trauma and disease lie the more subtle but equally painful symptoms of emotional suffering and neglect. Family disorganization and breakdown, personal despair and anxiety, depression fueled by an inability to deal with systems grown too large, alienation and anomie among the young, and a yearning for a sense of fulfillment and meaning on the part of many—these are only a few of the conditions that deserve social treatment, yet are often neglected because of insufficient programs or inadequate funding.

The targets for healing span all age groups, from pre-schooler to aged pensioner, and all classes, though many wear the double yoke of poverty and dysfunction. With so vast a need for change and so loud a call for help, one wonders at times if any degree of progress has been made or will be forthcoming. On reflection, all but the most biased reading of the last century's remedial efforts in the field of social welfare shows clearly that many advances have been made in child health and protection, in community programs for delinquents, in family counseling and mental hygiene: progress to be sure, but leaving so much still to be done. Equally difficult to assess is the reason for the insufficient action. Professional in-fighting, lack of financial resources, embryonic technologies of helping—all may be contributing causes. But perhaps in some later analysis the real impediment will be seen less as a shortcoming in finance or technology than a failure of will—a conclusion that seems more plausible with each commission report, each senate hearing, each social outcry against needs left unfulfilled. All of this makes extremely difficult the task of predicting where social treatment is headed. But while no one can be sure precisely where the field of interpersonal helping is going—one reading would see several vectors rather than a single direction —perhaps some sense of where we are going may be garnered from a careful analysis of where we have been.

Past Influences

The remedial field has always been truncated by gulfs and divisions. Presently they are philosophical and technological; previously they were geographical. Indeed, the bridging of distances between cities, states, and regions and the emerging recognition of a community of interest were central to the development of helping services in the final quarter of the last century. The period was also marked by a certain optimism and a special enthusiasm, almost as if the discovery of common problems and mutual interests, as well as the conquest of physical boundaries, portended solutions soon to be found.

If some differences of opinion existed about the causes of social problems—from moral turpitude to social influence to character defect—relatively little dissension could be found regarding what needed to be done. Families needed adequate food, clothing, shelter, and medical care. Children deserved a wholesome environment for growth and development. Those special children deprived of natural parents through death or desertion required devoted and loving foster families, or, as a last resort, homelike institutions for care. Nearly all remedial efforts involved some form of environmental manipulation: removing the waif from the city streets, finding a flat for a newly arrived immigrant family, converting the child care institution from barracks to cottage, placing the mental patient in uplifting surroundings, and removing the delinquent from his criminal associations. All of these efforts were based on a view of individual problems as greatly influenced (if not created) by social conditions.

It was natural, then, that along with individual casework there was a felt need for a more general societal effort directed at the root causes of specific problems. Poverty, inferior housing, overcrowded cities, poor health care—all required an attack along a broad front. What Mary Richmond called the "interdependence of individual and mass betterment" was a cornerstone of the emerging social work profession and was very much in evidence at professional conferences and symposia.[1] Social reform and social treatment went hand in hand into the new century in the belief that both were needed if truly efficacious solutions were to be realized. Much has happened between then and now. Counter-

1. See Richmond (1917, p. 365).

currents at times caused deep rifts between the two movements, and only recently has the old alliance been revitalized.

In the intervening years social work and the remedial field
got organized and went professional. Summer training institutes were replaced by graduate professional schools of
social work; loosely knit federations of friendly visitors became social welfare bureaucracies; common sense and dedi-
cation in charity workers were supplemented by a professional technology; problems once simply defined in social or
moral terms were seen as vastly more complex entities requiring sophisticated forms of intervention. By the late
1920s and over the vehement protestations of many of the
older social actionists, the shift had been made from cause to
function. Indeed, Porter Lee's 1929 presidential address to
the National Conference on Social Welfare couldn't have
more accurately described the differences between the new
helping professionals and their earlier counterparts: "an
embattled host for the cause, an efficient personnel for the
function."

Well before Lee's address, growing numbers of new professionals, heeding the criteria for professional advance-
ment suggested by Abraham Flexner at the 1915 National
Conference on Charities and Corrections, were hard at the
task of defining the new orientation to helping. And so much
needed to be done. Educational requirements were stiffened
and the two-year master's degree program became the entry
point to the new profession. National organizations were
formed to accommodate to the varying professional needs of
medical, psychiatric, and family social workers. Casework
and group work emerged as distinct methods of intervention
and various theoretical positions gathered their ardent sup-
porters. Chief among these was the new dynamic Freudian
psychology, which tended to view difficulties as internal and
emotional rather than external and social. The treatment of
choice shifted from environmental manipulation to insight-

producing counseling. No matter that the actual number of
psychoanalytically trained practitioners remained small;
theirs was still the model to be followed. In time the majority of professional schools of social work would adopt an essentially psychodynamic orientation to human development
as well as to practice. This new emphasis on the insight-focused interview conducted in an office, coupled with the
growing bureaucratization of social welfare agencies, with
the concomitant separation of function and division of labor,
tended to remove individual workers at least one step from
the intimate engagement between family and friendly visitor which had characterized earlier times.

A great deal of attention was paid to developing the new
technology of helping—psychosocial diagnosis, case planning, treatment intervention—as well as to delineating a
whole new taxonomy of human problems. The illness-treat-
ment model gradually grew in prominence, and adjustment
to (rather than changes in) social conditions became
the watchword.

Specifying the social worker's role and function—on the
psychiatric team, on the hospital ward, in the community
agency—became a preoccupying issue for the profession.
Again the new professionals were moving further from direct contact with the totality of the individual or family
problem. Precise role definitions and specification of function read well on the organization chart, but often ill
matched the multiple real-life problems of clients.

Whatever else one could say about the remedial segment
of the social welfare field from roughly the end of World
War I until relatively recently, it is certainly fair to charac-
terize it as having undergone a great turning inward upon
itself. It was a turning inward that had its salutary fea-
tures, to be sure—the development of professional standards, a greatly improved technology of helping—but it also

caused a kind of social myopia for which the profession was to be called to account in later years.

Present Influences

The remedial field today exists in a state of siege. So ubiquitous is the conflict, so intense the battle, that all but the loudest of salvos and the sharpest attacks go virtually unnoticed. The quest for professional normality has become the struggle for professional survival.

From without, the remedial field, in particular the social work profession, has been called to task by numerous client groups for being unresponsive to their needs and problems. Racial and ethnic minorities, among others, have challenged the helping professions to become more socially active on their behalf, to become far less ignorant of the cultures and values of the groups with which they work, and above all to direct change efforts not at individual pathology, but at the pathological social conditions in which clients must live, particularly if they are poor or members of a minority group. Especially telling is the charge that the very agencies and institutions once designed to alleviate human misery have grown to huge bureaucracies that now serve to perpetuate it. Clients are demanding more humane and relevant programs, more active participation in the helping process, and more control over the provision of services. Laudable aims, to be sure; but how are they to be incorporated into that now firmly entrenched professional role so long in the forging?

Other attacks come from the sources of support—public and private funding agencies. Disenchanted by promises never kept and expectations never realized, and faced with increasingly insufficient revenues to meet growing service needs, the funding agencies are turning from the helping professions to other quarters for aid in solving human problems. "Accountability" and "cost effectiveness" are the by-words of the new managerial orientation to human social problems. The private agencies, long accustomed to viewing themselves as the arbiters of innovative practice, are in particularly dire straits, struggling mightily to retain their autonomy and leadership and fearful of encroachment from the public sector. More generally, the entire remedial field suffers to an extent from a kind of post–poverty program hangover on the part of the public, causing, as the president of the National Association of Social Workers recently noted, the lowest degree of acceptance for social welfare programs and social work professionals that he could remember.

As if the wave of antiprofessionalism, the disenchantment of the public, and severe shortages in funding and client demands were not enough, other tremors emanate from within the remedial field itself. Some urge the almost total abandonment of palliative services in favor of action-oriented, system-focused strategies directed at the root causes of individual problems. We must make poverty, racism, inequality, and urban blight the major targets for the helping professions, the argument goes; to do otherwise is to offer a soporific when what is needed is major surgery. This particular thrust—really a whole series of separate pressure points within the field—multiplies considerably the range of possible targets at which already scant resources must be directed.

The plea to redirect resources to larger targets appears to be supported by a growing litany of research reports, all questioning the effectiveness of case-by-case intervention.[2] While some results can properly be attributed to faulty research design, the point seems to have been made that, by and large, individual attempts at remediation have not been

2. For example, see Berleman, Seaberg, & Steinburn (1972); Mullen, Chazin, & Feldstein (1972); and Wilkinson & Ross (1972).

successful to any appreciable extent. In the beginning, such studies served only to create spirited discussion in the professional literature; now they provide damaging evidence to those management-focused public officials seeking more cost-effective solutions to individual problems.

Partially as a result of these discouraging research reports, professional orthodoxy—particularly adherence to psychoanalytic theory—has been replaced by a theoretical pluralism unparalleled in the remedial field. Far removed from any kind of systematic eclecticism, the knowledge base of social treatment today resembles a collage of bits and pieces of theory, practice research, isolated techniques, and highly personalized approaches strung together by the flimsiest thread of professional ethics. Whatever common core of cumulative knowledge could have been assumed in the past has shrunk to minuscule proportions, as social work practitioners, theoreticians, and students battle with each other over who possesses the "truth." Perhaps most troubling in what could be a healthy ferment of new ideas is the social fervor with which many are pursued. One would have thought that after social work's almost total acceptance and later disenchantment with Freudian theory the profession would be more cautious about "granting the status of an axiom" only to snatch it away again later (Herzog, 1962).

Along with internal and external forces, the social treatment scene has been substantially altered in recent years by changing values and attitudes of the public at large. More liberal acceptance of out-of-wedlock pregnancy and single parenthood has forced many maternity agencies to alter their programs radically or go out of existence. In juvenile corrections and mental health, the trend toward more community-based forms of treatment signals major changes in the service structure—a bitter pill for some in the remedial field who for years have been arguing for more of the same facilities and programs.

New populations of clients, such as young drug users, and new forms of service delivery, such as crisis clinics, have given rise to a whole spate of agencies and programs, often staffed by nonprofessionals and operating outside of traditional social welfare agencies. Even private industry is now making inroads into the social welfare field, franchising service programs, training staff members, and offering consultation to government. Little wonder that some of the members of the old coalition—private agency executives, professional social workers, and public welfare personnel—feel at times as if events have passed them by, and that what was once solidly their territory must now be shared with considerable numbers of others. Faced with such formidable and diverse challenges, some yearn for the days of theoretical orthodoxy, client acceptance, and public support. Some, indeed, would view the current crisis in the remedial field as merely transitory—the result of, say, a hostile administration, or economic recession, or flash-in-the-pan new programs.

It is difficult to accept this position in light of what is now occurring in the remedial field. Basic structural revision rather than superficial change would appear to be the logical outcome of present trends. The critical question is, of course, what will the remedial field of the future resemble?

Future Directions

If one rejects out of hand the notion that things will remain exactly as they are in the field of interpersonal helping, or revert to some prior state of relative tranquillity, then the view that we are now witnessing the death of the entire remedial field must also be discarded. Two factors would seem to argue against this latter course. First, even with a totally new set of social institutions, such as many social actionists demand, there will still be a need for remedial services. Who will presume to suggest, for example, that new institutions will not in themselves create new problems of adjustment for individuals, requiring new methods of remediation? In truth, the problem with the whole remediation-reform question is that goals and means have become misplaced. Needed changes in present social institutions will not be brought about by remedial services, nor will the eventual realization of those systemic changes do away completely with the need for ameliorative programs. Clearly, both reform and remediation must proceed together in a manner similar to that envisioned by the social welfare pioneers of the early part of this century.

A second factor that seemingly will ensure the continuance of the remedial field in some form is the growing demand for more services of all kinds by a public that finds itself with the leisure time to become increasingly concerned with individual betterment and the overall quality of life. The demand for more parent education and the encounter group movement provide two fairly recent examples of the creation of new services by public demand. Assuming, then, the continuance of the remedial field in some form, what will it resemble? Cognizant of the risks inherent in hard-nosed predictions, we would perhaps do better to speculate on what *might* be true in the remedial field if a common effort were made to shape the casting of the future mold.

First among priorities would be a total rethinking of the values and ethos that inform the field of interpersonal helping. We need a value set that is in keeping with the principles of a sound ecology and which stresses the highest and best quality of individual, group, and community life. Specifically, this would entail an orientation to remediation—whether in corrections, health, or welfare—which stressed growth and development rather than illness and treatment, and sought to diminish rather than highlight the differences between the helpers and the helped. The recognition of the fullest potential of any client, whatever his diagnostic label, should be the primary goal of all remediation. This cannot and should not mean merely the readjustment of an individual to an essentially unhealthy social condition.

I further suggest that all remedial efforts be redirected at real-life problems of people in need and not at preconceived notions of what the difficulty is. In short, all attempts should be made to place renewed emphasis on the social aspects of remedial practice and make the method of helping conform to the client's problem and not vice versa. Central to the remedial process should be the joint efforts of helper and helped, pooling their resources in a voluntary relationship to achieve a commonly agreed-upon goal. This means that involuntary treatment, coercive practices, and anything less than a full sharing of confidence between client and worker will not be acceptable.

The problem of competing theories of change should be squarely faced in the full recognition that we remain far distant from anything resembling a unified theory of human behavior or a highly reliable solution to any of the multitude of problems with which we deal. Experimentation and eclecticism should be encouraged in social agencies and in professional training. Differences of opinion or theoretical persuasion should not assume the "thou-shalt-believe-all-or-nothing" quality they have in the past; we should attempt to build bridges rather than to shout across the chasm. Along with this eclectic approach to practice should go a thorough program of evaluative research to try to provide answers to the question, "what works best?" On this point it would be wise not to oversell whatever we have to offer. No single attempt at remediation will cure delinquency/ or completely solve a community's drug problems or minister to the total mental health needs of an area. Honesty and tempered optimism at the outset are probably the best antidotes to public distrust of professional intervention.

The area of service delivery is yet another quarter where major changes need to be made. First, and perhaps most troublesome, is the whole spate of categorical programs that have developed over the years, each with its own definition of problems and array of services. The hard question to be answered is whether our present method of defining problems makes sense any more, given what we now know about the interlinking of human difficulties. Kahn (1971) has pointed out that most categorical definitions of problems represented social advances when they were first promulgated: "orphan asylum" signified that homeless children would no longer be indiscriminately placed in almshouses and "mental illness" signaled a trend away from viewing certain behavior as morally reprehensible or subject to criminal penalty. The difficulty at present is that the remedial field is made up of a whole array of services clustered around certain problem definitions, usually with specific assumptions about etiology and amelioration. In light of what we now know about human behavior and in terms of an orientation to growth and development rather than illness and treatment, we must attempt to answer the question of whether these categories, these problem definitions, and these assumptions make sense any more. If they do not, then what better way can be constructed for dealing with problems of children and adolescents, or families in crisis, or the aged? These are extremely difficult questions to answer, and the more so because of the enormous investment of the present remedial establishment in the way it now views itself. The temptation always is to say simply that what we need is more of the same: more professionally trained social workers, more community mental health clinics, more institutions for delinquents. This approach, in the short view uncritical, could ultimately leave the social work profession mired in its cherished programs while the remedial field moves on to new modes of service delivery.

Another factor in the service delivery area concerns the continued existence of some of the old dichotomies: "public/private," "community/institutional." The era of the totally self-sustaining, voluntary agency appears to be drawing to a close. Rather than guard against the inevitable merger with the public sphere, private agencies might do well actively to seek linkages with the public sector, to fill needed service gaps and engage in joint attempts at service delivery. To those convinced that such a course would amount to the ruination of the voluntary agency, the question increasingly becomes "Which is more important—exclusivity or existence?" Finally, both voluntary and public agencies should prepare for the entrance of private industry and other vendors into the remedial field in the coming years. With this, as with the introduction of cost-effectiveness procedures and a new emphasis on accountability, the remedial field must choose between an essentially active or reactive position.

As with the public/private dichotomy, the traditional distinctions between community-based and institutional mental health and corrections agencies should give way to a conception of a single agency that offers a whole continuum of services ranging from totally institutional to totally community-based, with all variations in between. Diversification of services should be the watchword for those agencies now faced with going the route of single-purpose organizations or agencies (such as maternity homes for unwed mothers).

Finally, the remedial field might do well to think of restructuring services, bearing in mind only the factors of access and egress: How easy is it to obtain the needed service? How difficult is it to terminate it? Looked at in this manner, some services—for example, maternal and infant care, suicide prevention, and food programs for the elderly—should be structured in such a way that it becomes extremely simple to get in and out of the service network as the need arises. Others, like juvenile detention or involuntary hospitalization, might be set up in a way that provided for difficult access and easy egress along the way.

A final concern that needs to be addressed involves the whole question of client advocacy. In a general sense, the definition of the remedial helping role must be expanded to give equal weight to those actions taken on the client's behalf and those taken directly with him in the helping encounter. In a sense, this means no more than a return to the kind of collateral helping advocated by Mary Richmond at the turn of the century: helping the client negotiate a vast government agency, providing assistance in an employment search, negotiating with the courts over a custody problem working with a teacher to improve the home-school relationship. Social work professionals have always held these things to be important, but they were treated with somewhat diminished attention during the long infatuation with individual treatment. More specifically, when clients' rights are infringed through inhumane practices or punitive regulations, sufficient mechanisms should be developed through national professional organizations to provide the necessary support to both the aggrieved client and his worker.

In sum, the remedial field is likely to turn in several directions rather than only one: toward increased emphasis on cost effectiveness and accountability; toward a gradual blurring of distinctions between public/private and community/institutional programs; toward an orientation based on human potential and growth and development rather than on a narrow conception of illness and treatment; toward greater participation of consumers in remedial programs at all levels; toward a more systematic eclecticism in theory orientation underpinned by a substantial research endeavor; toward increased involvement of new vendors in the remedial field, including private industry and consumer groups; toward a rethinking of present problem categories

and accompanying service systems with the goal of providing an inclusive service net with little or no stigma attached
to the recipients; and, finally, toward a renewed social consciousness on the part of agencies and helping professionals
which places client advocacy at the heart of the remedial relationship. This could well be the form of the remedial field
of the future.

All this would appear quite curious to those prioneers who
journeyed to New York in 1874[3] to pool their ideas to provide better services to those in need, and later to Mary Richmond and others like her who knew of the importance of
such things as proper food budgeting and assisting families
in getting a load of fuel for cold winter nights; strange indeed to talk of "cost accountability" and "service networks,"
when it was abundantly clear what needed to be done: clean
and sufficient housing had to be provided for families, the
physical and mental health of children had to be seen to, offenders had to be worked with and returned to society. No
talk here of divisiveness: broad social reforms must of
course be mounted, and remedial programs as well, to aid
those who had already felt pain.

True, the numbers are now greater, the problems more
complex, the obstacles more awesome—but enough to damp-
en the enthusiasm or quell the spirit of those pioneers completely? I think not. For behind that enthusiasm lay something of a cause: "to raise life to its highest value." Perhaps
this is what is needed now, along with the efficient personnel, the programs, and the research; if not exactly an embattled host, then certainly an aroused and spirited coalition of
professionals, consumers, and laymen dedicated to raising
the quality of life for all, and in particular for those in special need of help. The remedial field of the future, whatever
its form, could only be better for the trying.

3. First National Conference on Charities and Corrections.

ADDITIONAL SOURCES

Agel, J. *The radical therapist*. New York: Ballantine, 1971.

Briar, S. Effective social work intervention in direct practice: Implications for education. In *Facing the Challenge*. New York: Council on Social Work Education, 1973.

Moynihan, D. P. *The politics of a guaranteed income*. New York. Random House, 1973.

Skinner, B. F. *Beyond freedom and dignity*. New York: Knopf, 1971.

Theobald, R. The survival of mankind. In *The social welfare forum, 1972*, pp. 20–33. New York: National Conference on Social Welfare, 1972.

Appendix:
Differential Approaches
to Social Treatment

If the social treatment practitioner at times feels over-whelmed by the complexity of the client problems he faces, the array of helping methods designed to solve them is equally confounding. Just as the base for much of interpersonal helping consists of untested and incomplete theory, the helping methods themselves are often poorly conceptualized, highly personalized, and unvalidated. Indeed, the pathways to social treatment are so numerous and diverse that the "treatment of choice" is more likely than not the "treatment of chance." Mastery of all methods of interpersonal helping has become a practical improbability, and rational choice of the helping method that best fits the client's problem is made more difficult by the fact that each method of social treatment comes complete with its own cohort of highly vocal exponents proclaiming the superiority of their approach over all others. In an area that so sorely needs dialogue and research that will eventually lead to the development of practice theory, openmindedness and rigor are in short supply.

Also discouraging is the fact that much of the evaluative research that does exist could be summarized (not too face-

Prepared with the assistance of Curtis D. Harstad, Asbjörn Osland, and Joyce Osland.

tiously) as suggesting that all approaches to social treatment appear to achieve equally minimal results. As one critical practitioner recently said, "No matter what theoretical approach is used, the results are always the same: one-third get better, one-third stay the same, and one-third get worse."

This is not meant to suggest an epistemological cynicism. We do know something about effectively helping clients master their problems, and this knowledge base is broadening each year. The point—for the practitioner—is action: clients have problems *now*, and they cannot wait for the final answer as to which set of helping techniques works best. It would be advantageous, however, to retain a healthy skepticism toward all claims of "success" and to avoid absolutes. No single approach to social treatment has yet proved to be effective with all clients.

The purpose of this section is twofold: (1) to suggest a framework for the critical appraisal of various approaches to social treatment, and (2) to identify briefly a select number of methods of social treatment.

Limitations of space do not permit a full elaboration of the various methods of social treatment, much less a critical review of their apparent strengths and limitations. Nor does the following summary include all helping methods. It is simply a brief description of some of the major approaches to interpersonal helping with individuals, families, and small groups. It provides a partial view of the range of social treatment methods and suggests some sources for further study. Many of the social treatment methods are based in part on one or more of the theories outlined in Chapter 4.

Choosing a Method of Social Treatment

Seldom have social treatment practitioners been confronted with so many different approaches to individual change: individual and group psychotherapy, behavioral treatment, encounter groups, traditional and radical approaches . . . the list (and the confusion) goes on and on. It is difficult for practitioners to separate fact from fancy, claim from counterclaim, and therapist from therapy. Too much technology of social treatment is proving almost as great a problem as too little.

One way to begin to make some sense of the various approaches to social treatment is to ask of each the same basic questions. While this in itself may not identify the approach that works best in each instance, it may at least point to important unspecified variables and unanswered questions. These areas of inquiry include the following:

Purpose. To what end is this helping approach designed. —behavior change, insight, alteration of the client's self-image, moral conversion, adjustment, other?

Knowledge base. From what theories, philosophical systems, or other sources does this approach draw—psychoanalytic theory, social learning theory, existential philosophy, communications theory, other?

Setting. Where is this method typically practiced—clinic or hospital, social agency, correctional facility, school, residential treatment center, the client's own home, community center, other?

Composition. Who are the *dramatis personae* in the treatment encounter—client, worker, client's family, spouse, peer group, relevant others? How is the composition decided—by the client, by the worker, by client and worker, by the agency, other?

Role of therapist or worker. What part does the worker play in the treatment encounter—counselor, therapist, teacher, behavior monitor, discussion leader, other? What are the requisite skills necessary to carry out this role—verbal, listening, group discussion, group activities, other?

Role of client. What part does the client play in the treatment encounter—active participant, codirector of treatment, student-learner, group member, other? What are the requisite client skills?

Strategies and techniques of helping. What actually occurs in the treatment encounter—confrontation, clarification, teaching, role playing and simulation, group discussion, behavior shaping, mystical experience, other?

Indications. With whom does this helping approach appear to work best—married couples, adolescents, children, acting-out delinquents, depressed clients, clients with limited verbal skills, whole families, psychotic clients, others?

Contraindications. Under what circumstances and for what type of client is this helping approach inappropriate or ineffective?

Empirical validation. To what extent has this approach been rigorously tested in field studies or in single case designs? Were significant results achieved? What are the implications of this research for the individual practitioner? What impediments to critical evaluation exist in the method (e.g., poorly defined techniques and objectives)?

In the final analysis, the question of empirical validation is the most important one. Effectiveness, rigorously demonstrated, should be the primary criterion for choice of helping method. Recent developments in research design, including the "case as own control" paradigm, provide the practitioner with the means for evaluating his own practice, in addition to keeping abreast of the results of larger field studies (Stuart, 1971). As each approach is identified and further elaborated through additional reading, perhaps these questions will suggest an order for subsequent critical analysis. For present purposes, discussion of each social treatment approach will be limited to (1) statement of purpose, (2) leading theoreticians, (3) description, and (4) selected references.

Methods of Social Treatment

ACTIVITY GROUP THERAPY

Purpose: The purpose of activity group therapy is to provide children with an opportunity to develop and improve
relationships with their peers by creating a setting in which
they may release tension, reduce anxiety, and spontaneously
act out their feelings in the presence of their peers and an
understanding adult. The group setting is designed to supply
substitute gratification, give vent to aggression, further
self-esteem, release blocks to expression in some children,
and build self-restraint in others.

Leading Theoretician: Samuel R. Slavson.

Description: Activity group therapy is used primarily
with children and young teenagers. Usually a group of five
to eight youngsters meets weekly for two hours. Their meeting room contains handicraft materials, group games, and
facilities for preparing food. Groups may also meet on play-
grounds or take field trips together. Samuel Slavson, foun-
der of activity group therapy, describes one of its major tenets as the belief that emotional disorientation and dissocial
behavior originate in family relations. Thus activity groups
try to approximate the ideal family and provide the positive
elements lacking in the group members' real families.

Activity group therapy attempts to meet what Slavson has
identified as the basic needs of young clients:
1. The need for unconditional love from parents and significant others.
2. The need for an increased sense of self-worth.
3. The need for genuine interests to occupy the child's leisure time.
4. The need for group acceptance to combat the loneliness
   experienced by the child.

Other assumptions of activity group therapy are that group members find relief through self-expression in activities, that activities themselves have therapeutic effect, and that these two functions are best carried out in a permissive democratic setting. Much emphasis is placed upon the need to develop self-esteem and ego strength in the group members. This is accomplished by the child's sense of belonging to a group, his sense of achievement from working on various projects, and the praise and support he receives from the worker.

The worker acts as a model of the ideal parent—a kindly, unpunishing, friendly, positive individual who respects each child and praises and encourages his efforts. The worker, who may be seen as a transference figure by the child, shows no favoritism in the group and encourages the members to handle situations that arise. Only when an individual member or physical property is in danger will the worker intervene. He provides assistance with activity projects when asked and may or may not join in group games. Because of his role as ideal parent, the worker does not become overly familiar with the group.

The first step in forming an activity group is to select the members carefully so that the various types of children chosen will have a therapeutic effect upon one another. At the first meeting the worker introduces the members and observes their behavior and activities. The manual arts are viewed as tools to aid interaction among group members by stimulating conversation, contact, cooperation, and mutual admiration. The worker does not initiate discussion or activities. Expression of hostile or antisocial behavior is ignored. At the end of each session, the worker prepares a meal or snack for the group. Of all of the group approaches with children, activity group therapy is perhaps the least directive. Neutrality and passivity are designated as two major facets of the worker's role.

Selected References:

Corsini, R. *Methods of group psychotherapy.* New York: Mc-Graw-Hill, 1957.

Meyer, H.; Borgatta, E.; & Jones, W. C. *Girls at vocational high.* New York: Russell Sage Foundation, 1965.

Scheidlinger, S.; Douville, M.; Harrahill, C.; & Minor, J. Activity group therapy for children in a family agency. *Social Casework,* 40, no. 4 (1959):193–201.

Silverstein, S. A work therapy program for delinquent boys. *Crime and Delinquency* 11, no. 7 (1965):256–64.

Slavson, S. R. *Introduction to group therapy.* New York: Commonwealth Fund, 1943.

——. The group in child guidance. In *Handbook of child guidance,* ed. E. Harms, pp. 402–412. New York: Child Care Publications, 1947.

——. *The practice of group therapy.* New York: International Universities Press, 1947.

——. *The fields of group psychotherapy.* New York: Wiley, 1956.

BEHAVIOR THERAPY

Purpose: Behavior therapy consists of the systematic application of the principles of learning theory for the purpose of therapeutic behavior change.

Leading Theoreticians: Teodoro Ayllon, Nathan H. Azrin, Donald M. Baer, Albert Bandura, Sidney W. Bijou, Charles B. Ferster, Israel Goldiamond, Leonard Krasner, Ogden Lindsley, O. Ivar Lovaas, Gerald R. Patterson, B. F. Skinner, Arthur W. Staats, Leonard P. Ullmann, Montrose M. Wolf.

Description: The roots of behavior therapy extend deep into the research related to the fundamental ways in which organisms acquire and alter their behaviors. Perhaps the contemporary researcher-theoretician who has made the greatest single contribution to behavior therapy is B. F.

Skinner, through his development of the operant conditioning model and the extension of the principles of learning to
teaching and living contexts. Behavior therapy is currently
being used with a whole spectrum of clients—juvenile delinquents, children with behavioral difficulties, couples with
marital problems, phobic persons, and countless others. In
addition, behavior therapy is used with individuals, families,
and small groups in a continuum of settings ranging from
closed (prison or mental hospital) to open (crisis clinic, client's own home).

In a very basic sense, most behavior therapy involves the
following:

1. Inventory of client problem areas.
2. Contract.
3. Problem specification (defining the target behavior[s]).
4. Determination of base line.
5. Determination of controlling conditions and reinforcement hierarchy.
6. Specification of behavioral change objectives.
7. Formulation and execution of modification plan (accel-
   eration of some behaviors, deceleration of others).
8. Objective evaluation.

Since behavior therapy involves only observable, measurable change goals, its outcome can be monitored rather readily. Some specialized forms of behavior therapy include systematic desensitization of phobic clients, token economies
(used primarily in total institutions and classrooms), group
behavior therapy, and implosive therapy.

For the behavior therapist, the client's problem is the behavior he would like to modify. If behavior can be altered,
the client's difficulty will be resolved. Behaviorists do not
typically speak of "underlying pathologies" or "symptoms"

Since behavior is the sum and substance of personality, change in behavior is as deep a change as one can talk about. Though the principles of learning have been known for some time, their clinical application is relatively recent. In many cases, behavior therapy was initiated with clients for whom traditional methods had failed: regressed psychotic adults, autistic children, the severely mentally retarded. Currently the application of behavior therapy is being extended to a far greater range of clients with less severe difficulties.

Selected References:

Ayllon, T., & Azrin, N. *The token economy.* New York: Appleton-Century-Crofts, 1968.

Franks, C. M. *Behavior therapy: Appraisal and status.* New York: McGraw-Hill, 1969.

Graziano, A. M., ed. *Behavior therapy with children.* Chicago: Aldine, 1971.

Klein, M. H.; Dittmann, A. T.; Parloff, M. B.; & Gill, M. M. Behavioral therapy: Observations and reflections *Journal of Consulting and Clinical Psychology* 33, no. 3 (1969):259–66.

Lovaas, O. I. A behavior therapy approach to the treatment of childhood schizophrenia. In *Minnesota Symposium on Child Psychology*, ed. J. P. Hill, 1:108–159. Minneapolis: University of Minnesota Press, 1967.

McPherson, S. B., & Samuels, C. R. Teaching behavioral methods to parents. *Social Casework* 52, no. 3 (1971):148–53.

Sarason, I. G. Verbal learning, modeling, and juvenile delinquency. *American Psychologist* 23, no. 4 (1968); 254–66.

Skinner, B. F. *Contingencies of reinforcement: A theoretical analysis.* New York: Appleton, 1969.

——. *Beyond freedom and dignity.* New York: Knopf, 1971.

Stampfl, T. G., & Levis, D. J. Implosive therapy: A behavioral therapy. *Behavior Research and Therapy* 6, no. 1 (1968):31–36.

Tharp, R. G. & Wetzel, R. J. *Behavior modification in the natural environment.* New York: Academic Press, 1969.

Ulrich, R.; Stachnik, T.; & Mabry, J. *Control of human behavior: From cure to prevention.* Glenview, Ill.: Scott, Foresman, 1970.

Wolpe, J. *The practice of behavior therapy*. Elmsford, N. Y.: Maxwell House, 1969.

CONJOINT FAMILY TREATMENT

Purpose: Conjoint family treatment is a form of therapy that includes all family members in the therapeutic encounter. The family system itself, as well as individual members, is seen as a target for change.

Leading Theoreticians: Nathan Ackerman, Jay Haley, Otto Pollak, Virginia Satir, Sanford Sherman.

Description: The central notion behind most conjoint family treatment is that pain and difficulty experienced by one family member will in some way affect the total family system, and conversely that successful remediation of an individual family member's problem will require alterations in total family functioning. The family system itself is seen as both the focus and locus of change. There are several approaches to conjoint family treatment; among the best known is that developed by Virginia Satir.

Satir views the family not merely as a collection of individuals, but as a dynamic system in which the marital relationship is the focal point around which all other relationships are formed. Central to this view of the family as system is the notion of family homeostasis: family members react to each other in a way that preserves a balance in their relationships. A good many family problems, according to Satir, may be traced to faulty communication between the family members. This includes incongruent communication and in particular "double bind" messages—messages that are closely related, but incongruent. For example, a teenager is told by a parent, "Why don't you act like a responsible adult?" but is treated as a much younger child incapable of making important decisions.

The conjoint family therapist presents a model of good communication to all family members by reacting, clarifying, and interpreting what he hears the family saying to him and to each other. Each family member's role is examined through an extensive family life chronology and the therapist concentrates a good deal of time on the "hurt" in the family. Family members are urged to share feelings with each other in the therapy session, and each family member's contribution, including that of the youngest child, is listened to and respected by the therapist.

Conjoint family treatment has grown in popularity in recent years, in no small measure because what at first appeared as an individual problem has so often, on closer examination, proved to be a family problem. Consequently, if the worker expects to ameliorate the client's problem, it becomes clear that the total family must first be engaged.

Selected References:

Ackerman, N. W. *The psychodynamics of family life.* New York: Basic Books, 1958.

——. & Beatman, F. L. *Exploring the base for family therapy.* New York: Family Service Association of America, 1961.

Bolte, G. L. A communications approach to marital counseling. *Family Coordinator* 19, no. 1 (1970):32–40.

Casework treatment of the family unit. New York: Family Service Association of America, 1965.

Expending theory and practice in family therapy. New York: FSAA, 1967.

Gehrke, S., & Kirschenbaum, M. Survival patterns in family conjoint therapy. *Family Process* 6, no. 1 (1967):67–80.

Hallowitz, D. The problem-solving component in family therapy. *Social Casework* 51, no. 2 (1970):67–75.

Leader, A. The role of intervention in family group treatment. *Social Casework* 45, no. 4 (1964):327–33.

Pollak, O. Disturbed families and conjoint family counseling. *Child Welfare* 46, no. 3 (1967):143–49.

Roberts, W. L. Working with the family group in a child guidance clinic. *British Journal of Psychiatric Social Work* 9, no. 4 (1968):175–79.

Sager, C. J. An overview of family therapy. *International Journal of Group Psychotherapy* 18, no. 3 (1968): 302–312.

Satir, V. *Conjoint family treatment.* Palo Alto: Science and Behavior Books, 1967.

———. *Peoplemaking.* Palo Alto: Science and Behavior Books, 1972.

Scherz, F. H. Family treatment concepts. *Social Casework* 47, no. 4 (1966):234–41.

Sherman, S. N. Family treatment: An approach to children's problems. *Social Casework* 47, no. 6 (1966):368–72.

Zuk, G. H. Family therapy: Formulation of a technique and its theory. *International Journal of Group Psychotherapy* 18, no. 1 (1968):42–58.

CRISIS INTERVENTION

Purpose. Crisis intervention is a method of social treatment designed to assist an individual in his efforts to cope with a critical incident or period in his life. Its basic goals are (1) to "alleviate the impact of disruptive stressful events" and (2) "to help mobilize the manifest and latent psychological capabilities and social resources of those directly affected (and often of the key persons in the social environment) for coping with the effects of stress adaptively" (Parad, 1971, p. 196).

Leading Theoreticians: Gerald Caplan, Erich Lindemann, Howard Parad, Lydia Rapoport.

Description: Typically, crisis intervention consists of a brief period of treatment including (1) an attempt to reduce the impact of the crisis event on the client's life (2) an effort to help the client regain former ego stability, (3) an attempt to identify and influence any specific problems that may have precipitated or currently surround the crisis situation, and (4) an attempt to help the client learn new coping skills or more efficiently mobilize existing skills in order to deal more effectively with future life situations.

Crisis intervention techniques are now used in a wide variety of traditional and nontraditional settings: mental health clinics, emergency rooms, crisis clinics, "hot lines," suicide prevention services, and community service centers. Many of the techniques of crisis intervention provide useful tools for the paraprofessionals and volunteers who often staff crisis-oriented services. Requisite worker skills include the ability to function effectively and efficiently in an emotionally tense atmosphere and to give support and direction while at the same time helping the client to develop autonomous coping skills.

Crisis intervention generally progresses in the following manner: (1) An attempt is made to alleviate the disabling tension through ventilation and the creation of a climate of trust and hope. (2) Next the worker attempts to understand the dynamics of the event that precipitated the crisis. (3) The worker gives his impressions and understanding of the crisis and checks out these perceptions with the client. (4) Client and worker attempt to determine specific remedial measures that can be taken to restore equilibrium. (5) New methods of coping may be introduced. (6) Finally, termination occurs—often after a predetermined number of interviews—when the agreed-upon goals have been realized. One of the advantages of crisis intervention is that it is a helping method designed for people acutely in need of help. Treatment is brief and often occurs during the period when the client is emotionally in desperate need and therefore forces the rapid and efficient use of client-worker resources.

Selected References:

Baldwin, K. A. Crisis focused casework in a child guidance clinic. *Social Casework* 49, no. 1 (1968):28–34.

Caplan, G. *Principles of preventive psychiatry.* New York: Basic Books, 1964.

Darbonne, A. Crisis: A review of theory, practice, and research. *International Journal of Psychiatry* 6, no. 5 (1968):371–79.

Duckworth, G. L. A project in crisis intervention. *Social Casework* 48, no. 4 (1967):44–52.

Feidan, E. S. One year's experience with a suicide prevention service. *Social Work* 15, no. 3 (1970):26–32.

Fox, S. S., & Scherl, D. J. Crisis intervention with victims of rape. *Social Work* 17, no. 1 (1972):37–43.

Golan, N. When is a client in crisis? *Social Casework* 50, no. 7 (1969):389–94.

Kaplan, D. M. Observations on crisis theory and practice. *Social Casework* 49, no. 3 (1968):151–55.

Klein, D. C., & Lindemann, E. Preventive intervention in individual and family crisis situations. In *Prevention of mental disorders in children*, ed. G. Caplan, pp. 283–307. New York: Basic Books, 1961.

Krause, E. A. On the time and the place of crises. *Human Organization* 27, no. 2 (1968):110–16.

Krider, J. W., Jr. A new program and its impact on a small agency. *Social Casework* 50, no. 9 (1969):508–512.

Morris, B. Crisis intervention in a public welfare agency. *Social Casework* 49, no. 10 (1968):612–17.

Oppenheimer, J. R. Use of crisis intervention in casework with the cancer patient and his family. *Social Work* 12, no. 2 (1967):44–52.

Parad, H. J. *Crisis intervention.* New York: Family Service Association of America, 1965.

——. The use of time limited crisis intervention in community mental health programming. *Social Service Review* 40, no. 3 (1966):275–82.

——. Crisis of intervention. In *Encyclopedia of social work* 1:196–202. New York: National Association of Social Workers, 1971.

Rapoport, L. Crisis intervention as a mode of brief treatment, In *Theories of social casework*, ed. R. W. Roberts & R. H. Nee, pp. 265–311. Chicago: University of Chicago Press, 1970.

Sachs, V. K. Crisis intervention. *Public Welfare* 26, no. 2 (1968):112–17.

EXISTENTIAL PSYCHOTHERAPY

Purpose. The goal of existential therapy is greater meaning, richness, and wholeness for the total human being, making him aware of and in greater harmony with the essence of his existence. The meaning of his life and his purposes and goals for living are central to the therapy. Treatment focuses on freedom of choice to act in the face of an absurd and often malevolent external reality.

Leading Theoreticians. Ludwig Binswanger, Medard Boss, Victor Frankl, Donald Krill, Rollo May.

Description: Existential psychotherapy is really more of an attitude toward treatment than a set of specific strategies or techniques. The therapist strives to maintain an "I-thou" relationship with the client in his search for "authenticity." He acts as a bridge between reality and nonreality and helps the client to identify those relationships (self-to-self, self-to-other, and self-to-world) which are not valid, not real, or distorted. The client is encouraged to open himself to an authentic human interchange with the therapist of all life events: joy, anger, weakness, strength, trust, mistrust. The therapeutic encounter is seen as an active journey toward meaning shared equally by both participants. There is some fusing of existences and yet a separateness of identities as both therapist and client move together toward authenticity and meaning. Since existential therapy is more a statement of philosophy than a set of strategies, it is particularly difficult to define in terms of practical applications.

Selected References:

Binswanger, L. Existential analysis and psychotherapy. In *Progress in psychotherapy*, ed. F. Fromm-Reichmann & J. Moreno. New York: Grune & Stratton, 1956.
Boss, M. *Psychoanalysis and daseinsanalysis.* New York: Basic Books, 1963.

Buganthal, J. F. T. *The search for authenticity.* New York: Holt, Rinehart & Winston, 1965.

Frankl, V. E. *Man's search for meaning: An introduction to logotherapy.* Boston: Beacon Press, 1959.

——. *Psychotherapy and existentialism.* New York: Washington Square Press, 1967.

Hartman, A. Anomie and social casework. *Social Casework* 50, no. 3 (1969):131–37.

Krill, D. F. Existential psychotherapy and the problem of anomie. *Social Work* 14, no. 2 (1969):33–50.

May, R. *Love and Will.* New York: Norton, 1969.

——, ed. *Existential psychology.* New York: Random House, 1961.

——, Angel, E.; & Ellenberger, H., eds. *Existence: a new dimension in psychiatry and psychology.* New York: Basic Books, 1958.

Sinsheimer, R. B. The existential casework relationship. *Social Casework* 50, no. 2 (1969):67–73.

Stretch, J. J. Existentialism: A proposed philosophical orientation for social work. *Social Work* 12, no. 4 (1967):97–102.

Weisman, A. D. *The existential core of psychoanalysis.* Boston: Little, Brown, 1965.

GESTALT THERAPY

Purpose. Gestalt therapy is designed to help people develop spontaneity, sensory awareness, freedom of movement, emotional responsiveness, expressiveness, enjoyment, ease, flexibility in relating, direct contact and emotional closeness with others, intimacy, competence, immediacy and presence, self-support, and creativity (Fagen & Shepherd, 1970, p. 2).

Leading Theoretician. Frederick S. (Fritz) Perls.

Description: Though countless practitioners have elaborated the art of Gestalt therapy, it is essentially the creation of one clinician, Fritz Perls. Synthesizing and integrating ideas from psychoanalysis (Perls himself was a training analyst) and Gestalt psychology, Gestalt therapy focuses on self-awareness and personal growth. Rejecting a illness/ treatment model of practice, Perls's therapy focuses on the person's present reality: "To me, nothing exists except the now. Now = experience = awareness = reality" (Fagen & Shepherd, 1970, p. 14). A central task of the Gestalt therapist is to help the patient overcome the barriers that block awareness. To accomplish this the therapist uses dream and fantasy material, present interaction, and reflection. In its essence, Gestalt therapy remains a psychoanalytic method of treatment.

Selected References:

Fagen, J., & Shepherd, I. L. *Gestalt therapy now.* Palo Alto: Science and Behavior Books, 1970.

Perls, F. S. *Ego, hunger, and aggression.* New York: Random House, 1969.

——. *In and out of the garbage pail.* Lafayette, Calif.: Real People Press, 1969.

——. *Gestalt therapy verbatim.* Lafayette, Calif.: Real People Press, 1969.

——; Hefferline, R. F.; & Goodman, P. *Gestalt therapy.* New York: Dell, 1965.

Pursglove, P. D., ed. *Recognitions in Gestalt therapy.* New York: Funk & Wagnalls, 1968.

GROUP COUNSELING

Purpose: Group counseling is a method of interpersonal helping which uses the small group as a context within which individuals may work on educational, vocational, or personal growth goals. Some examples are:

1. Groups to improve academic achievement.
2. Groups to aid in the development of interpersonal skills.
3. Groups with a major emphasis on career development.

Leading Theoreticians: G. M. Gazda, S. D. Glass, E. N. Jackson, C. G. Kemp, J. Munro, M. M. Ohlsen, O. H. Patterson.

Description: The distinction between group counseling and other forms of group therapy has always been a rather arbitrary one, often having more to do with the professional background of the group leader than with the actual focus of the group. Group counseling has tended to be practiced by counseling psychologists and guidance counselors, and has been largely developed in and around educational institutions: in student counseling services, vocational placement offices, and career counseling centers. Other practitioners of group counseling include clergymen, probation officers, vocational rehabilitation counselors, social workers, and educators. Other contexts include churches, prisons, private industry, and health and mental health care facilities.

Generally, groups are limited to eight to twelve members selected on the basis of similar problems or learning needs. Individual and group goals are developed in the early sessions. The group counselor functions in the role of discussion leader and helper, encouraging members' attempts to help one another and promoting the group as a forum for mutual problem-solving. Primarily (though this generalization is at best tentative), group counseling is designed for clients not too seriously impaired in the areas of social functioning and emotional stability.

Selected References:

Carter, W. Group counseling for adolescent foster children. *Children* 15, no. 1 (1968):22–27.

Danforth, J.; Miller, D. S.; Day, A. L.; & Steiner, G. J. Group services for unmarried mothers: An interdisciplinary approach. *Children* 18, no. 2 (1971):59–64.

Davis, J. A. The use of discussion groups in a military hospital in Japan. *Social Casework* 44, no. 2 (1963):74–80.

Elliott, M. A. Group therapy in dealing with juvenile and adult offenders. *Federal Probation* 27, no. 9 (1963):48–54.

Gazda, G. M. *Basic approaches to group psychotherapy and group counseling.* Springfield, Ill.: Thomas, 1968.

———. *Theories and methods of group counseling.* Springfield, Ill.: Thomas, 1969.

Glass, S. D. *The practical handbook of group counseling.* Baltimore: BCS Publishing Co., 1969.

Harms, E., & Schreiber, P., eds. *Handbook of counseling techniques.* New York: Pergamon Press, 1963.

Jackson, E. N. *Group counseling: Dynamic possibilities of small groups.* Philadelphia: Pilgrim Press, 1969.

Kemp, C. G. *Foundations of group counseling.* New York: McGraw-Hill, 1970.

Mandelbaum, A. The group process in helping parents of retarded children. *Children* 14, no. 6 (1967):227–32.

Mann, P. H.; Beaber, J. D.; & Jacobson, M. D. The effect of group counseling on educable mentally retarded boys' self concept. *Exceptional children* 35, no. 5 (1969): 359–66.

Munro, J., & Freeman, S. *Readings in group counseling.* Scranton, Pa.: International Textbook Co., 1968.

Ohlsen, M. M. *Group counseling.* New York: Holt, Rinehart & Winston, 1970.

Paull, J. E. Family group methods and structural change in child welfare. *Child Welfare* 48, no. 2 (1969):79–85.

Sarri, P. C., & Vinter, R. D. Group treatment strategies in juvenile correctional programs. *Crime and Delinquency* 11, no. 10 (1965):326–40.

Soden, E. W. Constructive coercion and group counseling in the rehabilitation of alcoholics. *Federal Probation*, September 1966, pp. 56–60.

GUIDED GROUP INTERACTION

Purpose: Guided group interaction utilizes the dynamics and strengths of a delinquent subculture to turn it full circle into a positive peer culture. It is assumed that the very dynamics, strengths, and values of the delinquent peer group can, through a supportive caring atmosphere, be used to establish a positive culture in which socially acceptable rather than delinquent behavior becomes the norm. Guided group interaction is a method of value and goal reversal. The energies and resources of the delinquent are tapped to provide exploration of alternative behaviors and attitudes.

Leading Theoreticians: F. Lovell Bixby, Albert Elias, Lemar Empey, Lloyd McCorkle, Saul Pilnick, Frank Scarpitti, Harry Vorrath.

Description: The technique of guided group interaction rests on certain assumptions about the functions of the adolescent peer group. The peer group (1) acts as the reinforcing agent for prevalent delinquent or positive social values, (2) sanctions conformity to the norms of the group, and (3) provides status and sexual identification to the group members (Pilnick, 1971, p. 181). Thus the delinquent peer group itself becomes the focus for change. Used largely in delinquency institutions, the group meets on a daily basis to discuss problems and positive development of the members. To a large extent the group members themselves are the therapists—confronting, challenging, supporting, and coaching one another—and the group metes out important rewards and sanctions to individual members. The notion of commitment to change is central to the method, and "conning" or refusing to accept responsibility for one's actions is strongly sanctioned by the group. Any problem of an individual member is considered a total group problem and every member is expected to help in its solution. The group strongly sanctions delinquent behaviors—running away, conning, stealing, physical aggression—and is equally supportive of all socially acceptable behavior.

The group leader treads a fine line between setting limits and listening sympathetically. He serves to guide, focus, or redirect the group's attention to certain key problems. He often questions the group about its problems, but does not attempt to answer questions for them; rather he refers them back to the members for resolution. At the end of each meeting the leader provides a summary of the important issues of the session and may recapitulate and define for the members their attempts to deal with common problems. Guided group interaction is currently in use in many juvenile correctional systems and is being adopted in more open community settings as well.

Selected References:

Elias, A. Group treatment for juvenile delinquents. *Child Welfare,* 47, no. 5 (1968):281–90.

Empey, L. T., & Lubeck, S. G. *The Silverlake experiment.* Chicago: Aldine, 1972.

—— & Rabow, J. The Provo experiment in delinquency rehabilitation. *American Sociological Review* 26 (1961):679–96.

Jones, H. *Reluctant rebels.* New York: Association Press, 1963.

Larsen, C. *Guided group interaction.* Minneapolis: Department of Court Services, Hennepin County, 1970.

McCorkle, E., & Bixby, F. L. *The Highfields story.* New York: Holt, 1958.

Miller, L. L. Southfields: An evaluation of a short term inpatient treatment center for delinquents. *Crime and Delinquency* 16, no. 3 (1970):305–316.

Pilnick, S. Guided group interaction. In *Encyclopedia of social work* 1:181–86. New York: National Association of Social Workers, 1971.

——; Allen, R. F.; Dubin, H.; & Youtz, A. *From delinquency to freedom.* Seattle: Special Child Publications, 1970.

——; Clapp, N. W.; Allen, R. F.; & Turner, L. T. *Guided group interaction.* Union, N. J.: Scientific Resources Inc. Press, 1968.

Scarpitti, F. R., & Stephenson, R. M. The use of the small group in the rehabilitation of delinquents. *Federal Probation* 30, no. 3 (1966):45–50.

Scott, J., & Hissong, J. Changing the delinquent subculture: A sociological approach. *Crime and Delinquency* 15, no. 4 (1969):499–509.

Vorrath, H. *Questions and answers for group leaders in positive peer group culture.* Red Wing, Minn.: Red Wing State Training School, 1970.

Weeks, H. A. *Youthful offenders at Highfields.* Ann Arbor: University of Michigan Press, 1963.

MILIEU TREATMENT

Purpose: Milieu treatment involves the creation of a living/learning environment that systematically uses the events that occur in daily living as formats for teaching alternative behavior.

Leading Theoreticians: August Aichorn, Teodoro Ayllon, Nathan H. Azrin, Bruno Bettelheim, Elaine Cummings, John Cummings, George Fairweather, Maxwell Jones, O. I. Lovaas, Howard W. Polsky, Fritz Redl.

Description: Milieu treatment approaches have been used with a variety of client populations, including emotionally disturbed children, juvenile delinquents, institutionalized adult mental patients, and mentally retarded children and adults. The commonality of all of these groups is their need for special care away from the natural home environment. The specification of milieu treatment has been difficult, since for obvious reasons no one would admit to having a nontherapeutic milieu. What constitutes a therapeutic milieu varies widely.

In reality, there are several models of milieu treatment, which, while not necessarily mutually exclusive, are distinguishable in their major emphases. Some milieu programs stress individual psychotherapy while others place heavy emphasis on dealing with behavioral and emotional problems in a group context. Still others—token economies, for example—attempt to maximize the potential for teaching behavioral alternatives in virtually all aspects of the living situation. Milieu treatment approaches draw on a variety of theoretical systems, including ego psychology, social learning theory, social systems theory, and small group dynamics. A number of professional disciplines are also involved in milieu treatment, including social work, psychiatry, clinical psychology, psychiatric nursing, special education, occupational therapy, and child care counseling, among others. Milieu treatment programs are typically residential (correctional institutions, mental hospitals, residential treatment centers), though day treatment programs are increasing in popularity with the trend toward community-based facilities.

Selected References:

Aichorn, A. *Wayward youth.* New York: Viking Press, 1935.

Allerhand, M. E.; Weber, R.; & Haug, M. *Adaptation and adaptability: The Bellefaire followup study.* New York: Child Welfare League of America, 1966.

Ayllon, T., & Azrin, N. *The token economy.* New York: Appleton-Century-Crofts, 1968.

Bettelheim, B. *Love is not enough.* Glencoe, Ill.: Free Press, 1950.

———. *The empty fortress.* New York: Free Press, Macmillan, 1967.

Browning, R. M., & Stover, D. O. *Behavior modification in child treatment.* Chicago: Aldine, 1971.

Cummings, J., & Cummings, E. *Ego and milieu.* New York: Atherton Press, 1963.

Fairweather, G. *Social psychology in treating mental illness.* New York: Wiley, 1964.

Frank, J. *Persuasion and healing.* Baltimore: Johns Hopkins University Press, 1961.

Goldfarb, W.; Mintz, I.; & Stroock, K. W. *A time to heal.* New York: International Universities Press, 1967.

Jones, M. *The therapeutic community.* New York: Basic Books, 1953.

Kesey, K. *One flew over the cuckoo's nest.* New York: Signet, 1963.

Maluccio, A. N., & Marlow, W. D. Residential treatment of

emotionally disturbed children: A review of the literature. *Social Service Review* 46, no. 2 (1972):230–51.

Mayer, M. F., & Blum, A. *Healing through living.* Springfield: Thomas, 1971.

Neill, A. S. *Summerhill.* New York: Hart, 1964.

Pizzat, F. *Behavior modification in residential treatment for children.* New York: Behavioral Publications, 1973.

Polsky, H. *Cottage six.* New York: Russell Sage Foundation, 1962.

Redl, F. *When we deal with children.* New York: Free Press, Macmillan, 1967.

—— & Wineman, D. *The aggressive child.* New York: Free Press, Macmillan, 1958.

Trieschman, A. E.; Whittaker, J. K.; & Brendtro, L. K. *The other 23 hours: Child care work in a therapeutic milieu.* Chicago: Aldine, 1969.

Whittaker, J. K. Group care for children: Guidelines for planning. *Social Work* 17, no. 1 (1972):51–61.

——. The child care continuum: New directions for children's residential centers. *Child Care Quarterly,* 2, no. 2, (1973): 124–135.

—— & Trieschman, A. E., eds. *Children away from home: A sourcebook of residential treatment.* Chicago: Aldine-Atherton, 1972.

Wolins, M., & Gottesmann, M. *Group care: An Israeli approach.* New York: Gordon & Breach, 1971.

PARENTAL EDUCATION

Purpose: The basic purpose of parental education is to provide insight into child behavior and to develop child-rearing skills.

Leading Theoreticians: Rudolf Dreikurs, Haim Ginott, Thomas Gordon, Gerald Patterson, Benjamin Spock.

Description: Approaches to parental education are many and varied. Some focus on developing effective communication with children; others develop specific behavioral techniques to use in daily living. Parental education also uses a variety of educational formats, including small discussion groups, short courses, and programmed self-instruction. As society becomes more complex and as traditional sources of child-rearing knowledge (extended family, friends) become increasingly unavailable as a result of high mobility, parental education assumes increasing importance in the field of community services.

Though the various approaches to parent education differ considerably, most group formats develop the notion of parents as teachers as well as learners and encourage sharing of information and knowledge. Discussions typically focus around such topics as active listening; monitoring and managing children's behavior, play, and activities; sexual awareness; sibling rivalry; and the development of responsibility and discipline. Most parental education is based on the assumption that raising children is a difficult and complex task for which the society ill prepares young people, and that to seek help with child rearing does not mean that parents are sick, neglectful, or bad.

Selected References:

Becker, W. *Parents are teachers: A child management program.* Champaign, Ill.: Research Press, 1970.

Button, A. *The authentic child.* New York: Random House, 1969.

Dreikurs, R. *Children, the challenge.* New York: Hawthorne, 1964.

Ginott, H. G. *Between parent and child.* New York: Macmillan, 1965.

——. *Between parent and teenager.* New York: Macmillan, 1969.

Gordon, T. *Parent effectiveness training.* New York: Wyden, 1971.

Holt, J. *How children fail.* New York: Dell, 1964.

Kurtz, D., & Palumbo, A. *The ABC's of child management.* Detroit: Infomatics, 1971.

Neill, A. S. *Freedom not license.* New York: Hart, 1965.

Patterson, G. R. *Families.* Champaign, Ill.: Research Press, 1971.

—— & Gullion, M. *Living with children.* Champaign, Ill.: Research Press, 1968.

Spock, B. *The common-sense book of baby and child care.* New York: Duell, Sloan & Pierce, 1957.

PLAY THERAPY

Purpose: Play therapy uses the child's play situation as both locus and focus of therapeutic behavior change.

Leading Theoreticians: Virginia Axline, Erik Erikson, Haim Ginott, Mary Haworth, Melanie Klein, Boris Levinson, Clark Moustakas.

Description: In many respects the child's world is a world of play and fantasy. The play situation provides the child experiencing behavioral problems with a rich context in which to work through his difficulties. While much has been written about the meaning of play for children and the therapeutic use of activities in groups, particularly in residential child care, classical play therapy is typically a specific method of treatment that takes place in a playroom, with an individual therapist. The roots of play therapy are deeply psychoanalytic, and in large measure the play situation may be viewed as a medium for developing understanding of problem behavior and aiding its resolution. Play therapy may serve multiple purposes, including diagnosis, relationship formation, ventilation of behavior, working through feelings, breaking down defenses, tapping the unconscious, and providing a format for modeling alternative behavior.

Play therapists vary on a continuum from almost totally nondirective to highly structured and directive. The therapist may use initial play sessions for diagnostic purposes to observe such things as relationship, attention span, areas of preoccupation, areas of inhibition, direction of aggression, wishes and fantasies, and self-perception. Depending upon orientation, the therapist typically encourages free play with a variety of available materials (paints, dolls, punching bags, puzzles, clay), interprets the child's affect to him ("You seem to be angry at the doll"), and finally offers insights into the child's behavior. The child may experience some regression to earlier levels of functioning while in the play situation, and also may practice newly acquired skills and try on new behaviors. A central notion of play therapy is that the child is expressing symbolically through play the conflicts he is experiencing in the outside world. In the relative safety of the play situation, these conflicts can be worked through and—so the theory goes—transferred to the child's real-life situation. While play therapy, as noted earlier, is typically a form of treatment derived from psychoanalysis, play situations have in some instances served as a locus for behavioral therapy with children (Patterson, 1965).

Selected References:

Axline, V. *Play therapy*. New York: Ballantine, 1969.

Erikson, E. H. *Childhood and society*, 2nd ed. New York: Norton, 1963.

Ginott, H. G. *Group psychotherapy with children: The theory and practice of play therapy*. New York: McGraw-Hill, 1961.

Hartley, R.; Frank, L. K.; & Goldson, R. *Understanding children's play*. New York: Columbia University Press, 1952.

Haworth, M., ed. *Child psychotherapy*. New York: Basic Books, 1964.

Klein, M. *The psychoanalysis of children*. London: Hogarth, 1932.

Levinson, B. M. Pets: A special technique in child psychotherapy. *Mental Hygiene* 48, no. 2 (1964):243–49.

Miller, S. *The psychology of play*. Baltimore: Penguin, 1968.

Moustakas, C. E. *Psychotherapy with children: The living relationship*. New York: Ballantine, 1970.

Patterson, G. R. A learning theory approach to the treatment of a school phobic child. In *Case studies in behavior modification*, ed. L. P. Ullmann & L. Krasner, pp. 279–85. New York: Holt, Rinehart & Winston, 1965.

Schiffer, M. *The therapeutic play group.* New York: Grune & Stratton, 1969.

PSYCHOANALYSIS

Purpose: The basic purpose of psychoanalysis is to uncover the past history of events, experiences, and early development of an individual in order to understand his present behavior. Once insight is achieved, the aim of the therapy is to establish new and adaptive relations between the components of personality—id, ego, superego—and external reality.

Leading Theoreticians: Classical psychoanalysis owes its existence to a single theoretician-clinician, Sigmund Freud. Freud's early work has been elaborated, expanded, and altered by countless clinicians, including Alfred Adler, Anna Freud, Erich Fromm, Karen Horney, Carl Jung, Otto Rank, and Harry Stack Sullivan.

Description: It is probably understating the case to say that no single clinician or clinical approach has had such far-reaching impact on the treatment field in the first three-quarters of the twentieth century as Sigmund Freud and psychoanalysis. Classical psychoanalysis, the second major contribution of Freud (the first was his psychoanalytic theory of development), has spawned many revisionist and derivative therapies and has held center stage in Western clinical thinking since early in the century.

The technique of psychoanalysis is based on five assumptions about human thought and behavior:

1. Existence of the unconscious.
2. To be fully understood, present behavior must be viewed in the light of experiences in early developmental stages: oral, anal, phallic, and latency.

3. Human behavior is the result of dynamic interaction between instinct and reason; i.e., gratification versus security and self-esteem.
4. Personality is a dynamic energy system.
5. Tripartite structure of personality: id, ego, and superego.[1]

Psychoanalysis typically takes place in an office, the patient lying on a couch with the analyst out of view. A key element in psychoanalysis is free association; that is, the free expression of thoughts, without regard to restriction, as they surface from the unconscious. The couch functions as an aid to relaxation and serves to reduce outside stimuli. During the process of free association, the analyst allows himself to become the target of transference; that is, feelings are displaced from significant figures in the patient's past and directed toward the analyst. The analyst offers certain interpretations of the patient's thoughts and defenses, aids the patient in working through the transference neurosis, and guides him in developing insight on his behavior.

Typically, psychoanalysis is a protracted (anywhere from two to ten years) and expensive therapy. The analyst's training is long and arduous (usually arranged through a psychoanalytic institute) and always includes personal analysis as one of its major components.

Selected References:

Adler, G., et al. *Collected works of Carl Jung*, trans. R. F. Hull, 20 vols., 2nd ed. Princetion: Princeton University Press, 1968.
Alexander, F. *Fundamentals of psychoanalysis*. New York: Norton, 1948.
Ansbacher, H. L., & Ansbacher, R. R. *The individual psychology of Alfred Adler*. New York: Basic Books, 1956.

1. See Chapter 4 for a more detailed view of psychoanalytic theory.

Eidelberg, L., ed. *Encyclopedia of psychoanalysis.* New York: Free Press, Macmillan, 1968.

Fenichel, O. *The psychoanalytic theory of neurosis.* New York: Norton, 1945.

Freud, A. *The psycho-analytical treatment of children.* New York: International Universities Press, 1946.

———. *The writings of Anna Freud.* New York: International Universities Press, 1968.

Freud, S. *An outline of psychoanalysis.* New York: Norton, 1949.

———. *The standard edition of the complete psychological works of Sigmund Freud,* 24 vols. London: Hogarth Press & the Institute of Psychoanalysis, 1962.

Fromm, E. *The forgotten language.* New York: Holt, Rinehart & Winston, 1951.

———. *The art of loving.* New York: Harper & Row, 1956.

———. *Escape from freedom.* New York: Avon, 1969.

Glover, E. *The technique of psychoanalysis.* New York: International Universities Press, 1955.

Horney, K. *Neurosis and human growth.* New York: Norton, 1970.

Jones, E. *The life and works of Sigmund Freud,* 3 vols. New York: Basic Books, 1957.

Marmor, J., ed. *Modern psychoanalysis.* New York: Basic Books, 1968.

Rank, O. *Will therapy and truth and reality.* New York: Knopf, 1945.

Sullivan, H. S. *The interpersonal theory of psychiatry,* ed. H. S. Perry & M. L. Gawel. New York: Norton, 1968.

Ticho, E. A. Differences between psychoanalysis and psychotherapy. *Bulletin of the Menninger Clinic* 34, no. 3 (1970):128–38.

PSYCHODRAMA

Purpose: the purpose of psychodrama is to allow the individual client or group to overcome problems through the use of drama, role playing, or action therapy. Through these media, clients are helped to express feelings of conflict, aggression, anger, guilt, and sadness. Psychodrama could be defined as a therapy that explores the truth by dramatic methods.

Leading Theoretician: J. L. Moreno.

Description. Psychodrama uses four major instruments: the stage, which is both psychological and physical living space for the subject or client; the director, or worker; the staff of "auxiliary egos," or therapeutic aides; and the audience. Both the auxiliary egos and the audience are made up of other group members. The strategy is to enable the subject to project himself into his own world and draw responses from fellow group members. Several commonly used techniques include:

1. Self-presentation. The client presents himself or a figure who is significant in his life.
2. Direct soliloquy. The client steps out of the drama and speaks to himself or to the group.
3. Double technique. An auxiliary ego acts with the client and does everything the client does and at the same time.
4. Mirror technique. An auxiliary ego acts in place of the client as clearly as he can. The client watches from the audience to see himself as others see him.
5. Role reversal. The client assumes the role of his antagonist and an auxiliary ego plays the client's part.

The director functions as producer, therapist, and analyst. As producer he guides and directs psychodramatic action; as therapist he provides the actors with support, confrontation, clarification; and as analyst he makes interpretations (often with the help of other group members) of the play action. Psychodrama is another derivative of the classical psychoanalytic approach.

Selected References:

Moreno, J. L. *Psychodrama.* New York: Beacon House, 1946.
———. *Who shall survive?*, 2nd ed. New York: Beacon House, 1953.

———. *The first book on group psychotherapy*. New York: Beacon House, 1957.

———. Fundamental rules and techniques in psychodrama. In *Progress in psychotherapy*, ed. J. Masserman, & J. L. Moreno, Vol. 3. New York: Grune, 1958.

———. Psychodrama. In *American handbook of psychiatry*, ed. S. Arieti, 2:1375–96. New York: Basic Books, 1959.

PSYCHOTHERAPY: INDIVIDUAL

Purpose: According to Wolberg (1967),

psychotherapy is a form of treatment for problems of an emotional nature in which a trained person deliberately establishes a professional relationship with a patient with the object of removing, modifying or retarding existing symptoms, of mediating distrubed patterns of behavior and of promoting positive personality growth and development.

Leading Theoreticians: R. D. Chessick, Carl Rogers, C. B. Truax, L. R. Wolberg.

Description: Psychotherapy is an umbrella term covering a host of individual therapies derived from an eclectic theory base. In common usage, however, psychotherapy suggests any of a number of methods of individual therapy derived from the classical psychoanalytic approach. While intervention in psychotherapy varies considerably according to therapist and therapy, some commonly used techniques include:

1. Development of a strong, empathic relationship with the client or patient.
2. Provision of emotional support.
3. Aiding the client or patient to develop insight into the causes of his behavior/feelings.

Schools of psychotherapy vary from highly directive and structured to nondirective and unstructured. Clients who enter psychotherapy are typically intelligent, reflective, motivated to change their behavior, and able to verbalize their feelings. Psychotherapy is usually practiced in mental health settings, though it may be found in a range of other community and institutional settings as well. Countless mental health professionals—psychiatrists, social workers, clinical psychologists, pastoral counselors—are engaged in the private practice of psychotherapy.

Selected References:

Chessick, R. D. *How psychotherapy heals.* New York: Science House, 1969.

Ford, D. H., & Urban, H. B. *Systems of psychotherapy: A comparative study.* New York: Wiley, 1967.

Gottschalk, L. A., & Auerback, A. H., eds. *Methods of research in psychotherapy.* New York: Appleton-Century-Crofts, 1966.

Haskell, D.; Pugatch, D.; & McNair, D. M. Time-limited psychotherapy for whom? *Archives of General Psychiatry* 21, no. 5 (1969):546–52.

Hersher, L., ed. *Four psychotherapies.* New York: Appleton-Century-Crofts, 1970.

Lemere, F. Brief psychotherapy. *Psychosomatics* 9, no. 2 (1968):81–83.

Lewin, K. K. *Brief encounter: Brief psychotherapy.* St. Louis, Mo.: Warren H. Green, 1970.

Paul, G. L. Insight versus desensitization in psychotherapy two years after termination. *Journal of Consulting Psychology* 31, no. 4 (1967):333–48.

Reisman, J. M. *Toward the intergration of psychotherapy.* New York: Wiley Interscience, 1971.

Rogers, C. R. *Client-centered therapy: Its current practice, implications, and therapy.* Boston: Houghton Mifflin, 1951.

Staines, G. L. A comparison of approaches to therapeutic communication. *Journal of Counseling Psychology* 16, no. 5 (1969):405–414.

Stollak, G. E.; Guerney, B. G., Jr.; & Rothberg, M., eds. *Psychotherapy research: Selected readings.* Chicago: Rand McNally, 1966.

Tarachow, S. *An introduction to psychotherapy.* New York: International Universities Press, 1963.

Truax, C. B. & Carkhuff, R. R. *Toward effective counseling and psychotherapy.* Chicago: Aldine, 1967.
Wolberg, L. R. *The technique of psychotherapy,* 2nd ed. New York: Grune & Stratton, 1967.

PSYCHOTHERAPY: GROUP

Purpose: The basic purpose of many approaches to group psychotherapy is the development of insight and the dynamic adjustment of the individual to his environment.

Leading Theoreticians: E. J. Anthony, Eric Berne, W. R. Bion, Raymond J. Corsini, Helen Durkin, Rudolf Dreikurs, S. H. Foulkes, E. V. Semrad, Dorothy Stock, Carl A. Whitaker.

Description: Like individual psychotherapy, group psychotherapy subsumes a wide range of theoretical orientations and leader styles. Psychoanalytic approaches to group psychotherapy (Foulkes & Anthony, 1965) parallel individual approaches with the exception that conflicts, transferences, and associations are displayed and dealt with on a group level. Other orientations include Adlerian approaches (Dreikurs, 1959) and client-centered approaches (Smith Berlin, & Bassin, 1963)

The leader—or therapist—in psychoanalytically oriented group therapy focuses on the total interactional field of the group, offers clarification when needed, and interprets unconscious or latent meanings of group behavior. He analyzes group processes and individual behavior, including defenses and transference relationships as they develop. In addition to a medium for individual change, the group typically provides a dynamic life of its own (including group structure and processes) which can be marshaled to alter individual behavior. Countless approaches to group therapy are, in effect, translations of the psychodynamic model and psychoanalytic techniques to a group situation.

Selected References:

Ackerman, N. Psychoanalysis and group psychotherapy. In *Group psychotherapy and group function,* ed. M. Rosenbaum & M. Berger, pp. 250–60. New York: Basic Books, 1963.

Anthony, E. J. The generic elements in dyadic and in group psychotherapy. *International Journal of Group Psychotherapy* 17, no. 1 (1967):57–70.

———. Reflection of twenty-five years of group psychotherapy. *International Journal of Group Psychotherapy* 18, no. 3 (1968):277–301.

Arsenian, J., & Semrad, E. V. Individual and group manifestations. *International Journal of Group Psychotherapy* 17, no. 1 (1968):82–98.

Berne, E. *Principles of group treatment.* New York: Oxford University Press, 1966.

Bion, W. R. *Experiences in groups.* New York: Basic Books, 1961.

Chance, E. Group psychotherapy in community mental health programs. *American Journal of Orthopsychiatry* 37, no. 5 (1967):920–25.

Corsini, R. J., & Rosenberg, B. Mechanisms of group psychotherapy: Processes and dynamics. In *Group psychotherapy and group function,* ed. M. Rosenbaum & M. Berger, pp. 340–51. New York: Basic Books, 1963.

Dreikurs, R. Early experiements with group psychotherapy. *American Journal of Psychotherapy* 13 (1959):882–91.

Durkin, H. E. *The group in depth.* New York: International Universities Press, 1966.

Epstein, N. Brief group therapy in a child guidance clinic. *Social Work* 15, no. 3 (1970):33–48.

Foulkes, S. H. & Anthony, E. J. *Group psychotherapy,* 2nd ed. Baltimore: Penguin Books, 1965.

Frank, M. G., & Zilbach, J. Current trends in group therapy with children. *International Journal of Group Psychotherapy* 18, no. 4 (1968):447–60.

Kraft, J. A. An overview of group therapy with adolescents. *International Journal of Group Psychotherapy* 18, no. 4 (1968):461–80.

Linden, M. E.; Goodwin, H. M.; & Resnick, H. Group psychotherapy of couples in marriage counseling. *International Journal of Group Psychotherapy* 18, no. 3 (1968):313–24.

MacLennan, B. W., & Levy, N. The group psychotherapy literature 1967. *International Journal of Group Psychotherapy* 18, no. 3 (1968):375–401.

Silver, A. W. Interrelating group-dynamic, therapeutic, and psychodynamic concepts. *International Journal of Group Psychotherapy* 17, no. 2 (1967):139–50.

Smith, A. B.; Berlin, L.; & Bassin, A. Problems in client-centered group therapy with adult offenders. *American Journal of Orthopsychiatry* 33, no. 3 (1963):550–53.

Stoller, F. H. Accelerated interaction: A time-limited approach based on the brief, intensive group. *International Journal of Group Psychotherapy* 18, no. 2 (1968):220–35.

Whitaker, C.; Stock, D.; & Lieberman, M. A. *Psychotherapy through the group process.* Englewood Cliffs, N. J.: Prentice-Hall, 1964.

REALITY THERAPY

Purpose: The purpose of reality therapy is to enable individuals to face reality and fulfill their basic needs in a socially acceptable manner.

Leading Theoretician: William Glasser.

Description: Reality therapy is the creation of a single individual, William Glasser. Though the literature on reality therapy is sparse, it is widely known among practitioners. Glasser's basic assumption is that everyone needing psychiatric treatment is unable to face reality and fulfill his basic needs. He rejects the notion of "mental illness" and suggests that all people have two fundamental needs: the need to love and be loved and the need to feel worthwhile to oneself and others. Reality therapy provides a context in which the individual learns to:

1. Face reality and accept responsibility for his behavior. Regardless of an individual's past or environment, he is still held responsible for his behavior.

2. Become more responsible. Responsibility is defined as the ability to fulfill one's needs and to do so in a way that does not deprive others of the ability to fulfill their own needs.

3. Distinguish between right and wrong. According to Glasser, people will not change until they begin to judge the morality of their own behavior. Right and moral behavior is defined as that which causes an individual to give and receive love and feel worthwhile to himself and others.

Glasser does not identify the knowledge base that supports his approach, but it would appear that it possesses aspects of learning theory and existential philosophy; that is, an emphasis on the here and now and on man's power to change his behavior. The necessity of dealing with the morality of behavior is also found in existential thought.

A reality therapist must be a strong, mature, warm person who can become involved with the client and make him feel worthwhile. He must be understanding and accepting while rejecting the client's irresponsible behavior. The worker relates to the client as himself, not as a transference figure. He must be a responsible person capable of fulfilling his own needs. Reality therapy demands that an individual become actively involved in solving his own problems. After a close relationship has been formed, the worker confronts the client with the reality of his irresponsible behavior. He rejects the client's irresponsible behavior, while continuing to accept him as a fellow human being. The worker teaches the client to behave more responsibly and fulfill his needs in socially approved ways.

Selected References:

Glasser, W. A realistic approach to the young offender. *Crime and Delinquency* 10. no. 2 (1964):135–44.
——. *Reality therapy.* New York: Harper & Row, 1965.

SELF-HELP GROUPS

Purpose: The basic purpose of self-help groups is to enable members to help each other deal with a common problem—alcoholism, drug addiction, single parenthood, mental illness, a physical handicap, a prison record, obesity, homosexuality, whatever. Self-help groups possess one or a combination of the following as primary group goals:

1. Individual change; self-improvement through consciousness raising, improved social functioning, or increased conformity to social norms.
2. Societal change; attempts to change societal norms through education, public speaking, legislative lobbying, and publication.

Leading Theoreticians: Alfred H. Katz, Abraham Low. Edward Sagarin, Harry Wechsler, Lewis Yablonsky.

Description: Most self-help groups are based on the following principles:

1. The belief that people with a common problem or status can best help one another.
2. The belief that people have responsibility for one another.
3. The belief that a group is an effective medium for helping its members accept themselves and solve problems, thereby enhancing their self-esteem.
4. The belief that people gain inner satisfaction and self-esteem from helping others.
5. The belief in the importance of the role model in the person of group members who are successfully handling their problems.
6. The belief that an empathetic group member should be on hand to help another member whenever needed.

Most self-help groups tend to deemphasize the role of the

leader and are organized on the principle of democratic group participation. Members are encouraged to take as much responsibility in the group as possible. Some common strategies and techniques of self-help groups are:

1. Providing acceptance and a sense of belonging to members.
2. Providing moral support in the knowledge that others share the same problem or status.
3. Providing an opportunity for members to ventilate problems, share feelings, and receive problem-solving advice from others.
4. Providing role models in the persons of group members who are successfully handling their problems or situations.
5. Providing an opportunity for members to take responsibility within the group which enhances their self-esteem.
6. Providing opportunities for group members to address other community groups in order to increase community understanding and aid. Such speaking engagements may also increase the self-confidence of the members and cement their loyalty to the group and its ideals.

Some well-known national self-help groups are Alcoholics Anonymous, Parents Without Partners, Recovery (former mental patients), Synanon (largely but not exclusively drug addicts), Weight Watchers, Gamblers Anonymous, and Neurotics Anonymous.

Selected References:

Barish, H. Self help groups. In *Encyclopedia of social work* 2:1163–69. New York: National Association of Social Workers, 1971.

Katz, A. H. Application of self help concepts in current social welfare. *Social Work* 10, no. 3 (1965):65–81.

Low, A. *Group psychotherapy.* Chicago: Recovery, Inc., 1943.
———. *The historical development of Recovery's self help project.* Chicago: Recovery, Inc., 1943.
———. *Mental health through will training.* Boston: Christopher, 1957.
Sagarin, E. *Odd man in.* Chicago: Quadrangle, 1969.
Vattano, A. J. Power to the people: Self-help groups. *Social Work* 17, no. 4 (1972):7–16.
Wechsler, H. The ex-patient organization: A survey. *Journal of Social Issues* 16, no. 2 (1960):47–53.
Weissman, H. *Individual and group services in the mobilization for youth experience.* New York: Association Press, 1969.
Yablonsky, L. *The tunnel back.* New York: Macmillan, 1964.

SOCIAL CASEWORK

Purpose: It is difficult to find a concise and inclusive definition of social casework, since there are several distinctive approaches under the general casework umbrella. Generally, social casework is a method or methods of helping developed within the profession of social work, the essential purpose of which is to help individuals and families resolve their social problems and achieve an adequate level of social functioning.

Leading Theoreticians: Scott Briar, Florence Hollis, Henry Miller, Helen Harris Perlman, William J. Reid, Ruth E. Smalley, Edwin J. Thomas.

Description: Among the more prominent approaches to helping individuals and families are:

1. *The problem-solving approach.* Developed and elaborated by Helen Harris Perlman, this approach to casework is essentially psychodynamic in orientation, though it rests on the basic assumption that all human living is a problem-solving process. Implicit in the problem-solving approach is the notion that a person's inability to cope with a problem on his own is due to some lack of motivation, capacity, or opportunity to work on, solve,

or mitigate the problem in appropriate ways (Perlman, 1971, p. 1207). The problem-solving approach is essentially educative in nature. The intricacies and interrelationships of person, problem, and place are explored and new alternative problem-solving solutions are examined in the context of a helping relationship.

2. *The Psychosocial approach.* Florence Hollis is the latest and best known current architect of the diagnostic, psychoanalytically oriented school of social casework. Treatment consists largely of helping the client develop insight into the causes of his behavior and its impact on relevant others. In addition to direct treatment, the Hollis model places considerable emphasis on environmental interventions taken on the client's behalf.

3. *The behavioral approach.* Edwin J. Thomas is the leading spokesman in the profession of social work for the practice of behavioral modification. Behaviorally focused social casework, drawing heavily on the principles of social learning theory, is virtually indistinguishable from other behavioral approaches to treatment. Must of the work being done in this area currently consists of the application of behavioral practice principles to the client populations served by social workers. From the mid-1950s, Perlman and Hollis, and more recently Thomas, has been among the most prominent and prolific casework theoreticians in the profession of social work.

4. *The functional approach.* Somewhat more circumscribed in influence is the functional approach to social casework, based in part on the early theoretical work of Otto Rank. Developed in the 1930s at the University of Pennsylvania School of Social Work, primarily by Jessie Taft and Virginia Robinson, the functional approach took essentially a more optimistic view of man's potential for change than did the orthodox Freudian

view. The functional approach stresses personal growth, the importance of social agency function as determinative of case work focus, development of self-direction and self-control, the importance of separations, and a view of the client-worker relationship as in a continual process of becoming.

5. *Other contributions.* In recent years the literature of social casework has grown considerably, particularly in the areas of crisis intervention, family treatment, existential treatment, and client advocacy.

Selected References:

Briar, S., & Miller, H. *Problems and issues in social casework.* New York: Columbia University Press, 1971.

Fischer, J. Is casework effective?: A review. *Social Work* 18, no. 1 (1973):5–22.

Hamilton, G. *Theory and practice of social case work.* New York: Columbia University Press, 1951.

Hollis, F. Explorations in the development of a typology of casework treatment. *Social Casework* 48, no. 4 (1967):335–41.

———. Social casework: The psychosocial approach. In *Encyclopedia of social work* 2:1217–26. New York: National Association of Social Work, 1971.

———. *Casework: A psychosocial therapy,* 2nd ed. New York: Random House, 1972.

Meyer, C. H. *Social work practice: A response to the urban crisis.* New York: Free Press, Macmillan, 1970.

Miller, H. Value dilemmas in social casework. *Social Work* 13, no. 1 (1968):27–33.

Mullen, E. J.; Chazin, R. M.; & Feldstein, D. M. Services for the newly dependent: An assessment. *Social Service Review* 46, no. 3 (1972):309–323.

Parad, H., & Miller, H., eds. *Ego oriented casework.* New York: Family Service Association of America, 1963.

Perlman, H. H. *Social casework: A problem solving process.* Chicago: University of Chicago Press, 1957.

———. Social work method: A review of the last decade. *Social Work* 10, no. 3 (1965):166–78.

——. Social casework: The problem solving approach. In *Encyclopedia of social work* 2:1206–1217. New York: National Association of Social Workers, 1971.

Rapoport, L. Social Casework: An appraisal and an affirmation. *Smith College Studies in Social Work* 39, no. 3 (1969):213–35.

Reid, W. J., & Shyne, A. W. *Brief and extended casework.* New York: Columbia University Press 1969.

Reid, W. J., & Epstein, L. *Task centered casework.* New York: Columbia University Press, 1972.

Roberts, R., & Nee, R. *Theories of social casework.* Chicago: University of Chicago Press, 1970.

Smalley, R. E. Social casework: The functional approach. In *Encyclopedia of social work* 2:1195–1206. New York: National Association of Social Workers, 1971.

Specht, H. The deprofessionalization of social work. *Social Work* 17, no. 2 (1972):3–16.

Thomas, E. J. Social casework and social group work: The behavioral modification approach. In *Encyclopedia of social work* 2:1226–37. New York: National Association of Social Workers, 1971.

——, ed. *The socio-behavioral approach and the interpersonal helping process in social work.* New York: Council on Social Work Education, 1967.

Wilkinson, K. P., & Ross, P. J. Evaluation of the Mississippi AFDC experiment. *Social Service Review* 46, no. 3 (1972):363–78.

SOCIAL GROUP WORK

Purpose: Social group work is a method of interpersonal helping developed within the profession of social work which uses the small group as both means and context for achieving individual and group objectives. Like social casework, social group work encompasses a number of different approaches, emphasizing a range of objectives including behavioral change, self-awareness and personal growth, interpersonal skills, group problem-solving, and social action.

Leading Theoreticians: James Garland, Ralph L. Kolodny, Gisela Konopka, Sheldon D. Rose, Emmanuel Tropp, William Schwartz, Robert D. Vinter, Hyman J. Weiner.

Description: Current attempts to conceptualize social group work practice have yielded at least three identifiable approaches, which, though distinctive in some respects, overlap considerably in many areas:

The *developmental* approach draws heavily from existential philosophy and stresses personal growth and self-awareness among its objectives (Tropp, 1971). The *rehabilitative* approach uses the small group structure and process for achieving treatment objectives of individual members. Drawing on a somewhat common base of small group dynamics, there is presently an ego-psychologically oriented (Garland, Jones, & Kolodny, 1965) and a behaviorally focused (Rose, 1972) approach to rehabilitative group work practice. The *interactionist* approach (Schwartz, 1971) views the small group as a social system in which group objectives are developed in a dynamic and changing context.

If the distinctions among current models of social group work are sometimes arbitrary, so are the distinctions among social group work and numerous other helping approaches that utilize the small group for purposes of client growth and change. Current trends in the practice of social group work include a renewed emphasis on the use of the small group for educational purposes and an attempt to translate research in group dynamics into practical applications with client groups.

Selected References:

Bernstein, S., ed. *Further explorations in group work.* Boston: Boston University School of Social Work, 1970.

Euster, G. L. Social learning in school groups. *Social Work* 17, no. 5 (1972):64–72.

Feldman, R. A.; Wodarski, J. S.; Flax, N.; & Goodman, M. Treating delinquents in traditional agencies. *Social Work* 17, no. 5 (1972):72–80.

Garland, J.; Jones, H.; & Kolodny, R. L. A model for stages of development in social work groups. In *Explorations in group work,* ed. S. Bernstein, pp. 12–53. Boston: Boston University Press, 1965.

Garvin, C. D., & Glasser, P. G. Social group work: The preventive and rehabilitative approach. In *Encyclopedia of social work,* 2:1263–72. New York: National Association of Social Workers, 1971.

Konopka, G. *Social group work: A helping process,* 2nd ed. Englewood Cliffs, N.J.; Prentice-Hall, 1972.

Northen, H. *Social work with groups.* New York: Columbia University Press, 1969.

Papell, C. B., & Rothman, B. Social group work models: Possession and heritage. *Journal of Education for Social Work* 2, no. 2 (1966):66–78.

A psychologist takes issue. *Social work* 14, no. 1 (1966):143–44.

Rose, S. D. *Treating children in groups.* San Francisco: Jossey-Bass, 1972.

Schwartz, W. Social group work: The interactionist approach. In *Encyclopedia of social work* 2:1253–63. New York: National Association of Social Workers, 1971.

―――― & Zalba, S. *The practice of group work.* New York: Columbia University Press, 1971.

Shulman, C. *A casebook of social work with groups.* New York: Council on Social Work Education, 1968.

Silverman, M. Knowledge in social group work: A review of the literature. *Social Work* 11, no. 3 (1966):56–62.

Tropp, E. Social group work: The developmental approach. In *Encyclopedia of social work* 2:1246–52. New York: National Association of Social Workers, 1971.

Vinter, R., ed. *Readings in group work practice.* Ann Arbor: Campus Publishers, 1967.

Weiner, H. J. Social change and social group work practice. *Social Work* 9, no. 3 (1964):111.

Whittaker, J. K. Models of group development: Implications for social group work practice. *Social Service Review* 44, no. 3 (1970):308–322.

Wilson, G., & Ryland, G. *Social group work practice.* Boston: Houghton Mifflin, 1949.

T-GROUPS AND ENCOUNTER GROUPS

Purpose: T groups and encounter groups fall under the general heading of human relations training groups. Their basic purpose is to use group dynamics as the data from which each individual group member learns about his own motives, feelings, and strategies in dealing with other persons, and in addition learns something of the reactions he produces in other people. Barriers to communication and relationship formation are identified and new behaviors encouraged (Colwell, Mauer, & Reaugh, 1972)

Leading Theoreticians: Kenneth Benne, Warren G. Bennis, Leland Bradford, J. R. Gibb, Ronald Lippitt, Edgar H. Schein, William Schutz, Lewis Yablonsky.

Description: In T-groups—often used in human relations training—an effort is made to create a climate of trust and openness which will be conducive to learning. The leader and members facilitate the creation of this learning climate through observation, analysis, and feedback of data from the transactions within the group. Within a present-focused context, the members grapple with issues of power, conflict, leadership, feelings, and values.

The encounter group, which has numerous variations, also strives to create a climate of openness and trust. Often encounter groups meet in marathon sessions to telescope group development and hasten the breakdown of defenses. Numerous exercises involving all manner of nonverbal and verbal communication may be used to facilitate interaction and feedback.

Selected References:

Alderfer, C. P. Understanding laboratory education: An overview. *Monthly Labor Review* 93, no. 12 (1970):18–27.

Argyris, C. On the future of laboratory education. *Journal of Applied Behavioral Science* 1, no. 1 (1965):58–83.

Bach, G. R. The marathon group: Intensive practice of intimate interactions. *Psychological Reports* 181 (1966):995–1002.

Bennis, W.; Benne, K.; & Chin, R. *The planning of change.* New York: Holt, Rinehart & Winston, 1969.

Bradford, L. P.; Gibb, J. R.; & Berne, K. D. *T-group theory and laboratory method.* New York: Wiley, 1964.

Burton, A., ed. *Encounter: The theory and practice of encounter groups.* San Francisco: Jossey-Bass, 1970.

Clark, J., & Culbert, S. A. Mutually therapeutic perception and self-awareness in a T-group. *Journal of Applied Behavioral Science* 1, no. 2 (1965):180–94.

Colwell, S.; Mauer, B.; & Reaugh, C. Approaches to group therapy. In Methods of interpersonal helping. Mimeo. Seattle: University of Washington School of Social Work, 1972.

Galder, J. Nonverbal communication exercises in groups. *Social Work* 15, no. 2 (1970):71–78.

Gibb, J. R.; Platts, G. N.; & Miller, L. F. *Dynamics of participative groups.* Washington, D.C.: National Training Laboratories, 1959.

Gifford, C. B. Sensitivity training and social work. *Social Work* 13, no. 2 (1968):78–86.

Goldberg, C. *Encounter:* Group sensitivity training. New York: Science House, 1970.

Gottschalk, L. A., & Pattison, E. M. Psychiatric perspectives on T-groups and the laboratory movement: An overview. *American Journal of Psychiatry* 126, no. 6 (1969):823–39.

Gunther, B. *Sense relaxation.* New York: Collier, 1968.

Jaffe, S. L., & Scherl, D. J. Acute psychosis precipitated by T-group experiences. *Archives of General Psychiatry* 21, no. 4 (1969):443–48.

Kuehn, J. L., & Crinella, F. M. Sensitivity training: Interpersonal "overkill" and other problems. *American Journal of Psychiatry* 126, no. 6 (1969):840–45.

Luft, J. *Group processes:* An introduction to group dynamics. Palo Alto: National Press, 1963.

Mintz, E. Time extended marathon groups. *Psychotherapy: Theory, Research, and Practice* 4, no. 2 (1967):65–70.

Ruitenbeek, H. M. *The new group therapies.* New York: Avon, 1970.

Schein, E. H., & Bennis, W. G. *Personal and organizational growth through group methods.* New York: Wiley, 1965.

Schutz, W. C. *Joy.* New York: Grove Press, 1967.

Yablonsky, L. *The tunnel back.* New York: Macmillan, 1964.

TRANSACTIONAL ANALYSIS

Purpose: The basic purposes of transactional analysis are:

1. To establish open and authentic communication between the cognitive and emotional aspects of personality.
2. To help individuals develop a freedom of choice to alter responses to stimuli.
3. To learn how to sort out the data that go into decision-making.

Leading Theoreticians: Eric Berne, Thomas A. Harris.

Description: Berne the originator of transactional analysis, drew on the work of Freud, W. Penfield, Harry Stack Sullivan, and Alfred Adler to develop his method. Central to transactional analysis is the notion that in each individual there are three identifiable ego states: parent, adult, child. By analyzing an interpersonal transaction, one can determine which ego states are active for the agent and for the respondent. Script analysis (determining the unconscious life plan of an individual) and game analysis are used to analyze the individual's characteristic ways of interpersonal functioning. Four basic life positions are identified:

1. "I'm not O.K.—you're O.K."
2. "I'm not O.K.—you're not O.K."
3. "I'm O.K.—you're not O.K."
4. "I'm O.K.—you're O.K."

The fourth life position represents the goal of transactional analysis. Berne's earlier work, popularized by Harris, has enjoyed widespread adaptation in therapy groups, church groups, and encounter groups. Institutes of transactional analysis offer didactic and laboratory training in the method and technique.

Selected References:

Berne, E. *Transactional analysis in psychotherapy.* New York: Grove Press, 1961.

——. *Games people play.* New York: Grove Press, 1964.

——. Principles of group treatment. New York: Oxford, 1966.

Harris, T. A. *I'm O.K.—you're O.K.: A practical guide to transactional analysis.* New York: Harper & Row, 1968.

Penfield, W. Memory mechanisms. *AMA Archives of Neurology and Psychiatry* 67 (1952):178–98.

Startz, M. R. Family services: Marital and premarital counseling. In *Encyclopedia of social work* 1:40–413. New York: National Association of Social Workers, 1971.

References

Ackerman, N. W. *Treating the troubled family.* New York: Basic Books, 1966.

Addams, J. Charity and social justice. In *Proceedings of the National Conference on Charities and Corrections,* p. 3. New York, 1910.

Ad Hoc Committee on Advocacy. The social worker as advocate. *Social Work* 14, no. 2 (1969):16–22.

Aronfreed, J., & Rever, A. Internalized behavioral suppression and timing of social punishment. *Journal of Personality and Social Psychology* 1 (1965):3–16.

Ayllon, T. & Michael, J. The Psychiatric Nurse as a behavioral engineer. In: *Case Studies in Behavior Modification.* L. P. Ullmann & L. Krasner, eds. New York: Holt, Rinehart & Winston, 1965, 84–94.

Baldwin, A. L. Sigmund Freud and the psychoanalytic theory of development. In A. Baldwin, *Theories of child development.* New York: Wiley, 1968.

Bandura, A. *Principles of behavior modification.* New York: Holt, Rinehart & Winston, 1969.

—— & Walters, R. H. *Social learning and personality development.* New York: Holt, Rinehart & Winston, 1963.

Becker, W. Consequences of different kinds of parental discipline. In *Review of child development research* 1:169–208. New York: Russell Sage Foundation, 1966.

249

Berelson, B. Beyond family planning. *Science* 163 (1969):533–43.

Berleman, W. C. Social welfare or conservation? Social Theory and Practice, 1972, 2, (2), 229–241.

———; Seaberg, J. R., & Steinburn, T. W. The delinquency prevention experiment of the Seattle Atlantic Street Center: A final evaluation. *Social Service Review* 46, no. 3 (1972):323–47.

Blake, J. Population policy for Americans: Is the government being misled? *Science* 164 (1969):522–29.

Boulding, K. The economics of the coming spaceship earth. In *Environmental quality in a growing economy*, ed. H. Jarrett. Baltimore: Johns Hopkins University Press, 1966.

Brager, G. Advocacy and political behavior. *Social Work* 13, no. 2 (1968a):5–16.

———. Our "organization man" syndrome. *Social Work* 13, no. 4 (1968b):101.

Brendtro, L. K. Establishing relationship beachheads. In A. E. Trieschman, J. K. Whittaker, & L. K. Brendtro, *The other 23 hours: Child care work in a therapeutic milieu*, pp. 51–100. Chicago: Aldine, 1969.

Brenner, C. *An elementary textbook of psychoanalysis*. New York: International Universities Press, 1955.

Briar, S. The current crisis in social casework. In *Social work practice*, pp. 19–33. New York: Columbia University Press, 1967.

———. The casework predicament. *Social Work* 13, no. 1 (1968):5–11.

———. Social casework and social group work: Historical foundations. In *Encyclopedia of social work* 2:1237–45. New York: National Association of Social Workers, 1971.

——— & Miller, H. *Problems and issues in social casework*. New York: Columbia University Press, 1971.

Browning, R. M., & Stover, D. O. *Behavior modification in child treatment*. Chicago: Aldine-Atherton, 1971.

Bruck, M. Behavior modification theory and practice: A critical review. *Social Work* 13, no. 2 (1968):43–56.

Buber, M. *I and thou*. New York: Scribner, 1958.

Cameron, N. *Personality development and psychopathology*. Boston: Houghton Mufflin, 1963.

Camus, A. *The rebel*. New York: Vintage, 1956.

———. *Resistance, rebellion, and death*. New York: Knopf, 1961.

Carter, R. D., & Stuart, R. B. Behavior modification theory and practice: A reply. *Social Work* 15, no. 1 (1970):37–50.

Chambers, C. A. *Seedtime of reform*. Ann Arbor: University of Michigan Press, 1967.

Chin, R. The utility of system models and development models for practitioners. In *The planning of change*, ed. W. G. Bennis, K. D. Benne, and R. Chin. New York: Holt, Rinehart & Winston, 1961.

Cloward, R. A., & Piven, F. F. *Regulating the poor: The functions of public welfare*. New York: Pantheon, 1971.

Commoner, B. *The closing circle*. New York: Knopf, 1971.

Crawford, B. Use of color charts in supervision. *Social Casework* 52, no. 4 (1971):220–22.

Dollard, J.; Doob, L. W.; Miller, N. E.; Mowrer, O. H.; & Sears, R. R. *Frustration and aggression*. New Haven: Yale University Press, 1939.

—— & Miller, N. *Social learning and imitation*. New Haven: Yale University Press, 1941.

—— & ——. *Personality and psychotherapy*. New York: McGraw-Hill, 1950.

Ehrlich, P. R., & Ehrlich, A. H. *Population—Resources—Environment*. San Francisco: W. H. Freeman, 1970.

Epstein, I. Organizational careers, professionalization, and social worker radicalism. *Social Service Review* 44, no. 2 (1970):123–32.

Erikson, E. H. *Identity and the life cycle*. New York: International Universities Press, 1959.

——. *Childhood and society*. New York:Norton, 1963.

Etzioni, A., ed. *The semi-professions and their organization*. New York: Free Press, Macmillan, 1969.

Franks, C. M., ed. *Behavior therapy: Appraisal and status*. New York: McGraw-Hill, 1969.

French, J. R. P., & Raven, B. The bases of social power. In *Group dynamics*, ed. D. Cartwright & A. Zander, 3rd ed., pp. 259–70. New York: Harper & Row, 1968.

Freud, A. *The ego and the mechanisms of defense*. New York: International Universities Press, 1946.

Freud, S. *The ego and the id*. London: Hogarth Press, 1950.

Gambrill, E.; Thomas, E.; & Carter, R. Procedures for socio-behavioral practice in open settings. *Social Work* 16, no. 1 (1971): 51–62.

Garland, J.; Jones, H.; & Kolodny, R. L. A model for stages of development in social work groups. In *Explorations in group work,* ed. S. Bernstein, pp. 12–53. Boston: Boston University Press, 1965.

Glasser, W. *Reality therapy.* New York: Harper & Row, 1965.

Glidewell, J. E. The entry problem in consultation. In *The planning of change,* ed. W. G. Bennis et al., 2nd ed., pp. 653–59. New York: Holt, Rinehart & Winston, 1969.

Goffman, E. *Asylums.* Chicago: Aldine, 1961.

Gordon, T. *Parent effectiveness training.* New York: Wyden, 1970.

Hamilton, G. *Theory and practice of social case work.* New York: Columbia University Press, 1951.

Handel, G., ed. *The psychosocial interior of the family.* Chicago: Aldine, 1967.

Harkavy, O.; Jaffe, F. S.; & Wishnik, S. M. Family planning and public policy: Who is misleading whom? *Science* 165 (1969): 367–73.

Hartmann, H. *Ego psychology and the problem of adaptation.* New York: International Universities Press, 1958.

Hearn, G., ed. *The general systems approach:* Contributions towards a holistic conception of social work. New York: Council on Social Work Education, 1969.

Herzog, E. Research demonstrations and common sense. *Child Welfare* 41 (1962):244.

Hollis, F. *Casework: A psychosocial therapy.* New York: Random House, 1964.

——. Social casework: The psychosocial approach. In *Encyclopedia of social work* 2:1217–26. New York: National Association of Social Workers, 1971.

Janchill, M. P. Systems concepts in casework theory and practice. *Social Casework* 50, no. 2 (1969):74–82.

Jarrett, M. C. Psychiatric social work. *Mental Hygiene* 2 (1918): 290.

Kahn, A. J. Summary statement. Unpublished remarks at the National Conference on Children's Residential Institutions, University of Chicago, April 1971.

Kazantzakes, N. *Zorba the Greek.* New York: Simon & Schuster, 1959.

Krill, D. F. Existentialism: A philosophy for our current revolutions. *Social Service Review* 40, no. 3 (1966):291.

——. Existential psychotherapy and the problem of anomie. *Social Work* 14, no. 2 (1969):33–49.

Kubler-Ross, E. *On death and dying.* New York: Macmillan, 1969.

Landy, D. Problems of persons seeking help in our culture. In *Social welfare institutions,* ed. M. N. Zald, pp. 559–74. New York: Wiley, 1965.

Langer, J. *Theories of development.* New York: Holt, Rinehart & Winston, 1969.

Leader, A. L. Current and future issues in family therapy. *Social Service Review* 43, no. 1 (1969):1–11.

Lee, P. R. Social work: Cause and function. In *Proceedings of the National Conference on Social Welfare.* New York, 1929.

Lippitt, R.; Watson, J.; & Westley, B. *The dynamics of planned change.* New York: Harcourt Brace, 1958.

Lubove, R. *The professional altruist.* Cambridge: Harvard University Press, 1965.

Maccoby, E. E. Role taking in childhood and its consequences for social learning. *Child Development* 66 (1959):126–35.

Maier, H. W. Application of psychological and sociological theory to teaching social work with the group. *Journal of Education for Social Work* 3, no. 1 (1967):29–40.

———. *Three theories of child development,* 2nd ed. New York: Harper & Row, 1969.

Meyer, C. H. *Social work practice: A response to the urban crisis.* New York: Free Press, Macmillan, 1970.

Miller, H. Value dilemmas in social casework. *Social Work* 13, no. 1 (1968):27–33.

Miller, I. Supervision in social work. In *Encyclopedia of social work* 2:1494–1501. New York: National Association of Social Workers, 1971.

Monane, J. H. *A sociology of human systems.* New York: Appleton-Century-Crofts, 1967.

Morrow, W. R., & Gochros, H. L. Misconceptions regarding behavior modification. *Social Service Review* 44, no. 3 (1970): 293–308.

Mowrer, O. H. *Crisis in psychiatry and religion.* New York: Van Nostrand, 1961.

Mullen, E. J.; Chazin, R. M.; & Feldstein, D. M. Services for the newly dependent: An assessment. *Social Service Review* 46, no. 3 (1972):309–323.

Mussen, P. H., *Carmichael's manual of child psychology,* 2 vols., 3rd ed. New York: Wiley, 1971.

Parke, R. D., & Walters, R. H. Some factors influencing the efficacy of punishment training for inducing response inhibition. *Monograph on Social Research in Child Development* 32, no. 1 (1967):1–45.

Patterson, G. R. *Families.* Champaign, Ill.: Research Press, 1971.

——— & Gullion, M. E. *Living with children.* Champaign, Ill.: Research Press, 1968.

Patti, R. J., & Resnick, H. Changing the agency from within. *Social Work* 17, no. 4 (1972):48–58.

Perlman, H. H. *Social casework: A problem-solving process.* Chicago: University of Chicago Press, 1957.

———. Social casework: The problem-solving approach. In *Encyclopedia of social work* 2:1206–1217. New York: National Association of Social Workers, 1971 (a).

———. Review of H. Bartlett, *The common base of social work practice. Social Work* 16, no. 1 (1971b):109–111.

Perls, F. S. *Gestalt therapy: Excitement and growth in the human personality.* New York: Julian Press, 1969.

Polsky, H. W. *Cottage six.* New York: Russell Sage Foundation; 1962.

———; Claster, D. S.; & Goldberg, C. *The dynamics of residential treatment: A social system analysis.* Chapel Hill: University of North Carolina Press, 1968.

———, *Social system perspectives in residential institutions.* East Lansing: Michigan State University Press, 1970.

Redl, F. Framework for our discussion on punishment. In *When we deal with children,* pp. 335–78. New York: Free Press, Macmillan, 1967.

Reid, W. J., & Shyne, A. W. *Brief and extended casework.* New York: Columbia University Press, 1969.

Rein, M. The social service crisis. In *Social policy,* pp. 47–70. New York: Random House, 1970a.

———. Social work in search of a radical profession. *Social Work* 15, no. 2 (1970b):12–28.

Richmond, M. *Friendly visiting among the poor.* New York: Macmillan, 1899.

———. *Social diagnosis.* New York: Russell Sage Foundation, 1917.

———. *What is social casework?* New York: Russell Sage Foundation, 1922.

References 255

——. *The long view*. New York: Russell Sage Foundation, 1930.

Robinson, H. B., & Robinson, N. M. *The mentally retarded child*. New York: McGraw-Hill, 1965.

Rose, S. D. *Treating children in groups*. San Francisco: Jossey-Bass, 1972.

Sarri, R. C. Administration in social welfare. In *Encyclopedia of social work* 1:39–48. New York: National Association of Social Workers, 1971.

Sarri, R. C., Galinsky, M. J., Glasser, P. H., Siegal, S., Vinter, R. D., Diagnosis in group work. In *Readings in group work practice*. R. D. Vinter, ed. Ann Arbor: Campus Publishers, 1967, 39–72.

Satir, V. *Conjoint family therapy*. Palo Alto: Science & Behavior Books, 1964.

——. *Peoplemaking*. Palo Alto: Science & Behavior Books, 1972.

Schwartz, W. Social group work: The interactionist approach. In *Encyclopedia of social work* 2:1253–62. New York: National Association of Social Workers, 1971.

—— & Zalba, S. *The practice of group work*. New York: Columbia University Press, 1971.

Sherman, J. A. & Baer, D. M. Appraisal of Operant Therapy Techniques with Children and Adults. In: *Behavior Therapy: Appraisal and Status*, C. M. Franks, ed. New York: McGraw Hill, 1969, 220–279.

Shulman, C. *A casebook of social work with groups*. New York: Council on Social Work Education, 1968.

Sinsheimer, R. B. The existential casework relationship. *Social Casework* 50, no. 2 (1969):67–73.

Siporin, M. Social treatment: A new-old helping method. *Social Work* 15, no. 3 (1970):13–26.

Smalley, R. E. Social casework: The functional approach. In *Encyclopedia of social work* 2:1195–1206. New York: National Association of Social Workers, 1971.

Solomon, R. L. Punishment. *American Psychologist* 19 (1964):139–253.

Specht, H. The deprofessionalization of social work. *Social Work* 17, no. 2 (1972):3–16.

Stein, J. W. *The family as a unit of study and treatment*. Seattle: Regional Rehabilitation Institute, University of Washington, 1969.

Stevenson, H. W. Social reinforcement of children's behavior. In *Advances in child development and behavior,* ed. L. Lipsitt & C. C. Spiker, vol. 2. New York: Academic Press, 1965.

Stuart, R. B. *Trick or treatment: How and when psychotherapy fails.* Champaign, Ill.: Research Press, 1970.

———. Research in social work: Social casework and social group work. In *Encyclopedia of social work* 2:1106–1122. New York: National Association of Social Workers, 1971.

Szasz, T. S. *The myth of mental illness: Foundation of a theory of personal conduct.* New York: Paul B. Hoeber, 1961.

———. *Psychiatric justice.* New York: Macmillan, 1965.

Thomas, E. J., ed. *The socio-behavioral approach and the interpersonal helping process in social work.* New York: Council on Social Work Education, 1967.

Thomas, E. J. Selected Sociobehavioral Techniques and Principles: an approach to interpersonal helping. *Social Work,* 13, no. 1 (1968):12–27.

———. Social casework and social group work: The behavioral modification approach. In *Encyclopedia of social work* 2:1226–37. New York: National Association of Social Workers, 1971.

——— & Goodman, E., eds. *Socio-behavioral theory and interpersonal helping in social work.* Ann Arbor: Campus Publishers, 1965.

Thorndike, E. L. *Animal intelligence.* New York: Macmillan, 1911.

Toren, N. Semi-professionalism and social work: A theoretical perspective. In *The semi-professions and their organization,* ed A. Etzioni. New York: Free Press, McMillan, 1969.

Trieschman, A. E.; Whittaker, J. K.; & Brendtro, L. K. *The other 23 hours: Child care work in a therapeutic milieu.* Chicago: Aldine, 1969.

Troop, E. *A humanistic foundation for group work practice.* New York: Selected Academic Readings, 1969.

———. Social group work: The developmental approach. In *Encyclopedia of social work* 2:1246–52. New York: National Association of Social Workers, 1971.

Ullman, L. P. & Krasner, L. *Case studies in behavior modification.* New York: Holt, Rinehart & Winston, 1965.

Vinter, R., ed. *Readings in group work practice.* Ann Arbor: Campus Publishers, 1967.

Walters, R. H., & Parke, R. D. The influence of punishment and related disciplinary techniques on the social behavior of children. In *Progress in experimental personality research,* ed. B. A. Maher, 4: 179–222. New York: Academic Press, 1966.

Watson, J. B. *Behaviorism.* New York: Norton, 1925.

White, R. W. Competence and the psychosexual stages of development. In *Nebraska symposium on motivation,* ed. M. R. Jones. Lincoln: University of Nebraska Press, 1960.

———. *Ego and reality in psychoanalytic theory.* New York: International Universities Press, 1963.

Whittaker, J. K. Mental hygiene influences in children's institutions: Organization and technology for treatment. *Mental Hygiene* 55, no. 4 (1971):444–50.

Wilkinson, K. P., & Ross, P. J. Evaluation of the Mississippi AFDC experiment. *Social Service Review* 46, no. 3 (1972):363–78.

Wineman, D. Ego function. Unpublished lecture, 1964.

——— & James, A. The advocacy challenge to schools of social work. *Social Work* 14, no. 3 (1969).

Witte, E. F. Profession of social work: Professional associations. In *Encyclopedia of social work* 2:972–82. New York: National Association of Social Workers, 1971.

World of behavior shapers. *Psychology Today* 6, no. 6 (1972): 28–77.

Name Index

Ackerman, Nathan W., 40, 170n, 209, 210, 234
Addams, Jane, 1, 24, 183
Adler, Alfred, 227
Adler, G., 228
Agel, J., 199
Agnew, P. C., 180
Aichorn, August, 221, 222
Alderfer, C. P., 245
Alexander, F., 228
Alexander, L. B., 42
Allen, R. F., 220
Allerhand, M. E., 222
Allport, Gordon, 99
Anderson, R. E., 109
Ansbacher, H. L., 228
Anthony, E. J., 233, 234
Argyris, C., 245
Aronfreed, J., 85
Arsenian, J., 234
Auerbach, A. H., 232
Axline, Virginia, 225, 226
Ayllon, Teodoro, 80, 83, 206, 208, 221, 222
Azrin, Nathan H., 206, 208, 221, 222

Bach, G. R. 245
Baer, Donald M., 79, 206

Baldwin, A. L., 83, 87
Baldwin, K. A., 212
Bandura, Albert, 78, 80, 82, 131, 138, 151, 153, 206
Barish, H., 238
Bassin, A., 233, 235
Beaber, J. D., 218
Beatman, F. R., 210
Becker, W., 224
Benne, Kenneth, 245
Bennis, Warren G., 92, 245
Berger, M., 234
Bergman, I., 99
Berleman, William C., 4, 6, 13, 61, 151, 190n
Berleson, B., 11
Berlin, L., 233, 235
Berne, Eric, 233, 234
Bernstein, S., 243
Bettelheim, Bruno, 221, 222
Bijou, Sidney W., 206
Binswanger, Ludwig, 99, 214
Bion, W. R., 233, 234
Bixby, F. Lovell, 219, 220
Blake, J., 11
Blum, A., 223
Bolman, W. M., 165
Bolte, G. L., 210
Borgatta, E., 206

260

Index

Kanfer, F., 165
Kaplan, D. M., 213
Katz, Alfred H., 237, 238
Kazantzakes, N., 98, 99
Kemp, C. G., 217, 218
Kesey, K., 222
Kierkegaard, S., 99, 100
Kindelsperger, K. W., 22
Kirschenbaum, M., 210
Klein, D. C., 213
Klein, Melanie H., 208, 225, 226
Kolodny, Ralph L., 3, 156, 242, 243
Konopka, Gisela, 242, 244
Kraft, J. A., 234
Krasner, Leonard, 206, 226
Krause, E. A., 213
Krider, J. W., Jr., 213
Krill, Donald F., 97, 98, 99, 101,
    102, 214, 215
Kubler-Ross, E., 138
Kurtz, D., 224

Landy, D., 117
Langer, J., 65, 66, 67, 71, 74-75
Larsen, C., 220
Lathrop, Julia, 24
Leader, A. L., 170n, 210
Lee, Porter R., 33-34, 37, 187
Lemere, F., 232
Levinson, Boris M., 225, 226
Levis, D. J., 208
Levy, N., 235
Lewin, K. K., 232
Lieberman, M. A., 235
Lieberman, R., 165
Lindemann, Erich, 211, 213
Linden, M. E., 234
Lindsley, Ogden, 206
Lippitt, Ronald O., 92, 94, 245
Litwik, E., 180
Locke, John, 75
Loomis, C. P., 92
Lovaas, O. Ivar, 206, 208, 221
Low, Abraham, 237, 239
Lubeck, S. G., 220

Lubove, R., 39

Mabry, J., 208
Maccoby, E. E., 82
McCorkle, Lloyd, 219, 220
McCormick, M. J., 61
McHarg, I., 22
MacLennan, B. W., 235
McNair, D. M., 232
McPherson, S. B., 208
Maier, H. W., 63
Maluccio, A. N., 222
Mandelbaum, A., 218
Mann, P. H., 218
Marlow, W. D., 222
Marmor, J., 181, 229
Mauer, B., 245, 246
May, Rollo, 99, 109, 214, 215
Mayer, J. E., 165
Mayer, M. F., 222
Merton, Robert K., 92
Meyer, Adolph, 39
Meyer, C. H., 61, 166n, 241
Meyer, J. B., 165
Meyer, H., 180, 206
Michael, J., 80, 83
Miller, D. S., 217
Miller, H., 20, 42, 239, 241
Miller, I., 166n
Miller, L. L., 220
Miller, Neil, 76
Miller, S., 226
Mills, P. R., Jr., 165
Milton, J. P., 22
Minor, J., 206
Mintz, I., 222
Mitchell, J. G., 22
Monane, J. H., 91
Moreno, J. L., 230, 231
Morris, B., 213
Morrow, W. R., 41n, 88n
Moustakas, Clark E., 225, 226
Mowrer, O. Herbert, 76, 99, 101
Moynihan, D. P., 199
Mullen, E. J., 165, 190n, 241

Subject Index